THE RISE AND FALL OF
BRITISH SHIPBUILDING

A Programmed Guide to Office Warfare (1969)
The Jones Report (1970)
The Canal Builders (1972)
The Reluctant Musketeer* (1973)
Canals in Colour (1974)
Remains of a Revolution (1975)
The Master Idol* (1975)
Josiah Wedgwood (1976)
Canal (with Derek Pratt) (1976)
The Navigators* (1976)
The Miners (1976)
Back Door Britain (1977)
Industrial Archaeological Sites of Britain (1977)
A Place to Stand* (1977)
The Green Bag Travellers (with Pip Burton) (1978)
The Past At Work (1980)
The Rainhill Story (1980)
The Past Afloat (1982)
The Changing River (1982)
The Shell Book of Curious Britain (1982)
The National Trust Guide to Our Industrial Past (1983)
The Waterways of Britain (1983)
The Rise and Fall of King Cotton (1984)
Walking the Line (1985)
Wilderness Britain (1985)
Britain's Light Railways (with John Scott Morgan) (1985)
The Shell Book of Undiscovered Britain and Ireland (1986)
Landscape Detective (with John May) (1986)
Britain Revisited (1986)
Opening Time (1987)
Steaming Through Britain (1987)
Walking Through History (1988)
The Great Days of the Canals (1989)
Cityscapes (1990)
Astonishing Britain (1990)
Slow Roads (1990)
The Railway Builders (1992)
Canal Mania (1993)
The Railway Empire (1994)

* novels

CONTENTS

ILLUSTRATIONS

First class luxury on the *Viceroy of India*
(Business Records Centre, University of Glasgow)
Employees, with bowler-hatted foremen at Readhead's, 1895
(Tyne and Wear Archives)

between pages 192 and 193

King George V with James Readhead, 1919
(Tyne and Wear Archives)
Shipbuilding on the Clyde *c*.1900
(University of Glasgow)
A boiler being delivered in the early 1900s
(Clyde Shipping Company Ltd)
One of the anchors of the *Titanic*
(Dudley Libraries)
Aquitania being prepared for the launch in 1913
(The Mitchell Library, Glasgow)
Women at work on machine tools during the 1914–18 war
(Business Records Centre, University of Glasgow)
A young rivet heater
(Tyne and Wear Archives)
Men at work on the turbo-steamer *Montrose*, 1919
(Strathclyde Regional Archives)
The *Queen Mary* under construction at John Brown's yard on Clydeside
(Scottish Record Office)
An aerial view of the Clyde in the 1930s
(Strathclyde Regional Archives)
A group of British shipbuilders
(Tyne and Wear Archives)
Stephen's of Linthouse in the 1950s
(Glasgow Museums: the Museum of Transport)
Automation at Readheads in 1963
(Tyne and Wear Archives)
Standard units being assembled on the berth at Readheads, 1964
(Tyne and Wear Archives)
An entire bow unit at Kvaerner Govan in the 1990s
(Kvaerner Govan Ltd)
Workers at Swan Hunter, May 1993
(North News and Pictures)
As the last ship left Cammell Laird in 1993
(Cammell Laird Archive, Wirral Museums)

[8]

PREFACE

As a child I have memories of walking along the river front at Stockton-on-Tees. There was still a sense of bustle, of movement down the river as ships made their way to the sea. I was then too young to know that my family had once had a part in this, to me, exotic and romantic industry. It began when one of my forebears, John Riley, had come from Leeds to superintend the construction of the Stockton gas works in 1853. He stayed on, and his three sons established a business building marine boilers. Today, they are remembered only in a street name, Riley Street. I knew none of this family history but I always felt a fascination with this world of ships, of swinging cranes and hammered metal. It excited me as a boy and still touches a nerve today. There remains something magical about the world of ships, something that pulls the imagination in the whole notion of a material as dense as iron remaining afloat in the limpid medium of water.

When, in later life, I became interested in the Rileys and their all too brief success in the world of shipbuilding, I began to contemplate just what it was that turned a seemingly prosperous and go-ahead firm into a financial failure. It soon became clear that the Riley Brothers' collapse was only a very minor part of a much more general decline in what had been one of the country's greatest and proudest industries. Its fame lingers on long after reality has presented a quite different version of events. Each year at the Proms, the crowd lustily sings 'Rule Britannia' but in truth Britannia rules nothing at all. Once that rule was absolute: no nation in the world could challenge Britain's maritime pre-eminence.

Now the industry has slid away to near oblivion. Perhaps this is only an aspect of an inevitable process of change that affects all societies at all times – but seldom can the collapse have been so swift, so dramatic. In this book, I have tried to look at how the failure occurred. The answer can be found in part in hard facts, of productivity, costs, availability of raw materials, but that is only a part of the story. I can just remember as a very young child feeling a sense of excitement, and certainly pride, that on this our local river ships were being built that would travel the oceans of the world. More than any other factor – loss of employment, loss of earnings opportunity – it is the lost pride that still hurts. Shipbuilding was never just another job: its demise was always more than just another closure.

A brief note is necessary about units. In general, I have used measurements of the period under discussion. Metric equivalents have – reluctantly – been added: reluctantly because they give a false sense of precision. A vessel described as 80 ft long or 200 tons is unlikely to have been exactly 24.38 metres and 203.2 tonnes. Metric units have been used when, for example, recent measurements have been made of archaeological finds and for the most modern ships built after metrication became general in the industry.

During my work on this book, I incurred a good many debts for help received, not least from my wife, Pip, who shared the research with me. Together we worked our way through archives, collecting materials, and in particular she took on the job of picture research. We were both helped by librarians and curators, and we should like to record a particular debt to the following: Alastair Smith, Curator, Science Department, Museum of Transport, Kelvin Hall, Glasgow; Miss Vanna Skelley, Manager, Business Records Centre, University of Glasgow; University Archives, Glasgow; Mitchell Library, Glasgow; Watt Library, Greenock; McLean Museum and Art Gallery, Greenock; Harry Fancy, Curator, Whitehaven Museum; Tyne and

Wear Archives Service, Newcastle upon Tyne; David Thompson, Birkenhead Reference Library; Merseyside Maritime Museum.

At the end, however, the selection of materials, the arguments and conclusions are, right or wrong, my own.

[1]

———— ❖ ————

RULE BRITANNIA

IN 1934 at John Brown's shipyard on the Clyde, Ship No. 534 was finally given a name: she went down the slip on 29 September with royal blessing as the *Queen Mary*. She was one of the grandest, fastest and for many the most beautiful of the great liners that week after week were to ply the Atlantic between Britain and America. So grand was the occasion of the launch that a special song was written to commemorate the event, words and music by Ina George.

> There were ships of oak in the days of old
> There are ships of steel today
> And the song is the same from the men who build
> 'God speed her on her way.'
> A Toast to the *Queen Mary*
> Long may she sail the sea
> Here's to the name she bears
> Here's to the course she steers
> We want her to sail the world
> With the flag of goodwill unfurled
> So shout hip-hip hooray
> For she's on her way
> Smooth sailing to the *Queen Mary*.

These were stirring sentiments that expressed not just good will, but a spirit of optimism and pride. The shipyards of Britain were still rated as among the best, if not the best, in the world and none stood higher and prouder than John Brown's on the Clyde. This was not a feeling confined to second-rate jingle writers: it was something known throughout the shipbuilding community. An old shipyard worker, interviewed in the 1960s, gave his view of the yard.[1] 'In my early days I was afraid to come to John Brown's because the requirements were so high, and I felt as a tradesman that I might not meet up with what they wanted. So that when I did come in here eventually I felt an immense pride.'

In 1930, four years before the launch of the *Queen Mary*, Mr G. McLellan began his working life as a Clydeside fitter. He too looked back with pride, but he also viewed the scene as he saw it half a century later.[2]

Oh aye there was plenty of work. Big change now. It's sad when you look at the riverside now all the cranes are disappearing. Scotts, the foundry, there's nothing there now at all. It's sad when you think on it, no work. They're talking about building ships at Lithgows' old place. They say they're still after orders but if they get an order who's going tae build it. They've got no workmen, they've got no apprentices, there's nobody knows anything about it now. They'll never build another ship on the Clyde.

The days of glory had gone and the yards had gone too. Scotts, Hamilton's, Lithgows and the rest: even mighty John Brown's had closed. Something, somehow, had gone terribly wrong. It might not have seemed that way when the greatest ship of its day entered the water, but, in truth, the seeds of destruction had already been sown.

The story of the building of the *Queen Mary* is an instructive one, for it shows just how thin was the dividing line between success and failure, and just how complex a business ship construction could be. The early negotiations in 1930 were largely concerned with the all-important specifications, defining the size, style and guaranteed performance of the ship. The ship was to have engines with a shaft horse power of 158,000. Regulations demanded that they should be capable of working at five to six per cent above that level for safety reasons: Brown's, however, preferred going well above that limit to a huge fifteen per cent margin, though they were at pains to point out that power at this level should only be used in genuine emergencies. No doubt they had visions of enthusiastic, record-breaking captains going at full blast all the way across the Atlantic. There was, in any case, no need to worry about speed records. Brown's also guaranteed that when the ship came to its speed trials off the coast of Arran, it would be able to sustain thirty and a quarter knots, putting it well beyond any obvious competitor. There was one other important clause in the contract: 'that the whole of the vessel's hull, machinery and equipment is to be of British manufacture'. Although the basic ship was John Brown's, there were some seventy subcontracts, bid for by over one hundred companies. From the first a good deal of British pride and prestige rested on the ship. In the course of construction, Brown's themselves had to make improvements to the yard, including acquiring new machinery and paying £10,000 as their contribution to widening the river at Clydebank. Negotiations were temporarily held up, as Cunard bargained for a berth at Southampton, but in May 1930, Brown's at last got their tender accepted. The price was set at £3,992,000.

It was an immense project, in every sense of the word. To describe a ship as being 80,774 tons or 82,066 tonne does not always convey her size very obviously, but when one thinks of the passengers she carried one realizes that the *Queen Mary* was regularly transporting the population of a good sized village across the Atlantic. In all there were 776 first-class passengers, 784 tourist and 579 third-class passengers. She was also to display her modernity in every department. There were the geared turbine engines driving four screw-propellers that gave the vessel her immense power, but they were hidden out of sight as far as most visitors and passengers were concerned. But what the passengers did see was kept resolutely up to date. It had long been the custom for luxury liners to disguise their state rooms. The *Mauretania*, for example, was designed as a floating palace. The grand entrances were in French walnut, and the designers bought veneers from all over France and Britain. The dining rooms were panelled in oak, the upper roofed by a huge dome in cream and gold. State rooms offered a choice of style – Sheraton or Adam – and carvings were never duplicated. Even the children got their own specially painted nursery rhyme pictures – though the play equipment appears to have been limited to one rocking horse. One sympathizes with the nursery staff, trying to arbitrate in quarrels over whose turn it was for a ride. For those who complained that it all looked more like a country mansion than a ship, the designers would point out that for the most part the last thing their customers wanted to be reminded of was the fact that they were at sea.

The patrons of the Grand Saloon were bejewelled ladies and white-tied gentlemen trying not to feel or look queasy – not hardened old sea dogs. The *Queen Mary*, however, offered something very different. No Sheraton elegance here, no glowering Tudor panelling, but crisp, clean Art Deco; light, bright and up to the minute. Not that the *Queen Mary* was to be anything other than wholly luxurious. Among the many jobs that went to outside contractors was the first-class swimming bath for £10,498 and the first-class Turkish bath for £4,050, both to Trollope and Sons, while the slightly inferior tourist swimming bath went to Wylie and Lockhead for £7,174. And thanks to a late decision in 1934 all the first-class accommodation and the tourist dining room had what was then still something of a novelty – air conditioning.

The ship was a prestige project in every possible way. But the times were not propitious. The Wall Street crash of 1929 still reverberated throughout the financial world, sending out waves of panic that lapped around the walls of the money markets. Confidence sank and the world slipped ever deeper into recession. Perhaps the last thing anyone needed was a new, very expensive luxury liner to link two increasingly impoverished countries. In December 1931, all work on the ship came to a halt. It was, in a way, remarkable that a vessel on which so much prestige rested should simply be allowed to rust and decay, unfinished. The government were at last persuaded to act and advanced a million pound loan to enable the ship to be completed. Brown's were anxious to get restarted and wrote to Cunard in March 1934:[3]

On going over matters carefully, we see plainly that after this 2¼ years delay, our men will neither be able nor capable at first of resuming work at anything like the pace with which the ship was being carried on in December 1931 when work was stopped, and hence if we delay any longer making a start on the vessel, the launch will not come off until November, which you would agree would be most regrettable from every point of view.

I quite understand that the adjustment of documents in connection with the government loan of One Million may extend over two or more weeks after Easter, so, as our Board now see their way to finance all expenditure that would be incurred on work on the ship for, at any rate, the month of April, we propose (unless you see strong objection against it) to start collecting men the day after the Royal Assent has been given, which both you and we trust will be on Wednesday evening.

Cunard's were equally keen to restart – and very anxious that the world should know all about it. There is a great contrast between the light-hearted enthusiasm of Cunard, when they sent off a booklet to a Sir Thomas Bell and the response[4]

Needless to say I do not expect that the even tenor of your life will be ruffled or that you will go into paroxysms of enthusiasm over the booklet, and would remind you that it is merely issued with the object of drawing the attention of the ordinary mortal. I rather hear you saying 'If we cannot build ships better than Cunard can produce booklets – Gawd help us!'

Brown's however were cool about any publicity at all during the construction period. Bell declared that the public would soon tire of 'technical pictures of a ship's skeleton' and that the only ones who would gain from their publication would be the French builders of the new 'Transatlantique'.[5] And a BBC suggestion that they might broadcast a discussion between two riveters was greeted with horror. 'I have discussed the matter with the Management and they are very strongly averse to such a procedure which, they think, would undoubtedly be prejudicial to the discipline in the yard.'[6] They seemed much happier discussing such vital matters as to whether the invitation cards for the launch should specify 'Undress Uniform' or 'Morning Dress' – they opted for the latter. This correspondence speaks volumes about attitudes at Brown's. It shows a certain stiffness and rigidity but, much more importantly, it shows a deep distrust, not untouched with contempt, for the work force. One suspects they were not so much afraid of what two riveters might say as alarmed at the notion that they should be permitted to express any opinion at all. This was a view which would have seemed entirely reasonable to most other shipbuilders in Britain at that time. The *Queen Mary* was a masterpiece incorporating the latest features of engineering and design, while back at the yard industrial relations were still those of the nineteenth century.

This is not perhaps too surprising. The idea that once the wonders of steam power were demonstrated the old age of sail power simply came to an end is completely wrong. If the *Queen Mary* is the most famous steamer to be built on the Clyde, then the *Cutty Sark* must be the most famous sailing ship. She was built at the Scott and Linton yard at Dumbarton in 1869. She continued to trade under sail right through to 1922, within a decade of work starting on the *Queen Mary*. In some ways, the two ships could not be more dissimilar: one a giant hull of steel powered by steam, the other a seemingly almost delicate hull of timber powered by sail. Yet, in other ways, there are points of similarity: both were designed to do a specific job of work for a specific trade, and both were designed for speed. The *Cutty Sark*, however, was destined never to achieve the role for which she had been intended. China tea was a luxury commodity, and there was a high premium paid for the first ship to arrive in London with the new harvest. *Cutty Sark* was built very specifically to claim that premium, but she had scarcely reached the water before the Suez Canal was opened, and the trade was taken from the old, elegant tea clippers and handed to the steamships. There was one trade left to the clippers – the wool run from Australia. Old rivalries were cheerfully renewed and the *Cutty Sark* showed her worth, creating a new record in 1895 when she completed the journey from Sydney to London in 67 days. For a long time, the lack of coaling stations *en route* kept the clippers in business – but they had to work for every penny they earned. Wool bales were loaded into the hold and crushed down by screw jacks until the entire space was all but filled with a solid mass of compacted wool. In her last voyages, the slender vessel was packed with 5,000 bales. No room on such a vessel for passengers – not very much for the crew. By the end of her working life, this complex vessel, able to carry up to thirty-four sails – representing three-quarters of an acre of canvas – was managed by just nineteen men.

The *Cutty Sark* also has its story to tell. The British were by no means the only innovators in ship design in the nineteenth century. The idea of a long, narrow hull with steeply raked hollow bows was developed in America. No doubt the Americans could have continued competing for the fastest clipper runs if all development had not been stopped by the outbreak of Civil War in 1861. So the British had every opportunity to dominate the world of fast, sleek sailing ships. What is most remarkable is that this was going on well into the steam age – not just a conservative tradition, but still innovative. So that in the second half of the nineteenth century one finds shipyards producing all types and varieties of vessels. At Liverpool, for example, James Quiggins and Co. were building sailing ships of all kinds. They provided whatever was needed for the ship to take to the seas ready for trade: the specification for their largest vessel, the 1,898-ton *Andromeda*, included everything from a carefully detailed suit of sails down to '1 clothes brush with handle'.[7] While across the Mersey at Birkenhead, Lairds were building a variety of vessels from an iron paddle steamer for South America, which came complete with a portable smith's hearth with bellows, anvil and tools for repairs at sea, to a barque for the emigrant trade, fitted out in spartan style, but with auxiliary steam engine and a lifting screw for when she was travelling under sail alone.[8] All these vessels presented their builders and designers with different challenges, different materials and different techniques – yet all were being built at the same time on the same river. And, most importantly, they were often being built by the same people. There was no sudden break as the world moved on from wooden ships driven by sail to iron ships powered by steam. There was a continuity of a kind, yet there were also conflicts between men brought up in the use of age-old skills and implements and those of the new age. These conflicts were never completely resolved. No history of modern shipbuilding makes sense unless one starts back not just in the nineteenth century but even earlier.

[2]

———— ❖ ————

THE WOODEN SHIP

I F one was setting out in the 1790s, instead of the 1990s, to write the story of shipbuilding, the tale that one had to tell would have been of steady, slow development in its technology, accompanied by an equally slow and steady development in the organization of the shipbuilders. Into this calm stepped a wheezing, huffing, puffing and – at first – not very efficient machine, the steam engine. The point about the steam engine was not that it provided a better means of moving a boat through the water – improvements to hull design, sail arrangements and many other aspects of ship design had done that. But they had all developed with the shipbuilding community: the steam engine was an outsider. The men who understood its workings and its manufacture were engineers and iron founders not shipwrights and carpenters. It was an alien force that brought new practices to disrupt the old ways – though not to destroy them. Men had been building wooden ships in Britain for over 3,000 years, and traditions built up over such a period of time do not vanish overnight. Much that was to happen in the years following the arrival of steam on the water makes no sense unless one has a notion of what went before.

There is a technical definition of a ship and an everyday definition, and here we are using the simplest of them all – 'a large seagoing vessel'. The record of the ancient past is hopelessly fragmented, offering no more than a glimpse here and there, with time lags in between that stretch for centuries. But one can at least say that the first known vessels that fit the definition are the three boats discovered in the mud of the Humber estuary at North Ferriby.[1] The third, excavated in 1974, has been more fully investigated. It qualifies as large with a 42½-ft (13-m.) keel, formed of two planks carved out of oak and sweeping upwards at either end. Around this solid base, the sides were built up of thinner planks. One can only guess at its shape, but everything about it suggests a seaworthy craft, and the site of the find would certainly indicate that the vessel was used on the adjoining Humber which can be as rough as any coastal waters. Its construction methods, in which the planks were sewn together with yew, was not one that would be found in later vessels – but here, undeniably, was a ship. And carbon dating suggests it was built around 1,500 BC in the Bronze Age. How many stages of development were there between this and the next vessel, the Saxon burial ship found at Sutton Hoo? No one can say, but by this time, a whole range of features was found that were to be a commonplace in shipbuilding for centuries to come.

We know a good deal about the Sutton Hoo vessel. It was approximately 90 ft (27.4m.) long with a maximum beam of 14 ft (4.3m.) and a midships depth of 4 ft (1.2m.). It was rowed by forty oars and steered using a single rudder or steering oar, hung over one side of the vessel at the stern. In time, this side of the ship – on the right looking towards the bows – became known as the steer-board, then starboard side. And because this was an awkward obstruction when coming alongside a wharf, the ship would normally berth with the opposite side against the quay – the port side. Already one begins to sense a real feeling for the continuity of maritime history. It is like the North Ferriby boat in that there is a stout keel at the bottom and a side built of planks, but there the similarity ends. Where the keel of the earlier boat simply curled upwards, here separate bow and stern posts rise up at the ends. The actual shell is an altogether more solid construction. The strakes, the length of planking running from stem to stern, overlap and are secured by metal rivets. This basic structure is then strengthened by twenty-six heavy wooden frames. This method of building with overlapping planks to create the hull is known as clinker building, and was to be used in virtually every wooden ship built in Britain from this time until around 1500 – and although it is no longer the only method used for building wooden hulls, it is still in use today.

The third archaeological excavation at Graveney in Kent revealed a vessel built in the century before the Norman Conquest. Again this was a clinker-built boat, but a good deal more sophisticated than Sutton Hoo. Here more details of construction emerged. Sutton Hoo existed only as a 'shadow' in the sandy soil. Here the actual wood was found preserved, if incomplete. The words of the old song 'Heart of oak are our ships' had a literal meaning for generations of ship-builders for whom English oak – and for most oak from the south of England – was the favoured building material. The strakes were joined to the ribs not by rivets, but by pegs made out of willow, known as treenails. This technique, too, has survived down the centuries, as has another that can be found in the Graveney boat. To keep the ship watertight, the space between the planks was packed with twisted hair. This is caulking: the hair, or oakum, in later vessels, would be placed along the seam and then rammed home with a caulking iron, a device looking somewhat like a large chisel. Extra protection was then provided by covering the outside with tar. It is not the differences between these and later building techniques that are so striking but the similarities.

Evolution continued for centuries, but the greatest change came in the development of the sailing ship. The earliest ships to sail in northern waters carried a square sail on a single mast, of which the Viking longship is the best-known example. This is not the place for a lengthy discussion of the development of the sailing ship, but over the years two traditions met: the northern square rig was joined by the Mediterranean lateen sail. The latter was triangular, and could be moved round the mast to take the wind on either side. The lateen sail made it possible for vessels to sail close to the wind and the combination of square sail and lateen sail culminated in the carrack. These were in their final phase of development, three-masted ships, square-rigged on fore and main masts with a lateen sail on the mizzen. With such a wide spread of canvas, a ship had become a complex machine, worked by a bewildering network of rigging, of

[23]

lines, blocks, dead-eyes and ratlines. Where the early vessels were made by craftsmen we would now call shipwrights, the medieval and Renaissance ship called for a greater array of workers – rope makers, block makers, riggers, metal workers and more.

The one factor that covers all the changes through the centuries is increase in size. The medieval vessel, whether officially a warship or not, might well be required to fight and the 'fighting castles' were added – the forecastle, the familiar fo'c'sle of modern ships, was joined by an after castle which became the poop deck. So the ship developed a new profile – high at bow and stern, low in the waist. And as size increased, so did the strength of the hull. The grandest of all clinker-built vessels of the age was Henry V's *Grâce Dieu* built at Southampton in 1418. The wreck was discovered in the Hamble in 1933, so that it was possible to find out a good deal about construction. This was a large vessel, around 1,400 tons (1,422 tonne), and it was clear that the frame had been added after the hull was completed. How this was achieved remains a mystery. Presumably some sort of templates were set in place at regular intervals to define the hull shape. At least the details of the planking are known. It had three layers of oak planking of which the inner plank was four inches narrower than the other two. These were held together by treenails. At the seams, the two outer planks of the upper strake overlapped the next three planks of the lower strake, while the narrow inner plank rested on top. Each seam was thus five planks thick – approximately 7½ inches (19 cm.). They were fastened together by iron bolts. The new ship showed a number of factors that were not present in the earliest ships – notably the replacement of the old steerboard by a rudder and tiller, making it altogether more manageable.

The next, most important stage in development came with the abandonment of clinker building for large ships in favour of carvel building. If clinker building can be thought of as construction from the outside in, then carvel building is construction from the inside out. First the skeleton was built. The keel was laid, with the keelson above it for extra strength, and to these were added the stem at the bows and the stempost at the stern. In between were the ribs that defined the shape of the hull. The planking was then added, giving a smooth surface to the outside of the hull, instead of the corrugated overlapping of the clinker-built ship. Further strength was supplied by beams supported on timber 'brackets' or knees, which ran across the vessel and supported the deck planking. Wales, wooden bands running right round the hull, gave yet more strength and protected the outer planking from damage. This method of building was to remain more or less constant throughout the age of the wooden sailing ship. There were still many advances to be made. The invention of the steering wheel made ship handling altogether more precise, so that sail designers could confidently plan for systems that would allow vessels to sail ever closer to the wind. This was achieved by using a combination of square and triangular sails – employed as staysails and jibs. The changes may have come slowly but they were none the less real.

This very condensed, and greatly simplified, story of ship development does at least bring out the most important features as far as the shipbuilding industry was concerned. The more complex a vessel becomes, the more specialist workers are required to build it, and this whole intricate frame of ribs and planks, knees and beams, masts and spars would involve the use of a vast amount of timber. It is difficult to say just how much was required, partly because the 'standard unit' was 'a load', defined unhelpfully as the quantity of timber one horse could pull in a cart. Even given the vagueness of the definition, the estimate for a medium-sized warship of Nelson's age, such as the 64-gun *Agamemnon*, was for 2,000 loads and that is a very large number of trees. Not all woods were equally suitable. Oak was always first choice, especially for 'compass timber' used where the wood had to be cut on a curve, as in the supporting knees. The oak, its branches growing out more or less horizontally from the trunk, was ideal. Wood could be taken from the junction point and the grain would then always run true.

It is difficult now to appreciate the sheer volume of timber that went into a large ship. As early as 1506 there were problems with the biggest ships. That was the year the *Great Michael* was built in Scotland, a truly massive vessel, 240 ft (73m.) long, 36 ft (11m.)

deep with wooden walls built 10 feet (3.05m.) thick to withstand bombardment by cannon. Charnock in a history of marine architecture written in 1801 recorded that the ship 'was of so great stature and took so much timber, that she wasted all the woods in Fife which were oak wood, with all timber that was gotten out of Norway'.[2] By the time of the Napoleonic Wars, a ship was perhaps a more complex affair, but the basic requirements remained the same: immense quantities of timber of all kinds. The specification for a 74-gun ship, built in 1801[3], listed 'timber, thick stuff, 4-inch [10 cm.] plank, 3-inch plank, thin plank, knees, elm timber, East Country plank, Dantzic deals, fir timber'. Oak still dominated. A ship built in 1805 cost £62,430 of which £18,000 went on 2,400 loads of oak, compared with 230 loads of knees, 80 of elm and 35 of firs. The other major costs were labour, with shipwrights £6,824 and smiths £3,838. Not surprisingly, the ready availability of timber was a very important factor when it came to siting a shipyard. A builder, J. Graham of Harwich, wrote to the Admiralty in 1805, offering to build a seventy-four-gun ship:[4]

> Permit me, honourable Sirs, to offer a few words in explanation, and as reasons for requesting being indulged with the small addition of six months more time than is allowed to the builders on the River Thames; they have a large proportion of their timbers and all other materials delivered to them by land carriage and barges, which do not depend on such contingencies as I am exposed to; all materials whatever, must be brought to this yard by sea, of course dependent on winds and weather, which often occasion several weeks delay, the effects of which in the course of 24 years, I have fully experienced and severely paid for.
>
> Although ships cannot be completed at this place so quick as in the Thames ... yet I have the satisfaction to know the ships of war I have had the honour to build are among the best and more durable in the Navy.

Timber supply was a preoccupation of shipbuilders wherever and for as long as wooden ships were being built. Builders in the north-west in the 1830s were complaining bitterly about the duties payable on imported timber from the Balkans, and even more bitterly about what they saw as an unfair advantage given to their offshore neighbours. The Whitehaven newspaper waxed indignant:[5]

> Among the other bungling measures of the Whig Ministers, we last week alluded to the shameful law by which ship-builders in the Isle of Man are allowed to import Baltic timber used in the construction of vessels, upon paying *one-eighth of the duty required in any other port* of the united kingdom. We then recommended that a petition on the subject should be prepared and sent from this port, and we are happy to find that our advice has been anticipated, for a petition on the subject was signed by all the ship-builders at this port, and transmitted to London, on Monday last, for presentation, by our member, Mr. Attwood, who we have no doubt will enforce it with that zeal for the welfare of the shipping interest of the northern ports which has ever distinguished his exertions in the House. Upon further enquiry on this painfully interesting subject, we learn that by a ship of 300 tons, the builders in the Isle of Man *make a profit of above one thousand pounds* in the mere difference in the duties upon oak and pine timber and plank, of which a vessel of that tonnage is composed, between this port and the Island. We subjoin a copy of the petition, and trust that every port in the kingdom will take the matter up zealously, and complain of this most unjust preference, which must, if persevered in, spread ruin on every side.

Nothing happened, and the subject was still being aired a decade later, even if circumstances had by then been dramatically changed. Shipyards in Douglas were described as 'being in a most disastrous state'. The Whitehaven view was not notably charitable.[6]

> When we consider the unfair advantage possessed by the rival ship-builders, in obtaining their timber nominally duty free, we must confess that we have no sympathy whatever with them, and

[27]

therefore we will not hypocritically pretend to condole with them in their misfortunes.

One would have to search hard to find any trace left of these warring yards where rivalries were so bitterly fought out in the nineteenth century. There are even fewer traces of the private eighteenth-century yards which built the ships that made up Nelson's navy.

One such place which has survived remarkably unchanged right up to the present day is Buckler's Hard on the Beaulieu River. It was not originally intended as a shipyard at all. In 1709, the Duke of Montagu had an ambitious scheme by which he would establish a colony on St Lucia in the Windward Islands to grow tropical produce which would be sent back to his new port on the Beaulieu. He started in England, establishing Montagu Town with a grand main street, 80 ft (24m.) wide, flanked with houses and leading down to what he hoped would become a huge wharf. Sadly his expedition reached St Lucia only to find it had been annexed by the French. With no produce, there was no port – but there was a deep river location on the edge of the New Forest, and the broad street was an ideal thoroughfare for cartloads of timber. Montagu Town became Buckler's Hard, and was leased to a series of shipbuilders, the most famous of whom was Henry Adams who stayed from 1747 until 1805.

It is hard to imagine this spot – not a town, scarcely a village, but more a hamlet – as a major shipbuilding centre, yet in Adams' time, it ranked in importance not far behind the yards on the Thames and ahead of such other important centres as Harwich. A shipyard such as Buckler's Hard had few distinguishing features. A ship would either be set up on a slipway or in a primitive dry dock scooped out of the mud of the river bank, drained and blocked with mud until the dam was broken for the launch. Timber would stand in piles around the gradually growing hull: almost everything required for a ship was brought in at the last moment, then left out in the open air until it was needed. It was certainly quite common for the timber that was to go into the making of a ship still to be growing in the forest while the plans were being drawn up. And such yards were to continue in existence, using much the same methods into the present century.

James Goss was just one of any number of small shipwrights building barges together with ketches and schooners for the coastal trade.[7] His yard was at Calstock on the banks of the Tamar, and it was here that he built his first barge in 1891 and continued building wooden ships right up to 1920. Goss selected his own timber from the nearby Cotehele estate, and it was brought back to be sawn into planks in the saw pit. The log to be sawn was rolled across the top of the pit and the two sawyers set to work. One was at the bottom of the pit pulling down on the seven-foot-long saw in the cutting stroke, and receiving a fine fall of sawdust at each stroke. His partner stood above, helping to guide the down stroke and pulling the saw back up again. Frank Booker, describing the technique, wrote of the ferociously hard work involved.[8]

This sawing often went on for days from dawn to dusk, and when in hot weather the sweat and friction rubbed the sawyers' armpits raw, fuller's earth was dabbed on them. Goss never used a pencil on timber, but indicated the measurement with a scratch of his thumb-nail, and their accuracy was never in question.

Goss was very much the old style of craftsman, who carried his trade secrets secure inside his own head, and who sketched out his plans on a piece of old board propped up against his kitchen wall. He was a product of the old system, where one became a master shipwright by learning all aspects of the trade in a wholly practical way. In his time he too would have taken his turn in the saw pit and worked all the other jobs that went into shipbuilding. He survived as a successful builder until his retirement in 1920, but when he went the yard went with him, and it has scarcely left a mark behind. He represented the end of an old tradition, which had already begun to change over a century before he began work. Increasing ship size had called for ever greater yards, and the chief customer for the big ships was the navy.

Quite when Britain can be said to have acquired anything that might be described as a navy is difficult to determine. Traditionally, Alfred the Great has been called the founder of the navy, and he is certainly one of the first kings to order ships to be built. These were designed to combat the raids of the Viking long boats. In the fourteenth century Edward I used ships in his war against Scotland, but these would have been requisitioned merchantmen rather than specially built warships. Richard I was arguably the first to establish a genuine naval base when he assembled a fleet at what is now Portsmouth in 1194 to attack the French, but when the excitement died away, the infant naval base died with it, not to be resurrected until the end of the fifteenth century when Henry VII decided that a strong fleet was an essential requirement for a small island with pretensions to being a major power.[9] Henry V is said to have had a fleet of over a thousand vessels to carry his army to France, and it was Henry who first began ordering big, impressive ships – as much for prestige as for use in war. As well as the *Grâce Dieu* there were the equally grand and piously named *Holy Ghost* and *The Trinity*. But it was under the Tudors that the navy began to acquire its official status, with its own shipyards, building and repairing its own ships. Henry VIII established dockyards at Woolwich and Deptford and began improving long-forgotten Portsmouth. This was not an age when Britannia ruled the waves, very far from it. The great age of exploration had involved ships from Spain and Portugal, while northern waters and the trade to the east were dominated by the Dutch. Each was to develop a characteristic vessel. The galleon, first seen in the Mediterranean, was a compromise between the old rowed galley and the big sailing carrack. The union was seen most clearly in the bows with the sharp 'beak' borrowed from the galley united with the superstructure of the forecastle from the carrack. These were the vessels designed to protect the trade routes between Spain and the New World. The Dutch, meanwhile, concentrated on trade. The *flyut* or flyboat was bluff-bowed and rounded in the stern, with a very full section and almost flat bottom. Everything was sacrificed to maximize cargo space: the elaborate, gilded cabins and galleries of the galleons were replaced by altogether more spartan accommodation, and it was rare for them to carry more than perfunctory armament. Britain had nothing comparable to either, and Henry VIII turned to Europe to recruit shipwrights to build up his own navy. Even so, by the end of his reign, the navy could boast no more than seventy vessels, of which fifteen were then already outmoded galleys, used mainly for towing.

In these times, apart from the Dutch flyboats, the distinction between warships and merchantmen was not always obvious – and was to become ever less clearcut in Elizabeth I's reign. At its start, Britain was as far from being a major mercantile force as she was from being foremost in the ranks of naval power. It was estimated that the country had a modest 50,000 tons (50,800 tonne) of merchant shipping of which there were only twenty vessels of 200 tons (203 tonne) or more. Looking simply at the Baltic trade, the difference between, for example, the British and the Dutch was extraordinary: fifty-one English ships plied the trade against over a thousand from the Netherlands.[10] Change, however, was on its way, boosted by two forces: the coastal trade of coal from the north-east, especially between Newcastle and London, and the fishing fleets that made ever longer voyages to the North Sea, Iceland and the Newfoundland Banks. It was the latter trade that was to be particularly important for it was from the fishing ports of the south-west – from Devon, Cornwall and Dorset – that the new generation of great Elizabethan sailors was to come. A third trade soon joined the other two, at once more profitable and more warlike. The attempt of the Dutch to establish their homeland as a Protestant state, free from the influence of Catholic Spain, led to closure of the great northern port of Antwerp, and a general division of the European nations on religious lines. It gave the British, at least as they saw it, *carte blanche* to wage an unofficial war against the trade of the Spanish and Portuguese colonies. Whether the men who carried out these raids were privateers or pirates, heroes or villains, depended on which side of the religious divide one happened to be standing. But the result of all this great flurry of maritime activity was a demand for more and bigger ships.

Queen Elizabeth was very conscious of the threat to Britain from the European powers and of the importance of maintaining control

of the seas and the coast. Her efforts to extend the Navy were hampered by divisions in the Privy Council, with the powerful Cecil
faction favouring a policy of appeasement towards Spain. And even
when the political will and the money were both available, she had
to contend with inefficient and notably corrupt naval dockyards. She
dealt with the latter in a very practical way by establishing pensions
for her leading shipwrights, enabling them to plan for old age by
rather more acceptable methods than accepting bribes and robbing
the royal stores. Matthew Baker was one of the beneficiaries – the
first named master shipwright in the records, who was to build excellent ships, notably for Sir John Hawkins. Elizabeth also gave her
encouragement to merchant venturers, of which by far the most
important was the East India Company, granted a charter in 1598.

In the career of Sir John Hawkins, all facets of this extraordinary
age seem to meet in this one man. As plain John Hawkins he made
a fortune trading with his brother between Britain and the Canaries.
Then he turned to an even more lucrative trade established by the
Portuguese and – in theory – monopolized by them and the Spanish:
the slave trade. In 1562 he set out on his first voyage, calling first at
Teneriffe to pick up a Spanish pilot, then moving down to Sierra
Leone where, by a mixture of purchase and kidnapping, he acquired
some 300 Africans. He set sail for Hispaniola, modern Haiti, where
he sold the slaves and used the money to buy hides and sugar which
he was to sell in Britain – what was to become the classic triangular
trade of the slaver. His second trip was semi-official. The venture
was backed by the Queen. Hawkins sailed in the royal ship *Jesus of
Lubeck* and flew the royal standard. This was a blatant flaunting of
Spanish and Portuguese laws which banned foreign vessels from shar-
ing in their vilely lucrative trade. Hawkins was to pitch his luck too
far. On his third trip, with his cousin, Francis Drake, he was forced
by bad weather to take cover in Vera Cruz, at precisely the moment
that the official Spanish convoy arrived several weeks before it was
expected. In the ensuing battle, three of the English ships were lost
and Drake and Hawkins were lucky to limp home. Hawkins was
then an implacable opponent of Spain, and he was able to plan
for both personal and official revenge. In 1577 he was appointed

Treasurer of the Navy and set about a much needed programme of improvement – building faster, better armed ships which were to prove their worth against the Armada in 1588. The following year he became Comptroller of the Navy. It was he more than anyone who helped establish Chatham as a major naval dockyard. He was also a man who showed deep concern for the ordinary seaman: he built almshouses at Chatham and established a special fund, the Chatham Chest for disabled seamen. He died in 1595 on his last expedition to the West Indies. He was an extraordinary man – great seaman, brilliant administrator, ruthless slaver and benevolent patron of his men. Yet it was out of just such a bizarre mixture of piracy, honest trade and official duties that the navy was changed and the dockyards which were to build its ships were born.

The first of the naval dockyards began its days of glory in the early sixteenth century even though its history stretched back a good deal further. In 1212, orders went out from King John to the Sheriff of Southampton to 'construct a good and strong wall round our dock at Portsmouth without delay so that when winter comes, we may avoid damage to our vessels and their appurtenances'.[11] Storehouses were built around the new wet dock, but it was not until 1495 that a dry dock was built. It was excavated, lined with wood and, when a vessel entered, the entrance was plugged with clay and the water pumped out. Although there are few written records of shipbuilding at Portsmouth at this time there is at least some physical evidence that can suggest what went on, and the most impressive single piece of evidence is the salvaged hull of the *Mary Rose*, raised from the Solent in 1982.

The *Mary Rose* was built between 1509 and 1510, one of the first warships to take advantage of the newly developed idea of gun ports to mount no fewer than eighty weapons. These were classified under such alarming names as 'murderers' and 'grete murderers'. She was one of the first vessels to be built to fire broadsides, and set a pattern that was to be followed for another three centuries. More importantly, as far as the history of shipbuilding is concerned, enough of the hull survived to give a good idea of how the vessel was built. As in other early warships, oak predominated – an estimated thirty-six acres of woodland would have been felled to provide the timber. The keel, however, was made up of two pieces of elm, scarfed together to create a length of 105 ft (32m.). Then stem and stern posts were added, together with keelson and floor timbers, the latter fastened with iron bolts. After that the ribs of the hull were built up, creating the basic form and shape of the ship. This required something more than just the traditional 'good eye' of the master builder. Each rib would have to have been built to just the right size and in just the right shape, and it is impossible to see how this could have been done without first drawing up plans and then constructing templates from these plans. As the ship grew, so it would have been propped up in position by a framework of timber. Once the planking was added to the frame, further strength was provided by riders and braces bolted to the hull. It is unfortunate that those who go to see *Mary Rose* at Portsmouth today cannot make a direct comparison with her famous neighbour, *HMS Victory*, for visitors do not usually get a chance to visit the very bottom of the ship where the construction methods are revealed. Those who are lucky enough to be taken down will be struck by the similarities: the same basic method of construction – the scarfed joints, the treenails and iron bolts, the frame defining the shape. A closer inspection will reveal other similarities. The surface of the curved futtocks shows the characteristic marks of the adze, that quintessential tool of the shipwright, used for shaping timbers. She is notably larger – the keel is 186 ft (56.7m.), nearly twice as long as the *Mary Rose* – but otherwise construction techniques seem scarcely to have changed. One important difference is certainly not shown: the *Victory* was built not at Portsmouth but at Chatham.

In 1547, it was decided that Portsmouth was too far from London and the fleet was moved to the Medway. The fleet was anchored at 'Jillyingham Water' and storehouses were set up at what was then the hamlet of Chatham. At first it was no more than a victualling station, but soon repair facilities were added, starting with a mast pond where up to seventy-seven masts could be kept, to be followed in 1581 by a dry dock. Some idea of the relative importance of the naval dockyards can be gained from the wage bills for 1584.

Chatham	£3,680
Deptford	£205
Portsmouth	£30
Woolwich	£18

It is at this time that shipbuilding begins to take on a more human aspect. In 1572, Matthew Baker, son of Henry VIII's ship designer James Baker, was appointed Master Shipwright. Some of his ship drawings and drafts are preserved in the Pepys Museum in Cambridge – and were referred to by Pepys as 'Fragments of Ancient Shipwrighting'. One of his detailed drawings of a ship's hull shows a fish superimposed on the section below the water line. The shape is what came to be known as 'cod's head, mackerel tail', with blunt bows and a sharp narrowing in at the stern. Whether Baker was consciously studying the shape and form of the sea's natural residents, or whether this was a conceit to suggest that his vessels could move as smoothly as any fish, is something we shall probably never know. We do know a great deal about his working methods and his contribution to the craft of the shipwright. It was Baker who introduced the idea of measuring a ship's size by recording its tonnage. He measured the number of tunns or casks of Bordeaux wine that could fit into the hold. It is unfortunate that the tunn, a measure of volume, sounds so similar to ton – a measure of weight – even though the two are connected. But 'tonnage' is not a standard measure. Naval vessels, for example, are measured by displaced tonnage, which is the weight of water displaced by the ship – which is the same as the weight of the ship itself. A merchant ship can be measured empty or full of cargo and the difference between the two, the weight of cargo, is the measure usually referred to, the deadweight tonnage. So a warship of say 10,000 tons (10,160 tonne) will not be the same size as a merchantman of 10,000 tons – and to add to the complication modern measures use the metric ton, the tonne. But, if Baker's innovation was not to lead to any universal standards of measurement, it was at least a start in indicating the size of a ship. Of more lasting importance was his method of laying out a ship's lines on paper. He set out cross sections at various points along the length of the ship, based on a variety of curves, but all based on segments of a circle. These were drawn in by apprentices using compasses, not the small folding instruments of the school geometry set, but vast implements often taller than the apprentices who wielded them. These drawings could be used to construct templates for shaping the ships' timbers. A study of the drawings shows him designing vessels 100 ft (30m.) long, around 500 tons (508 tonne) burden. Baker, the master shipwright, was the technical ruler of the shipyard.

The master shipwright was more than just the designer. Once his drawings were complete, light battens were made to correspond to the shape and these were taken off to the forest so that suitable 'compass timber' could be selected. He oversaw the work on a ship and took the all-important decision as to whether the finished hull was ready for sea. It was not unknown for him to call for extra timber for added strength or even demand virtually a complete rebuild. His rule stretched beyond the shipbuilders to encompass the design of dry docks, wet docks and stores. Baker was immensely influential, and one of his most famous successors, Phineas Pett, wrote to him in 1603:[12] 'although I served no years in your service yet I must ever acknowledge what ever I have of any art (if I have any) it came only from you ... whose ever memorable work I set before me as a notable precedent and pattern to direct me'.

Yet the pay of master shipwrights remained low. As late as 1695 the pay of the men in charge of the three major dockyards – Chatham, Woolwich and Portsmouth – was only £200 a year, supplemented by premiums paid for taking apprentices. The opportunities for adding to that income by other means were however very large, as was amply demonstrated by the next in a line of famous shipwrights, Phineas Pett.

Pett was born at Deptford in 1570, where his father was master shipwright. It seemed that he was intended for 'better things' and took his MA degree at Cambridge. This did not, however, lead to any obvious career: he was a young man with fine qualifications, but no trade. He set out, after all, to follow his father, but needed practical experience. He took an apprenticeship with Richard

Chipman, but when no shipyard work appeared he signed on as ship's carpenter on a privateer. As a result he at least gained two years' experience of a ship at sea, under the most severe conditions. He did not, however, gain much in the way of wealth: on his return to Britain his brother had to lend him cash for clothes. He decided that if hard work was not going to lead him to the top, he might ascend with the help of a noble patron. His family connections brought him into contact with the navy hierarchy and he assiduously courted the favours of Lord Howard, the Lord High Admiral. In 1607 he aimed higher still.[13]

> I began a curious model for the Prince my master, most part whereof I wrought with my own hands; which being most fairly garnished with carving and painting, and placed in a frame, arched, covered, and curtained with crimson taffety, was, the 10th day of November, by me presented to the Lord High Admiral.

Howard showed the model to the king, and the king at once proposed that Pett should build the ship itself. Unfortunately, Pett had no previous experience of building a ship of this size; he had leapt over competent shipwrights by patronage not ability. When the ship was ready, it was universally condemned. The lines were bad, the timber poor. It was, declared the assembled shipwrights, 'altogether imperfect'. Pett, not for the last time in his career, survived the accusations. More serious charges followed. He was accused of taking bribes, a custom so widespread as to have hardly merited a comment, but he went even further and, whatever one might think of his morality, one has to admire his brazen audacity.

In 1608, he was said to have used timber discarded as too rotten for the navy, to build a 160-ton (162.5-tonne) ship of his own. Masts and rigging were 'borrowed' and as if that were not enough she was sailed away from Chatham with a hold full of naval items. He received a reprimand from the king and went back to work. He was soon back to his old ways, and an official enquiry of 1618 found him guilty of inefficiency and overcharging. Whether the enquiry was generally thought to be guilty of malice and envy, whether Pett's patrons were too powerful or whether Pett himself was simply too good a man to lose, the damaging criticism had no effect on his career. In 1619 he was put in charge of building a new dockyard at Chatham, which was to include a dry dock capable of building the biggest warship of the day. Chatham was now firmly established as a major shipbuilding centre. Pett proudly noted that the king 'privately acquainted me with his princely resolution for the building of a great new ship, that he would have me to undertake'. This was the *Sovereign of the Seas*, hugely expensive and very ornate – her figurehead showed King Edward on horseback trampling over seven defeated kings. Although Phineas Pett designed her, it was his son Peter who was to oversee construction. She was launched in 1637 and twice rebuilt, in 1659 and 1680, before she went up in flames in 1696, not as a result of enemy action but of a fire in the galley.

In 1647 Peter had taken over control of the dockyard, but when the Dutch swept up the Medway and destroyed a large part of the fleet in 1667, he was held personally responsible and was turned out of office. The long reign of the Petts had ended. Given the substantial evidence of corruption, it is amazing that it lasted so long. Patronage alone was not the answer. In spite of their shortcomings, they designed and built some splendid ships. Shipbuilding was a mystery in the medieval sense of the word – it was a craft without precise rules, and such rules as there were were closely guarded. A master shipwright laid out his plans, and no one could be sure how the actual vessel that was built from them would perform – except, everyone fervently hoped, the master shipwright. It was certainly in the interest of the master shipwright to maintain the mystique, to build up the notion that he, and he alone, was in possession of important secrets. This was an element built into apprenticeship agreements. When young Alexander Stephen, who was to go on to found his own very successful business, signed up as an apprentice in 1787, the agreement contained this clause.[14]

> I do hereby oblige my self to pay you the fee of three pound sterling money for teaching me the art of ship drafting as you produce it yourself, the one half when entered to said drafting and the other

when I can lay down a draft by my self. I also bind my self to teach no other person the same under the fine of ten pound sterling money.

Many were sceptical about the nature of this specialist knowledge. As late as 1852, the *Nautical Mirror* wrote of wooden shipbuilding in these terms.[15]

Science has comparatively little to do with the matter. A few general principles, no doubt, gave a basis, but the superstructure was greatly an affair of guess-work and eye-work. Frames were laid down from 5 to 10 feet apart, near the centre of the vessel. Others were then placed at a distance of 20 feet or so, from the bow and stem; and all the rest of the work was done at the arbitrary pleasure of the builder, by his individual caprice or conjecture.

By 1852, it might have seemed obvious that there was something lacking in the old methods, but that was certainly not clear two centuries earlier. The first-rate master shipwright continued to be a figure who was held in awe, and who could be forgiven almost anything. Standards of honesty only improved when a new man was appointed as Clerk to the Navy Board in 1658 – the man who was largely responsible for Peter Pett's dismissal, Samuel Pepys.

Pepys was concerned to stamp out dishonesty, and had to abolish the time-honoured practice by which important posts went to those who were prepared to pay the most for them. He encouraged true talent but had to contend with the incompetence of many who held high office. At times he was able to encourage the best and was rewarded with success: even if the old sense of mystery still remained.[16]

Mr. Deane and I did discourse about his ship Rupert, built by him there, which succeeds so well as he hath got great honour by it, and I some by recommending him; the King, Duke, and every body, saying it is the best ship that was ever built. And then he fell to explain to me his manner of casting the draught of water

[39]

which a ship will draw beforehand: which is a secret the King and all admire in him; and he is the first that hath come to any certainty beforehand of foretelling the draught of water of a ship before she be launched.

Sir Anthony Deane was appointed master shipwright at Harwich, and was one of a new breed of shipwright, prepared to look to theory as well as rely on practices handed down over generations. Pepys persuaded him to set out his theories.[17]

At noon home to dinner and Captain Deane with us; and very good discourse, and particularly about my getting a book for him to draw up his whole theory of shipping; which at my desire he hath gone far in, and hath shown me what he hath done therein to admiration.

The book, *Doctrine of Naval Architecture*, duly appeared in 1670. But Pepys was still faced by the ignorance of the Board.[18]

To the Council-chamber, where the Committee of the Navy sat; and here we discoursed several things, but, Lord! like fools, so as it was a shame to see things of this importance managed by a Council that understand nothing of them.

All the time, the royal dockyards were growing both in size and complexity. When Daniel Defoe began his travels round England in 1722 he visited Chatham, still 'the chief arsenal of the royal navy'.[19] He was overwhelmed by the scale of the enterprise.

The buildings here are indeed like the ships themselves, surprisingly large, and in their several kinds beautiful: The ware-houses, or rather streets of ware-houses, and store-houses for laying up the naval treasure are the largest in dimension, and the most in number, that are any where to be seen in the world: The rope-walk for making cables, and the forges for anchors and other iron-work, bear a proportion to the rest; as also the wet-dock for keeping masts, and yards of the greatest size, where they lye sunk in the water to preserve them, the boat-yard, the anchor yard; all like the whole, monstrously great and extensive.

He went on to list the stores collected for ships under construction, and then went on to list all the other items kept at the yard, ready for use.

for this purpose there are separate and respective magazines of pitch, tarr, hemp, flax, tow, rosin, oyl, tallow; also of sail cloth, canvas, anchors, cables, standing and running rigging, ready fitted, and cordage not fitted; with all kinds of ship-chandlery necessaries and gunners stores, and also anchors of all sizes, grapnells, chains, bolts, and spikes, wrought and unwrought iron, cast-iron work, such as potts, caldrons, furnaces, &c. also boats, spare-masts and yards; with a great quantity of lead and nails, and other necessaries (too many to be enumerated) whose store looks as if it were inexhaustible.

To observe these things deliberately, one wou'd almost wonder what ships they were, and where they should be found, which cou'd either for building, or repairing, fiting, or refiting, call for such a quantity of all those things; but when, on the other hand, one sees the ships, and considers their dimension, and consequently the dimension of all things which belong to them; how large, how strong every thing must be; how much of the materials must go to the making every thing proportionable to the occasion, the wonder would change its prospect, and one would be as much amaz'd to think how and where they should be supply'd.

He went on to visit Portsmouth which was then growing again in importance, and the area around the shipyards was developing into a separate town. Continuing west, he found much the same was true of the rapidly expanding facilities at Plymouth. The scale was changing, but the working methods were still those of the previous century. Yet already in Britain, change was underway. The Industrial Revolution was about to turn many old crafts into industries. In the

[41]

conservative world of shipbuilding, the sense of continuity was to be stronger than any great sense of change; but there were to be differences – differences not just in the work itself but in the attitude towards it.

❖

TRADE, INDUSTRY AND SCIENCE

A LMOST all forms of manufacturing changed in the course of the eighteenth century. In textiles, where for centuries women had spun at the cottage door while the men worked at the loom, the new age saw the establishment of the mills, powered first by water, then by steam. The forges and foundries used improved methods to deliver iron in almost unlimited quantities. Inevitably some of the new technological advances had their effect on shipbuilding. The manufacture of the miles of rope needed for sailing ships had much of the character of the old woollen trade. Here the job of aligning the fibres, hackling, went mostly to the women, while the men and boys did the work of turning the fibres into rope and cord.

Bridport was one of the great centres of rope making, largely because the surrounding countryside was ideal for growing hemp. In the first process the fibres were greased with oil, then pulled through a series of steel pins stuck to the hackling board. After that the 'streak', as the bundle of fibres was called, went for turning into yarn. The spinner carried the streak round his waist. He twisted the fibres together and attached them to four hooks set on the spinning wheel. He then walked slowly backwards feeding out the flex while a young boy turned the wheel at a steady rate. At the end of the walk, the rope was removed from the spinning wheel and attached to a reel. Now the walker returned, keeping the rope taut as it was reeled in. A spinner might walk many miles in the course of a day. The yarn then had to be laid in strands to create rope. Here a machine was used to pull out and twist the rope, in a process not dissimilar to the previous one, except that here it was the board with the hooks that was moved along the length of a long building, the rope walk.

The ropewalks are among the most striking features of the naval dockyards. The Great Ropery at Portsmouth, for example, built in 1770, is 1,095 feet (334m.) long. Just as the cotton and woollen mills were taking work from the domestic workers, so too the families of Bridport saw their trade vanishing to the new, efficient dockyard roperies. It was industrialization, not so drastic as that seen elsewhere, but industrialization none the less. In other industries, mechanization came hand in hand with standardization, but in the shipyards each ship was a one-off. So, even in the machine age, a dockyard depended mainly on manpower. What was new was the scale at which that manpower was employed. In 1774, Portsmouth, which had been so long in decline, boasted a work force of 2,883 men. The largest single group, and half the total, were shipwrights, but there were also sawyers, spinners, smiths, carpenters, caulkers, scavelmen who worked the dry docks, riggers, joiners, bricklayers, sailmakers and more. It is doubtful if any other enterprise but a naval dockyard could have mustered such a force of workers. Could some of the work be turned over to machines? It was happening everywhere else, so why not here as well? The problem remained that shipbuilding was still seen as a craft or even an art form, not as an industrial process. Few shipwrights had any concern with theory; they worked on the basis of practical experience. But there were attempts to apply science to questions that now would seem obvious candidates for scientific theory – for example, what is the most efficient hull shape for a particular type of ship?

In the eighteenth century two scientists, an Englishman, Sir Isaac Newton, and a Dutchman, Christian Huygens, had formulated the law which said that the resistance to a body travelling through water increases as the square of the velocity – in other words if you double the speed, you quadruple the resistance. The interesting point here is that Huygens reached his results by towing objects through a tank full of water, which remains the standard method of testing hull design. But it was not until 1746 that a Frenchman, Pierre Bongeur, thought of using tank tests in this way, and the idea only reached Britain in 1758. The Society of Arts put up a premium of £100 to anyone who could produce a hull design 'that would soonest pass through a given space of water driven by a given weight'. The applicants were required to supply plans and quarter-scale models.[1] The Society of Arts were nothing if not ambitious. The models were to be tested to see how they performed in calm water and in rough; speed was to be tested as well as ability to sail close to the wind. To ensure that no factor other than hull design was being measured, each of the models was fitted out with one of two standard sail arrangements: a two masted schooner rig for the models of 74-gun ships and a sloop rig for the smaller frigates. Various types of test were devised, including an ingenious water-tunnel, the marine equivalent of a wind tunnel. The main tests, however, involved towing by engines, using falling weights to provide control power. There were trials in smooth water at Peerless Pond in London to test speed of the different designs using what was then something of a novelty – a stop watch. The sheltered pond was not suitable for rough water trials, so the teams took the models out to the Great Pond in Epping Forest. The tests were not a great success, and it is not difficult to see why. The models used were basically little different from what one would expect, in that they were made by amateurs who simply followed normal practice. There was no theory involved and professional shipbuilders would be most unlikely to enter such a competition when the prize was £100, but with no guarantee that any vessel would ever be built on the basis of the models. Indeed the Society left it to the winners to find their own way to the Admiralty doors. It was a serious attempt to use scientific methods to evaluate ship design, but it came from outside the ranks of the professionals and could be – and was – dismissed as irrelevant by the practical men in the yards. There was to be another attempt in 1791 to bring the techniques of science to bear when a Society for the Improvement of Naval Architecture was set up. It had no more success than the Society of Arts and ten years later the society was no more. So the eighteenth century ended with British shipbuilding scarcely advanced from the position it had held for many hundreds of years.

What was true of the British was not true of everyone. The French in particular took science seriously, and published a number of learned papers and books on naval architecture. Early in the nineteenth century Abraham Rees set out to produce his *Cyclopaedia* which in a series of articles commissioned by leading men of the day was to summarize the current state of craft and industry.[2] The section on shipbuilding begins

> Ship-building, or *Naval Architecture*, is the art of constructing and raising, or building that noble fabric called a ship.
>
> This science, or whatever relates to navigation, is, without doubt, one of the most important and most useful employments of the human mind; especially in a country whose marine is its bulwark, and its commerce the admiration, and, we may add, the envy of the world.
>
> Nevertheless, the scientific part of ship-building has been too much neglected; and although some few years have elapsed since mathematicians (particularly in France) have laboured with some success, yet their discoveries are so much enveloped in profound calculations, that shipbuilders, in general, have scarcely been able to derive any advantage from them.

Nevertheless, the author attempts to set out the latest thinking in the subject and begins with an explanation of what had by then become the standard way of presenting the design of a ship in drawings. There are three basic plans, representing slices through the vessel in three planes. One, the sheer plan, shows vertical sections running from stem to stern – as the ship is symmetrical it is only necessary to show one half. The body plan represents vertical planes at right angles to the sheer plan, so that it shows the shape of the frames. Conventionally, the left-hand side of the diagram shows sections from midship to bows, the right-hand side, midship to stern. The third drawing represents horizontal sections through the ship. Between them these three plans completely define the shape of the hull. In a shipyard they would be taken to the moulding loft, where they would be drawn out on the floor, so that templates could be constructed. Then the templates could be used to shape the main timbers. At first glance, the rest of the account with its formulae and mathematical equations suggests that what follows is a scientific treatise. Closer inspection shows that it is nothing of the sort — the various formulae are simply methods of calculation. What is lacking is any scientific basis. In effect, it tells a shipwright, once you have decided the shape you wish the hull to be, this will show you how to set your ideas down on paper. There is no hint as to how to decide on the shape in the first place, except in the most general way. At the time of writing there was some controversy as to whether a higher length to breadth ratio might not improve sailing characteristics. Here is the author's view.

Those who would diminish the breadth have alleged, and truly, that a narrow vessel meets with less resistance in passing through the water, and by increasing in length, the vessel will drive less to leeward, and the water-lines consequently be more delicately formed to divide the fluid; that a long narrow ship will require less sail to gain velocity, consequently the masts will be lower, the rigging lighter, and the vessel navigated by fewer hands. On the contrary, a ship's being broader at the line of floatation will admit of being narrower on the floor, particularly at the fore and after parts; that by being broader it can carry more sail, and more readily rise upon the waves than a narrow one.

All this may or may not be true, but it is no more than a bald assertion with no attempt to back it with facts, figures or experiments. There was an effort at this time to put shipbuilding on to a more scientific basis. The Admiralty established a school of naval architecture at Portsmouth in 1811, but the establishment took little interest in its graduates. It was only in mid century when it became clear that French warships had become in every way superior to their British counterparts that some began to believe that perhaps the French did have something to teach after all.

[47]

If the navy was slow to change, commercial yards were not necessarily much more forward looking, though they seem to have been readier to try new ideas. The Scott family began in a modest way constructing herring busses and other small craft at Greenock in 1711.[3] They continued a long period of slow development until, at the end of the eighteenth century, they began building vessels for trade with the West Indies and America, then later with India. This brought them into direct competition with American shipbuilders who, whatever the writer of Rees's *Cyclopaedia* might say, were proving that their long, lean clipper ships were the fastest vessels afloat. Scotts followed this lead: they built clippers of a five or six to one length to beam rate as against the four to one of the East Indiaman. And in the 1840s they were testing hull shapes using models in one of the graving docks. Handling characteristics were also tested using models, but this time on Loch Thom in the hills above Greenock, where conditions for a model were in scale for those experienced by a ship at sea. Scotts were a lively innovative company. They were, for example, the first on the Clyde to send a ship along the slipway already fully rigged. This may not sound such a great advance, but launches were nerve-racking times at the shipyard. In a description of the Southwick yard on the Wear, there are accounts of some quite hair-raising launches. On one occasion, two ships were launched simultaneously, one to each side of the slipway. The friction was so great that teams of men had to run behind the sliding vessels hurling buckets of water as the wooden rails caught fire. On another occasion the restraining ropes broke and the vessel shot across the river, its bowsprit going straight through the window of a house on the opposite bank and out of the wall on the other side. So to launch a fully rigged ship was a very real gesture of confidence.

Inevitably, new technologies found their way into the shipyards. The availability of iron in vast quantities made a difference to the way in which ships were built. Indeed, given the steady and alarming depletion of the old oak forests, iron arrived only just in time. It was not so much that there was a general shortage of timber: wood was available in seemingly unlimited quantities from northern Europe and America. There was, however, a real shortage of good compass timber. *Victory*, for example, had 438 knees of oak, and it was no great feat of imagination to see that these could be replaced by iron with a huge saving of timber. In many early ships, going back indeed as far as the *Mary Rose*, the hull was strengthened by diagonal braces. These too could be replaced by iron. By the end of the Napoleonic Wars, such changes were regularly being made, and can still be seen in the frigate *Unicorn*, started just as the wars were coming to an end. The ship was 'mothballed' and the hull remains just as it was when built, providing a beautiful example of the composite ship, using a combination of timber and iron in the hull.

The man who introduced the system of iron bracing was Robert Seppings who began his working life as an apprentice at Plymouth Dockyard and rose to become Surveyor of the Navy in 1813. In later life he was honoured with a knighthood and a Fellowship of the Royal Society. At first, the replacement of wooden braces by iron might seem a minor affair, but it enabled hull lengths to be increased from around 200 to 300 ft (61m. to 91m.), and as a longer waterline length also means increased speed, the efficiency as well as the size of the ship was transformed. But that, as far as the navy was concerned, marked the end of innovation in hull design until the second half of the nineteenth century.

No one would describe the naval yards as centres of innovation, yet there was one quite remarkable exception. At Portsmouth a system was introduced that looked forward to the industrial processes of the twentieth century. The navy brought in mass production. The system came about because two men were in the right place at the right time. In 1796, Samuel Bentham was appointed Inspector-General for the naval dockyards. He came from a wealthy background, served a full apprenticeship as a shipwright and travelled widely in Europe to see what others were doing. He was responsible for many improvements, including a better system of closing off dry docks, but as well as being an innovator in his own right, he was quick to see the value of ideas put to him by others, even if they were strangers to the closed world of the yards.

[49]

An essential feature of the Industrial Revolution was the replacement by machines of repetitive tasks carried out by hand. Every sailing ship carried a vast array of blocks. They might be small or large, used singly or in combination, but their fundamental shape and method of construction scarcely varied. The block was the ideal object for making by machine rather than hand. The inventor of block-making machinery was an engineer, the famous father of an even more famous son, Marc Brunel. It was Brunel who made the first approach, and Bentham was an instant enthusiast. Between 1802 and 1806, forty-five different machines were introduced to the dockyard at Portsmouth, and when they were all at work ten men could turn out 140,000 blocks a year, where 100 men had worked before.[4] The machines themselves were made by another great engineer, one of the pioneers of machine-tool manufacture, Henry Maudsley. The story of the block-making machines was one of success and failure. That the machines worked is beyond dispute. That the three men most closely involved were among the great innovators in that most exciting time in engineering history is equally indisputable. The failure was not theirs. It was the failure of the vast and weighty Admiralty bureaucracy. Change was quite simply not wanted. Bentham was sent off to St Petersburg for two years in 1805, and when he returned he found his old job had gone to that last refuge of a conservative administration – a committee. He was a member, but a single voice in favour of progress and development. His views of the Admiralty bureaucrats are not recorded, but Marc Brunel's son, Isambard Kingdom, made his known with typical forthrightness. He had sent an idea for a new gunboat to General Sir John Fox Burgoyne at the start of the Crimean War. To Brunel's extreme annoyance the plans were forwarded to the Admiralty.[5]

You assume that something has been done or is doing in the matter which I spoke to you about last month – did you not know that it had been brought within the withering influence of the Admiralty and that (of course) therefore, the curtain had dropped upon it and nothing had resulted? It would exercise the intellects of our acutest philosophers to investigate and discover what is the powerful agent which acts upon all matters brought within the range of the mere atmosphere of that department. They have an extraordinary supply of cold water and capacious and heavy extinguishers, but I was prepared for and proof against such coarse offensive measures. But they have an unlimited supply of *some negative* principle which seems to absorb and eliminate everything that approaches them.

It was, sadly, all too true. The Admiralty and innovation were strangers. But the sheer scale of their operations and the growing strength of the commercial yards meant that those who worked there saw themselves as under threat. For centuries the shipwrights had regarded themselves as an élite, craftsmen in a long and noble tradition. Increasingly they were being classed as industrial workers, units in the productive process. It was not a change that they relished. It was not simply a matter of jobs – though the hundred blockmakers who found themselves unemployed when Brunel and Bentham brought the new machines into Portsmouth could hardly have been very happy. Just as important was the question of status. They were not hired off the street and put to work. They had served a long and arduous apprenticeship. They had earned their privileges, however petty and small those privileges might be. In the changing attitudes between employers, whether civil or military, there was now seemingly unlimited scope for disagreement. Take one very simple case, the men's allowance of 'chips'. Inevitably, in the course of cutting and hacking up timber, a great deal would be left over that was useless for construction, but which would blaze cheerfully in the hearths of the dockyard workers. These were the chips that the men were allowed to take home with them, but inevitably perhaps the authorities complained that the privilege was being abused.[6]

Let the reader fancy . . . 2000 men leaving off work at ½ past 11 o'clock, to make up their bundle of chips. Nor were the chips made in the fair processes of their labour, sufficient to satisfy them; they actually employed themselves in cutting up good and serviceable spars, even under the eye of their officers. But that was not all – these precious bundles contained copper bolts and other valuable articles concealed in them. It is true that these bundles went through a sort of professional examination at the dockyard gate, where a subordinate officer had an iron rod in his hand, with which he occasionally pierced a package here and there; to perform the operation on all would (allowing one minute on each) have occupied upwards of thirty-three hours.

Compared with the wholesale removal of official stores by men such as Phineas Pett in an earlier age, this was quite small scale, but was punishable by at best the lash and at worst transportation. To the poorly paid dock worker, a little small-scale larceny was a compensation for poor pay: to the dockyard manager, a lot of small thefts added together made a large hole in the stores. It was the same with other misdemeanours, which the men regarded as unimportant but which carried heavy penalties. There were complaints of drunkenness at Portsmouth as early as 1689.[7]

Whereas it has become too common a practice in this Yard for the workmen of all sorts to keep Ill companies in the tapp house drinking and Tippling to the loss of their time and great disservice to their majesty and that ye tapp house is appointed and ordained for to give a pinte of drinke to a man at a time when a dry and that but midling not strong beere which they daily sell here in the tapp house, it being a common practice for ye men to be drunk with it.

In fact, the naval dockyards generally had some sort of beer house within the walls – working hours were long, and breaks short. They were set up by the porters as a very useful additional income. It was a commonplace for working men to be given a beer ration to help them through the long working days – some trades, such as those of the foundry workers, were notorious for the vast ale consumption of the hot, weary furnacemen. Even in the dockyards there were official allowances of beer. This seems odd today, but one has to remember that whatever the ill effects of a pint or two of beer might be, the effects of drinking the local water were likely to be a good deal worse. The trouble was that instead of dishing out small beer to the thirsty men the porters were 'dosing them and making them unfit for labour to their Majesties great disservice as well as the poor men's waste of their wages'.[8]

Ale was also handed out in the commercial yards. William Stephen of Greenock frequently sent a cask along to the men, and on one occasion when the men were working in particularly bad conditions, he took along a bottle of whisky and a bucket of water and mixed the drams himself. Remarkably, he combined this largesse with regular religious meetings. He would arrive at dinner time and deliver a sermon, and if the bell went for work to resume he would say, 'Na, na, lads, you're in my time now – stay where you are'. Apprentices studied the scriptures hard, mainly it was said to locate difficult questions for extending the break time.[9] Stephen was a notably honest employer and straight with the men. There was none of the hypocrisy which one finds in Admiralty pronouncements. The concerns of their Lordships for the waste of men's wages sits uneasily with their own methods of payments which forced families into debt, with the ale house often the only source of funds.

Rates of pay for the dockyards were set in 1650 and remained unchanged until 1788. They ranged from 6d. a day for the oakum boys to 2s. 1d. for caulkers and shipwrights and a top rate of 2s. 4d. for plumbers. This covered a working day of six in the morning to six at night in winter, with an hour off at midday, and sunrise to sunset in summer, with half an hour for breakfast and an hour and a half for dinner. Overtime was paid either for 'tides' of half-hour periods or 'nights' periods of five hours. It was a system that had no provision for checks and was open to abuse. In Plymouth, a clerk claimed for 94 nights and 151 tides in one quarter. Even the Admiralty was not prepared to accept that, since as the official report pointed out ''tis impossible for him to attend so much extra time for that he could not have had above 2 hours in 24 to eat and sleep'.[10] It was not low wages and long hours that brought about abuse; they were common enough in eighteenth-century industry. It was the method of payment. Men received pay quarterly in arrears, and new men starting in the yard had a quarter's pay kept in hand, so that they worked for six months without any payment at all. With such a start, it was almost impossible to break out of debt, and the dockyard workers were prey to loan sharks and local inn keepers. There was a great deal of petitioning before the Navy Board agreed to set up a 'Subsistence Allowance' – official, interest-free loans, which were deducted from the quarterly pay. It was still far from satisfactory, but it was not until 1814 that weekly wages were introduced.

The pay system was never entirely uniform. In place of fixed rates, men were often put on 'task and job', a form of piece work, where 'task' was work on new ships and 'job' repairs to old. It was almost as unpopular as the quarterly payments since the rates were seldom fully explained and seemed to the men to be completely arbitrary. In 1780 new Task rates were introduced, which were thinly disguised drops in pay – too thinly disguised, for the men saw straight through them. Spontaneous riots broke out in the yard and spread beyond the dockyards to Plymouth itself. After thirteen weeks the authorities capitulated, but the system remained, no more popular then than it had been before. In 1801, there was a severe food shortage and with it a rise in food prices. At the same time, the yards stopped overtime and tried to introduce ever more rigorous Task and Job rates. The result was inevitable and there was a rough justice in the response. At Devonport, the men broke open the Admiralty stores and sold off the victuals at cheap prices to the townspeople of Plymouth. Again the disturbances went on for weeks, and the unfortunate Town Commissioner who was given the job of reading the Riot Act was pelted by the locals and driven off before he could utter a word. Once again authority had to give in and agree to pay a special allowance to tide people over the hard times.

This story is by no means untypical of industrial life in the eighteenth century. In the absence of any organized labour groups, people put up with bad conditions, often eking out low payments with a little pilfering. Then, when the situation became wholly intolerable, there were no paths open for discussion and arbitration, so they turned to the only route left open. They rioted. It was a method of getting grievances settled that was almost as unsatisfactory for the abusers as it was for the abused. There were organizations of skilled workers, but they were looking back to the old craftsmen's guilds rather than forward to the trade unions that were to grow in numbers and strength through the nineteenth century.

Commercial yards did not operate in the same way. In the early years on the Thames, for example, shipbuilders worked on the 'gang system'.[11] The owners supplied all the material for the ship, together with heavy equipment such as cranes. The men owned their own tools and formed gangs of twenty to thirty who elected a 'leading hand' who acted as the spokesman and negotiated a fixed price for the job. Unlike the Royal Dockyards, the Thames yards paid a fixed daily rate at regular intervals. If the work finished ahead of time, then the remainder of the cash due under the contract was shared out. If, however, it took longer than expected and all money due on the fixed price was paid, then the men had to work on for nothing. In practice, owners and men had a pretty clear idea of how long a job should last, so that negotiations were in effect over what the daily rate should be. There were, as the masters saw it, a number of advantages to the system. Before they started work, they knew the price of materials and the price of labour, to which they would add their own profit and give the resulting estimate to the shipowner. It was neat and tidy, but it was a system which offered no great incentive for cost-cutting and efficiency, as long as competition was not too fierce. Everyone could get along together quite cosily. It worked well enough, when jobs were modest and yards small, but as ships and businesses grew, it became unworkable. Like their counterparts in the naval yards, the Thames shipbuilders had to look for new ways to secure pay and conditions.

The earliest groupings of workers were self-help societies, often set up with lofty principles. In part this was to keep them within the law, and clear of prosecution under the Combination Acts. In the preamble to the rules for the Shipwrights Union Society established in South Shields in 1734, the members

taking it into our serious consideration that man is formed a social being, and that the Sovereign Ruler of the World has been pleased

[55]

to place us in life dependent on each other, and in continual need of mutual assistance and support, Do severally agree to bind ourselves into a Friendly and Benevolent Association.[12]

By 1824, another union had been formed, the Shipwrights Provident Union of the River Thames. The preamble begins with an altogether sourer note.[13]

Destitute of that sympathy of feeling which ought to subsist between brother workmen, every man following the impulse of his own mind; all his actions regulated on no other principle than self; hypocrisy and deception making rapid inroads on the little integrity that was left. Men acting under those influences, was kept aloof from each other; all was Confusion and disorder; masters and men were in constant contention, in consequence of the invasion of what was considered the rights of each other.

It then continues by taking a very different view from that of the eighteenth-century society, a view which for all its wrapping-up in phrases of mutual help, peace and goodwill is actually setting out something new: the rights of the men to have a voice in their own affairs.

The operative shipwrights anticipate a cordial co-operation of the master shipwrights of the River Thames in the furtherance of their views of reciprocal interest, as it is their intention in future, not to be made the cat's paw of any one, but that the fitting and repairing of ships shall be done in proper places and by proper persons, such as have premises, and have followed the profession of a shipwright seven years, and to prevent any future inroads on that harmony, which is so conducive to a good understanding between masters and men, a regular system of prices will be formed, by which a uniform mode of proceeding will be adopted in every yard. Masters will, from these measures, be able to calculate, with precision, the several estimates of jobs they may be called upon to give in.

Should our society flourish, and become united from such a

heterogeneous mass of discord, confusion, hypocrisy, and self-interest, we may become the greatest, the most prosperous, the happiest, and the most valuable part of the British Empire.

There are two quite distinct elements to the proclamation. One is the insistence on proper qualifications for the job – a full seven-year apprenticeship with everything that entailed.

To an extent, the owners were happy with the system. Even owners expected their sons to serve their time. Alexander Stephen signed up with his father in 1809 for seven years, promising

> not to absent himself from his said service at any time by night or by day, week day or Sabbath day, without liberty asked and under the penalty of paying his said master three shillings sterling or serving him two days at the expiry hereof, for each day's absence in his master's opinion: to abstain from all gaming, drinking, and all immoral and debauched company.[14]

He also went through the crude initiation ceremonies that all apprentices suffered, such as having his head washed in scalding water. And like other apprentices he had seven years of low pay, starting at 5 shillings a week and rising to 7 shillings. In the early days, this was a system that ensured that master and men had skills in common, and that the master was able to turn his hand to any job that his men were asked to do. Again this worked well for small yards, but as business grew and processes became ever more complex, it became less and less tenable. To the workers it was important. It gave them a special status. The shipwright who had served an apprenticeship had certain rights as a craftsman, with seven years' training behind him. It seemed self-evident that he had special abilities and skills which meant that he alone could tackle certain jobs. This, one has to remember, may have been the nineteenth century, but the shipyard was still using the old methods of hand working. Brunel's block-making machines at Portsmouth were virtually unique as far as ship-yards were concerned. The craftsman ruled and expected his skills to be given due recognition.

[57]

The owners of the Thames yards were brought up with this system and had no quarrel with it. The union, however, wanted it all set down so that there could be no doubts as to the importance of maintaining the status.[15]

> That is the building and repairing of ships should, in all cases, be performed on scientific and mathematical principles . . . it is therefore necessary . . . that proper persons should be employed for that purpose; and it is equally necessary that the employer should, at all times, be a regular bred shipwright, so as to be a competent judge of the good or bad quality of work performed . . . It is the intention of the members of this society, by a moral system, to support their respectability in society, and keep up the rights of their 'trade'.

They insisted again that they would only work for qualified builders, and they were equally concerned that work that should be given to journeymen should not be handed over to apprentices.

The owners might, if they had given it careful consideration, have felt that to have a trade closed and defined for all times was an impossibility, even if it was considered desirable. But it was not such clauses that excited them. The new union wanted to see the prices for works set out in a book, and they also wanted an agreement that in return for not demanding a rise when labour was scarce, the employers in turn would not drop rates when it was work that was in short supply. The answer of the owners was uncompromising. They wanted nothing to do with the price book.

> To the completion of this book, we are told the labours of the union committee have been some months devoted, and to ensure its perfection the best authorities consulted; yet it is the unanimous opinion of such of the ship-builders as have had opportunity for its inspection, that it would be utterly impossible to act on it.[16]

And, they wanted nothing to do with allowing any Union to interfere with the setting of pay and conditions.

We must unequivocally declare, that under whatever variety of practice, work may have been let to shipwrights in different dock-yards, we have always considered our rights of selection and rejection of the men to be employed on our premises, paid from our funds, and subjected to our personal superintendence, to be sacred.

This was the start of a confrontation which was to be typical of relations between employers and men for the next 150 years and more. The men made demands, the employers declared that they would not be dictated to by anyone, and the Union called a strike. In the case of the Shipwrights Provident Union of the Port of London, the first issue was that of working hours. The union asked for a twelve-hour working day, the owners refused and the ensuing strike lasted for two months. On this occasion it was the men who won.

All this flurry of activity has to be seen against the background of the Combination Acts, which had prevented unions being formed in the eighteenth century, but were largely ignored by the 1820s. The shipwright's 'book of prices' had a precedent in 'The London Cabinet-makers' Union Book of Prices', published first in 1811 and 1824, by a Committee of Masters and Journeymen – a combination which was undoubtedly illegal under the Act. But as George White, a Commons Clerk wrote in the 1820s, the Act of 1800 had

been in general a dead letter upon those artisans upon whom it was intended to have an effect – namely, the shoemakers, printers, papermakers, shipbuilders, tailors, etc., who have had their regular societies and houses of call, as though no such Act was in existence; and in fact it would be almost impossible for many of those trades to be carried on without such societies, who are in general sick and travelling relief societies; and the roads and parishes would be much pestered with these travelling trades, who travel from want of employment, were it not for their societies who relieve what they call tramps.[17]

The Acts were in any case about to be repealed, and as unions formed in shipyards throughout the country, so battle lines were drawn and views hardened. A dispute that broke out in Whitehaven was initially about pay, but soon became involved with that far more intractable problem – the question of principle. It all began with attempts by the Union to press for higher wages and enforce a closed shop. One answer of the employers was to attempt to bring in outside workers, a move which was fiercely, and on some occasions violently, resisted. The local paper reported an incident involving the apprentices at Brocklebank's yard, who had already booted out one would-be employee.

> In a short time they bethought themselves of another freak. A marked man – one who did not belong to the 'Union' and had not conformed, we presume, to their regulations, was picked out by them as a *scab* – he, too, was hoisted upon a pole, shoulder high, and they were boisterously proceeding with him into the town, when they were met at the foot of Duke-street by Mr. Brocklebank, who endeavoured to prevail upon them to liberate the man, but in vain – a scuffle ensured, Mr. B. pressed in among them, and was either knocked or thrown down by one of his own apprentices! and he did not rise again without soiled apparel, and a bloody face![18]

Justly incensed, Mr Brocklebank immediately proceeded to his yard, and dismissed every man and boy employed in it, and shut it up.

It was now the turn of the employers to take up their battle positions, and they placed an advert in the paper.

> That in consequence of the late tyrannical and disorderly conduct of the Members of the 'CUMBERLAND SHIPWRIGHT'S UNION,' this Meeting consider it a duty they owe to the Public, the general Interests of Society, and to themselves, to make this PUBLIC DEC-LARATION – That from and after Saturday the 29th inst. no Shipwright, so long as he shall continue a Member of, or connected with, the existing Union, will be employed by us, or any of us.

> resolved unanimously,

[60]

That all such Men as shall offer themselves for Employment, free from, and unconnected with the Union, will be paid as Wages at the Rate of four Shillings per Day, which for the present, shall be considered as the general Rate of Shipwright's Wages in this County. And further, this Meeting earnestly hope that the Shipwrights will not hesitate at once to conform to these Resolutions, in order that the Ship Building Business of the County may continue to be conducted with that character and respectability which it has hitherto maintained, and that peace and good order may at once be restored to Society.[19]

There was no return to work. By February the next year, the paper was bemoaning the folly of the men. 'If they prefer loitering about and leaving their families depending upon the miserable pittance of their Club Fund, which has been extorted by a coercive system, from the families of industrious workmen in other quarters, no one will be found to commiserate the wretchedness brought upon themselves by refusing the liberal offer of *twenty-four* shillings per week.'[20] By now the strike had lasted twenty-five weeks. By April, the protest inevitably began to crumble, as men drifted back into work.

It is a story that could be repeated in many industries at that time: a test of strength between the newly legalized unions and the employers. To one side expressed in the excited capital letter and italic bedecked prose of the *Cumberland Pacquet*, the issue was simple. 'It has let the men see the folly of ATTEMPTING TO RULE THEIR MASTERS, *and made them resolve* NOT TO OFFEND SO AGAIN(!!!)' To the shipyard workers it was a question of whether they should have a voice in their affairs and a say in the conditions that ruled their working lives. Such disputes and arguments are still with us today, but there was another factor which was to make arguments in the shipbuilding industry different from those in others, even unique.

It might have seemed to contemporaries on both sides of the divide that the arguments about craft status, apprenticeship and qualifications were little more than rhetoric. Those were the issues that could be largely passed over with a few meaningless words and phrases. Had the industry stayed on its course producing sailing ships with wooden hulls, that could well have been true for generations to come. But even while the bitter battles were being fought in the yards of Whitehaven, the world of shipbuilding was beginning to change. The ancient craft was about to be dragged within the ambit of the Industrial Revolution. Science, heavy engineering, mechanization had been kept at bay for a surprisingly long time. Now their hour had come.

[4]

❖

THE STEAM AGE

T HE steam engine had been in existence for almost a century before the first steamboat set off across British waters. This is not surprising, given the nature of the early experiments with steam: the growth of the steam engine was the reverse of more familiar processes. The infant was vast and shrank with maturity. It was only after it had shrunk a good deal that it could be fitted into any vessel then in existence.

Once again, early ideas came from the Dutch inventive genius, Christian Huygens. It was already known that air pressure represented a considerable force — in fact a force of around 14 pounds per square inch (psi). It was thus obvious that if you had a piston inside a cylinder and you created a vacuum within the cylinder, air pressure would drive the piston in. Huygens's rather alarming idea was to create a partial vacuum inside a cylinder by using gunpowder. Valves would allow some of the hot gas to escape, but on cooling the valves would close, the gas would now occupy a smaller space and air pressure could move the piston. The theory was sound as far as it went, but no practical machine could be devised which could be charged with gunpowder after each stroke: the idea of using explosives inside a cylinder to drive a piston had to wait for the invention of the internal combustion engine. But Huygens's assistant, Denis Papin, had an alternative idea. His plan was to condense steam inside the cylinder to create the vacuum. This was a very early example of a theoretical problem being solved by scientists, and then being taken up and developed as a practical working machine.

Papin put forward his ideas in 1690, and in 1698 Captain Savery invented what he called 'the Miner's Friend' – though as it involved lighting fires in coal mines, it was the sort of friend most miners would have been happy to do without. Basically, the engine was a pump. It consisted of a vessel in which a vacuum was formed by condensing steam. Atmospheric pressure would force water up towards the vessel and steam pressure was then used to lift the water still higher. Papin suggested various improvements, but this deflected him from following his own ideas. It was Thomas Newcomen, acting quite independently, who put the Papin notion to practical use. He was concerned with the great effort involved in pumping water from the tin mines of Cornwall. Pump rods would descend in a mine shaft under their own weight: he was looking for a means of pulling them back up again. If the rods were fastened to an overhead beam, then all that was needed was a force acting on the opposite end of the beam. At that far end he set the cylinder and the piston, which was attached to the beam. Steam was passed into the cylinder below the piston and condensed by spraying with cold water, thus creating a vacuum. Air pressure pushed the piston in, one end of the beam was lowered and the other raised, dragging up the pump rods as it came. When pressure was equalized, the rods again descended and the whole cycle could be repeated. The beam nodded as the pump rods rose and fell.

In 1712, a Newcomen engine was set to work at coal mines in Dudley, and soon spread throughout Britain and Europe. As a pump it undoubtedly worked, but could scarcely be called efficient – in fact, modern calculations suggest that it had a thermal efficiency of around 0.5 per cent and it was huge. As there was no way of increasing the air pressure, the only way to get more work was to make the machine bigger: by the middle of the century, cylinders were being built that were six feet and more in diameter and over ten feet high. John Scott Russell, who was in later life to become involved in some of the greatest steamships of his day, recalled seeing a Newcomen engine at work, and described seeing the beam emerging from the engine house with its long rods leading down into the mine shaft:

An illustration from Matthew Baker, *Fragments of Ancient Shipwrighting,* showing a shipwright at work in the 1580s. The section shows the 'tumblehome' shape. The man is carrying a knee.

Tudor shipwrights laying out a ship's lines using a large pair of compasses from Baker 1586.

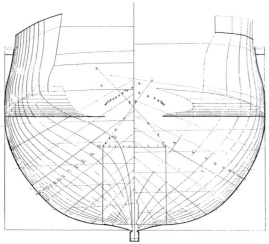

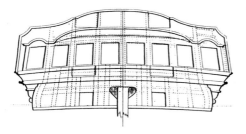

The body plan for a 74-gun ship, showing the lines from the stern to the left, and from the bows to the right, with details of the stern gallery below. From *Rees's Cyclopedia* of 1819-20.

Wooden shipbuilding at
David Williams' yard,
Porthmadog in the 1900s.
Traditional tools on view
include an adze and a
caulking mallet.

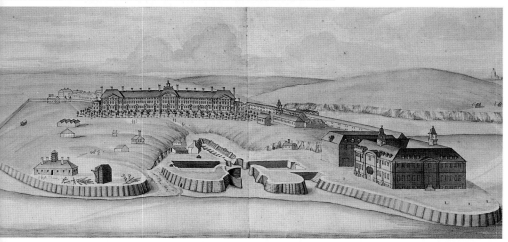

Plymouth Dockyard at the end of the seventeenth century just after completion. It shows
wet and dry docks, with the impressive officers' terrace in the background.

The simple shipyards of Belfast c.1800, before the arrival of Harland and Wolff.

Rigging the *Thirlmere* in 1874.

The Barclay Curle yard on the Clyde in 1845, with a mixture of sailing ships and paddle steamers. Painting by William Simpson.

Preparing for the abortive launch of Brunel's *Great Eastern* in 1857. The picture shows the stern checking drum wheel which failed, killing one of the men.

Among those watching the attempted launch of the *Great Eastern* were, on the left John Scott Russell and, cigar in mouth, Isambard Kingdom Brunel.

Rolling armour plate at Charles Cammell's Sheffield steel works, 1861.

Yarrow's yard on the Isle of Dogs where the company began building steam launches in 1865.

The Denny Tank. The first commercial test tank in the world built in 1884. A wax ship model is being pulled along, while instruments measure hull resistance.

289

The preparations for the launch of the battleship *Blanco Encalada* built for the Chilean
navy by Armstrong and Elswick in 1894.

First class luxury on the *Viceroy of India*.

Employees, with bowler-hatted foremen predominant at Readhead's 1895.

'a gigantic, deformed elephant's head, black and clumsy, it used first to stoop its head very slowly, gradually down, reaching with its long trunk as far as it could stretch into the well of the mine; once down it took a long rest, and then, with a painful, slow, creaking, complaining, jerking motion, gradually and fitfully got its head up again'.[1] It was not exactly a machine that one would think of in terms of any transport system. In any case, it only worked because movement in one direction was caused by gravity acting on heavy rods. That changed in the 1760s.

James Watt, who was working as an instrument maker at Glasgow University, was sent a model of a Newcomen engine which was not working very well. He realized that it was not a mechanical fault but a fundamental flaw in the design. Because the vacuum was created by cooling the cylinder, energy had to be wasted heating up the cylinder all over again for every stroke of the piston. Why not, argued Watt, condense the steam in a separate vessel: the cylinder could be kept hot, and the condenser kept cool. This made a big difference to the efficiency of the engine, but one logical step took the whole process into a different world. If the engine had a separate condenser, steam could be condensed on either side of the piston by closing off the cylinder. Air pressure was irrelevant – steam pressure alone could provide the power. And that meant that weighty pump rods need not be a factor either: steam alone could drive the piston up and down. This was revolutionary – literally revolutionary, for all you had to do was attach the piston rod to a crank, and the engine could turn a wheel. The pumping engine could now drive machinery. It could turn a wheel that would work the machinery of a textile mill, or a saw mill, almost any type of machinery. It could also be used to turn a paddle wheel on a boat.

The idea was tried out first in France, and after one unsuccessful attempt in 1775, the resoundingly named Marquis Jouffroy d'Abbans tried out a paddle steamer, the *Pyroscaphe*, on the Saône near Lyons in 1783. The French could easily have established a lead in this new and exciting technology, but their industrial and scientific revolution was about to be swamped by the far greater upheavals of the political revolution. It removed an important element from the world of technology, as the fashion swung away from theory and science towards pragmatism and empiricism. It was a world in which the British were well placed to make their mark. In the next two decades, Britain was to be at the forefront of development together with America. The Americans were bold in their experiments. In the 1780s they tried using a steam pump to pull in water at the bows of a boat and throw it out at the stern. This primitive form of jet propulsion was too far beyond the available technology. British inventors then showed their mettle. William Symington built an engine which he used to work a small boat on a lake near Dumfries in 1788, which had the distinction of being the first steamer to transport a poet. Robert Burns was among the passengers, but however he might have been moved over the water, he was not moved to verse. But the experiment did have a practical outcome. Symington was encouraged to build a steam tug, the *Charlotte Dundas*, for use on the Forth and Clyde Canal. Steam was supplied by a crude 'waggon-boiler', with the flues, somewhat surprisingly for a small boat, encased in brick. The engine had a single 22-inch (56-cm.) diameter cylinder, set horizontally. The mechanism was as simple as could be and a connecting rod fastened to a crank was all that was needed to turn the paddle wheel. The engine was a somewhat puny affair, developing only 10 horse power. Nevertheless in March 1802 the *Charlotte Dundas* hauled two 70-ton (71.1-tonne) barges for twenty miles up the canal against a strong headwind in about six hours. In spite of what was a very promising start the canal authorities decided that the water churned up by the paddles would erode the banks and the steamer never saw commercial service. In fact, no one in Britain seemed to take very much notice. It was an American observer, Robert Fulton, who carried on the idea. He tried out a number of variations in a series of experiments on the Seine, before returning to America to begin the first ever regular steamer service. In 1807, the paddle steamer *Clermont* was set to work between New York and Albany and though the British were still lagging behind, it was powered by a Boulton and Watt engine. Five years later, Britain too got a commercial steamer service. The story of its development is not just of technical interest: it shows shipbuilding starting the move towards a whole new way of working – and a whole new group of designers and builders.

One of the new men was David Napier. In his short autobiographical notes[2] he describes his own background. His father ran a forge and foundry, first at Dumbarton, then at Glasgow. He had two steam engines, one a blowing engine for supplying a blast to the cupola furnace, the other for working machinery for boring cannon. As a boy, David Napier had seven years at school, but from the age of twelve he spent most of his time at the works. At school he had learned French, Latin and Mathematics, but now he began a very different type of education. 'I never served a regular apprenticeship to anything but put my hand to everything, and by the time I was twenty years old I had the complete charge and control of my father's business in every respect. Shortly after this my father died.'

The young man found time to marry – and raise fifteen children. They seem to have been equally prolific. Napier was clearly defeated by sheer numbers and simply referred to them as 'a swarm'. Around 1812, Henry Bell was a frequent visitor to the foundry. He was a hotel proprietor from Helensburgh, who was having some building done which involved ironwork. He had heard of Fulton's success in running steamers in America, and saw no reason why he could not run an equally successful service on the Clyde. Napier was given the job of casting the engine and manufacturing the boiler. The engine, though modified over the years, is preserved at the Science Museum in London. Again the design is simple, but a little more complex than that of *Charlotte Dundas*. Here the 12.5-inch (31.75-cm.) diameter engine is vertical, so the drive is transmitted through a pair of side-levers to the crankshaft which has a 6-ft (1.8-m.) diameter flywheel. Again power is low – 4 hp – and, like other early steamers, the vessel was helped on its way by a sail. A contemporary illustration shows a single square sail which is using the tall funnel as a mast. Napier's account of boiler making shows just how empirical so much early development was.

I recollect that we had considerable difficulty with the boiler, not having been accustomed to make boilers with internal flues, we

[67]

made them first of cast iron but finding that would not do we tried our hand with malleable iron and ultimately succeeded with the aid of a liberal supply of horse dung in getting the boiler filled.

The vessel, the *Comet*, worked very successfully, first on the Clyde then along the west coast until she ran ashore at Creignish Point at the northern end of the Sound of Jura in 1820 on a voyage from Fort William. Its fate was no doubt regarded as divine intervention by a local minister, whose views were expressed to a fellow divine. Of Henry Bell, he wrote[3]

> He, being puffed up in pride of his abilities, did lately conceive a ship to go upon the waters, not by dint of the clean winds of the air as ordained by God, but by means of fire which burned and a great smoke which issues from the bowels thereof. Not content to keep his unholy devices in the scene of their conception, this man must needs sail or propel his creature even under Crinan itself, near to which place your servant labours in the Gospel both in Gaelic and English.
>
> And so to Fort William, with much effusion of stinking vapour and great hurt to the light-minded of this congregation and of the Christian consciences of the people of Argyll, the Isles, and even Inverness.

Whether or not it was a financial success, David Napier wryly noted that he still had Bell's promissory note for the work, and he never got paid. It did not, however, prevent Napier from getting more deeply involved in steam navigation, and his account of his early years gives some idea of how the new technology sputtered into action.

> Seeing steam navigation was likely to succeed I erected new works at Camlachie for the purpose of making steam engines where the engines were made for the 'Dumbarton Castle' the first steamer that went up Loch Fyne and for the 'Britannia' the first that went to Campbeltown. Although these vessels did not venture outside

the Cumbraes in stormy weather, they suggested the idea to a company in Dublin of having steamers between Holyhead and Howth, for which purpose two vessels were built at Greenwell, no expense being spared to ensure success – The engines were made by Mr. James Cook at that time the oldest and most respectable engine maker in Glasgow, but when tried on the station the engines were so complicated and cumbersome that they broke down almost every gale of wind, and ultimately were laid up in Kingston Dock near Dublin, as useless, and the idea of making machinery of any kind that would withstand the shock of a heavy sea in a gale of wind was put down an impossibility – Whether it was from pique and not having been employed to make the engines of these vessels or from a conviction that the ocean could be safely navigated by steam, I cannot now say, but I commenced I think about the year 1818 to build a steamer on my own account for that purpose called the 'Rob Roy'. I recollect the day before starting on the first trip from Glasgow to Dublin Mr. Chas. McIntosh, the celebrated chemist and inventor of water 'proof cloth', saying we should all be drowned.

In the event they survived a gale that battered them all the way from Glasgow to Belfast and back again, and soon he was heavily involved in building steamers for the Irish Sea crossing.

Napier continued to work at improving the steam engine. His main contribution was the steeple engine, which had two cylinders in line with the overhead crankshaft, and each cylinder had two piston rods. The guides for the crossheads were so high that they poked up through the deck planking – hence the name 'steeple'. This type of engine became very popular on the Clyde. David Tod, who was to become co-founder of the engine builders, Tod and McGregor, was working in the millwright's shop at Napier's at the time. Napier was said to have thought of the idea in the night, promptly got out of bed, gone down to the dining room, cleared out the furniture, rolled back the carpet and drawn his plans in chalk on the floor. Next day Tod and a pattern maker were called in to start preparing the first model.[4]

[69]

A feature of all the early steamers was the use of steam at what would now be thought of as very low pressure. There are two ways of increasing the power of a steam engine: increasing pressure or making it bigger. The ships' engines of the first half of the nineteenth century opted for the latter. As a result a comparatively small vessel such as the Nubia built by Laird Brothers for P & O in 1854 had a very big engine. The Nubia was a modest 2,227 tons (2,263 tonne), but the engine had a 78-inch (195-cm.) diameter cylinder and a 5-ft (1.5-m.) stroke, working at 15 psi to generate 450 hp.[5] Size was not the only problem: these big engines were inefficient. By the middle of the century it still needed at least 4 lbs (1.8kg.) of coal to maintain 1 hp for an hour. So the Nubia at very best would have needed around 20 tons of coal a day. It was felt by many that because of the huge amount of coal required, long voyages by steamer would never be a practical proposition. Ironically, one of those who held that view was Marc Brunel.

One method of improving efficiency and cutting down on fuel was to improve hull design. Conventional wisdom among designers of wooden sailing ships was that a full round bow and a clear run were the best features for moving a vessel rapidly through the water. These allowed the ship to carry a good deal more canvas than if she had more pointed bows, which could plunge dangerously deep. On the other hand, problems arose from the great swell of water pushed in front of the bows which slowed the ship down. This latter problem simply did not occur with a steamer – even when, as was usual, carrying sail as well as an engine. David Napier was again one of the new generation of builders who came from an engineering rather than a shipbuilding background. Tradition was of less interest to him than science and experiment, as he explained in his memoirs. His doubts were first roused by reading the mathematical theories of French engineers. Then, having decided that in theory a finer bow would be preferable, he set out to test the idea using a model on a mill pond, much as the eighteenth-century experimenters had done. Unlike the gentlemen of the Society of Arts, however, he was able to put his experiments to immediate practical advantage when building the Rob Roy. 'When it was launched nautical people said I had put the wrong end foremost, however when tried it was found they were wrong, and the old boats were put into dock to have their bows sharpened which was found invariably to increase their speed.'

A sense of continuity can be seen developing among that new generation of engineer-shipbuilders, just as it had among the old master shipwrights. David Napier moved his works to Lancefield and let his old to his cousin Robert Napier, who 'obtained the assistance of a clever mechanic by the name of Elder'. These two were to be responsible for many more important advances. Robert Napier continued the family tradition of taking an interest in science, and the scientists responded by showing how their theories could be made the basis of practical improvements. He met some of the leading men of the day, including James Joule, who first established the laws for the mechanical equivalent of heat. They talked over 'thermodynamics, surface condensers etc', and Joule not only provided the scientific basis on which Napier could develop his idea, but also proposed a better form of water injection.[6] Not all industrialists showed such a keen interest in theory, but the Napiers and those who came within their influence seem always to have been interested in the latest scientific ideas. Meanwhile David Napier moved yet again to Millwall on the Thames. This time his two assistants, Tod and McGregor, struck out on their own, and made a successful career as engine builders, and when it came time for Napier himself to retire, he let part of the Millwall works to Scott Russell 'for the purpose of building a monster steamer'. The monster was Brunel's giant the *Great Eastern*. But there were to be other changes in ship design and development before that stage was reached, and Brunel was at the heart of them.

The shipwrights who chose to ignore the pontifications of scientists were not necessarily reactionary or foolish. Scientists were quite capable of making the most absurd statements, and none was more prone to this vice than Dr Dionysius Lardner, author of one of the most popular encyclopaedias of the day. He 'proved' to a meeting of the British Association that transatlantic steamer travel was impossible, because no steamer could profitably carry enough coal for the crossing. It seems, and he was by no means alone in this,

[71]

that he had failed to understand the fundamental advantage of building big ships. Resistance to movement through water depends on surface area, but when you increase ship size, the volume does not go up in the same proportion. If you are trying to move a cube through water, the resistance depends on the area of the face of the cube. If that has sides of one unit, and you double them, then the area increases from one unit to four units, but the volume of the cube goes up to eight units. In terms of ships, you gain a lot of storage space for cargo and fuel if you increase the size, but you do not need that much more force to move it through the water. Brunel set out to build his first big ship.

One of the best known of all engineering stories tells how Brunel was being quizzed by Doubting Thomases on the Board of the Great Western Railway about the practicality of building a railway that would stretch all the way from London to Bristol. Brunel, in a typical outburst of bravado, declared that he saw no reason at all why the route should end at Bristol. Why not, he declared, extend it across the ocean, all the way to New York? Only one member of the GWR board took the idea seriously, Thomas Guppy – it is not even certain that Brunel himself took it seriously. It was a characteristic of the man that if anyone challenged one of his extravagant ideas, he would counter with one yet more extravagant. But it was equally typical that if the new idea fired his imagination, he would carry it forward in the face of all opposition. Once Guppy had taken his conversational gambit seriously, there was no turning back. Brunel was now wholly committed to the notion of transatlantic travel. He was also already committed to just about the most adventurous and time-consuming project in the whole world of engineering at that time: the construction of the Great Western Railway. But challenges were potent drugs to Brunel and wholly irresistible. A committee consisting of Guppy, a former naval officer, Captain Christopher Claxton, and a third GWR visionary, Peter Maze, was formed and out of it grew the Great Western Steamship Company. Brunel was to design the ship and William Patterson of Bristol to build it. This was an age of rare excitement and bold endeavour. Here was a small group of men, consisting of a brilliant engineer, but one whose practical experience lay entirely with building railways and bridges, a pensioned-off naval officer, two amateur enthusiasts and just one experienced shipwright setting up to create something that the scientific establishment of the day declared was impossible. The only precedent was a single voyage by a small vessel, the *Savannah*, which had made the trip from America to England using steam power. But steam was only used for a part of the journey. The paddle wheels were collapsible and could be lifted out of the water and carried on board. The whole journey had taken 659 hours, and steam power had only been responsible for about eighty-five of them. The voyage had done nothing to settle the argument either way.

Work began on the *Great Western* in 1836. The ship was very large for her time at 1,340 tons (1,361 tonne), and she was going to need a correspondingly big engine, particularly as steam pressure was to be a niggardly 5 psi. It was of a form already well established for paddle steamers, with two cylinders, which could work independently or together. Steam was to be supplemented by sail carried on four masts. Brunel was well aware of the need to have a rigid hull, not just to help the vessel withstand the pounding of Atlantic gales. There is a tendency for frames and planking to 'give' in all wooden ships – indeed, this helps to absorb the stresses and strains. But a steam engine needs to be kept steady, so that the metal moving parts move easily together. Brunel used the latest in marine technology, with iron strapping and iron knees to hold the hull together – the system developed for the navy by Seppings.

The *Great Western* was destined not to be the first to make the Atlantic crossing under steam power: the honour went to the comparatively small *Sirius*. But the triumph was all Brunel's. *Sirius* left Cork on 4 April 1837, and the *Great Western* left for the longer crossing from Bristol on the 8th. All the way across the great ship gained on her tiny rival, but *Sirius* kept ahead and reached New York first, if only by a matter of hours. It was no doubt galling to Brunel and his associates, but it was their ship that showed the way forward. *Sirius*'s voyage had been a wild adventure. They had arrived in New York virtually cleaned out of fuel – more or less confirming Dr Lardner's view that such voyages, even if they were achieved, could have no practical future. Passengers could hardly be expected to travel in a steamer that might well end up with no fuel to complete the voyage. Brunel's ship was bigger, quicker – and had arrived in New York with nearly 200 tons (203 tonne) of coal on board. The way forward was clear – or nearly so.

What Brunel had proved beyond any shadow of doubt was that commercial long-distance steamer traffic was viable. But to a mind as hyperactive as his it must have been equally obvious that this was a start not a conclusion. In his marine engineering career he suffered from what might have seemed an overwhelming disadvantage: he had had virtually no training in the subject. In an age of innovation and rapid change this lack of tradition was, in fact, a positive advantage. Where traditionalists tended to rely heavily on precedent, Brunel and his associates Guppy and Claxton could look at a question of ship design much as they would any other piece of industrial design. And Brunel's contacts tended to be with men who were in the forefront of industry, who had been brought up to accept development and wider change as the norm. Brunel was never afraid to follow an idea through to its logical conclusion, even if that conclusion seemed bizarre to everyone else.

After the success of the *Great Western*, the Bristol papers carried an announcement of a new venture, on 29 September 1838:

> The Great Western Steamship Company are about to build another vessel of equal size to the *Great Western*; she will be called the *City of New York*. A large cargo of African oak timber has been purchased for this and further ships.[7]

That, no doubt, was what the Great Western Steamship Company thought they were getting, but they should by now have realized that Brunel was not a man for standing still. He now began to think about improving performance and increasing size. Plans changed at a bewildering rate. Within two months of the first announcement, the keel had grown from 205 ft (62.5m.) to 254 ft (77.3m.), the breadth from 35 ft 4 ins (10.7m.) to around 40 ft (12.2m.); only the depth of hold remained constant at around 23 ft (7m.). Already, however, he must have had doubts about the possibility of endlessly extending the wooden hull. An alternative material was available: iron.

Brunel did not invent the iron ship, but he was perhaps the first to see that it opened the way forward to a new generation of big ships. In fact, the technology of boat building in iron was already over half a century old and, as with so many other developments of this crucial period, the initial impetus came from outside the ship-building industry.

The iron ship was a true child of the Industrial Revolution. It was born out of the huge expansion of iron production that was a mark of the eighteenth century. At first the changes only increased the supply of cast iron, which was of little value in shipbuilding. Then in 1784, Henry Cort, who had taken over a small ironworks in Hampshire, patented his puddling furnace for transforming pig iron into wrought iron. At much the same time he brought in grooved rollers to turn his iron into bars. Rollers could also be used to squeeze and flatten the iron to create sheets; the basic materials for the building of an iron ship were at hand. Ultimately of course, the supply of wrought iron depended on there being enough pig iron available in the first place. One of the men who made that possible was a Shropshire iron master, John Wilkinson, who had introduced a steam engine to provide the blast for his furnace in 1776. All the Shropshire furnaces depended more or less on water, the River Severn and its canal links for transport, and it was Wilkinson again who made the first trial with an iron barge. Not many had confidence in the idea, but his first vessel, appropriately named *The Trial*, was launched into the Severn at Coalbrookdale in July 1787. 'It answers all my expectations,' he wrote, 'and it has convinced the unbelievers, who were 999 in a thousand.'[8] It seems a long way from a modest river barge to an ocean-going liner, but once something has been achieved in the field of technology, it is seldom very long before someone does it better.

A number of iron vessels, all quite small, were built over the next few years, but there was one very significant event in 1822 — and it occurred about as far from the sea as one can get in Britain, at

[75]

Tipton, in the heart of the watery tangle of the Birmingham canal system. Charles Manby had taken out a patent for an iron steamboat and formed a steamboat manufacturing society. His first vessel was named after his father, the *Aaron Manby*. She was not a big vessel, 180 ft (55m.) long by 17 ft (5.2m.) broad and only 3 ft 6 ins (1.06m.) draught, but too large for the English canals. She was sent to London in sections, assembled and set off on her first voyage, down the Thames and across the Channel to Le Havre and on again to Paris. Now the iron ships had passed another important landmark – an iron hulled steamer had crossed the seas. It is also a characteristic of the age that apart from being the first iron steamship, she was also built with an entirely new type of feathering paddle wheel: the paddles were at right angles to the rim for maximum thrust when they were in the water, but lay flat against it to reduce air resistance at the top of the cycle.

The advances were slow but significant. Among the early champions was the Laird family. William Laird had arrived on Merseyside in 1810 at the age of thirty, trying to win orders for his father's rope works at Greenock. Instead he stayed and began planning for the establishment of a new port at what is now Birkenhead, which was to be linked to the Dee by canal. That scheme came to nothing, but he did stay and establish the Birkenhead Iron Works, around which he laid out a model town with wide streets and an elegant central square. Everything was built to a remarkably high standard; there were gas lights in the streets and pumped water in every house. The works at first specialized in building boilers, but by 1829 he had built his first iron vessel, a lighter for Ireland. In that year, his son John joined him in the works and together they decided that the future lay in iron ships. It perhaps seems obvious now, but at the time there was widespread distrust and a number of problems still remained unsolved. Some were more apparent than real.

The one essential item for navigation was, as it had been for centuries, the compass – the magnetic needle that points the way north. Unfortunately, the needle is also attracted to iron, and this was thought to make long voyages in iron ships impossible. The iron of the ship does not skip around but stays put. It was the astronomer,

Professor Airey, who showed that because the ship's own magnetic effect was constant, it could be corrected by positioning counter-balancing magnets alongside the compass.

The problem of fouling, however, was to prove far more difficult to eradicate. In the wooden ship, copper sheathing, originally designed to protect against the marine worms proved equally efficient at preventing the build-up of weed. Fouling was to be a problem for far longer in the iron ship. Nevertheless, the use of iron was given the official seal of approval when Lloyds registered the *Sirius* built in 1837.

In October 1838, Brunel, Guppy and Claxton were already discussing the use of iron when the Lairds' Channel packet, the *Rainbow*, steamed into Bristol. It was a perfect opportunity to study an iron ship at sea and Claxton made a number of voyages, investigating many of the features of the ship, notably seaworthiness. He became a convert. The iron ship was better in every way and he noted one feature that is now perhaps immediately obvious. Because iron beams, knees, bulkheads and so on took up less space than their wooden equivalents there was more room in the hull for cargo. Or as he himself put it:

Suppose all the angle irons or ribs the shelves etc. were all rolled out flat and added to the thickness of the plates forming her sides, when an average thickness of 2 ft. [.61m.] of timber would be replaced by an average thickness of 2½ in. [6.25cm.] of iron, with far better ties, a more compact framework and greater strength, than wood can under any circumstances.[9]

In July 1839, the keel of the new ship was laid down: the wooden *City of New York* was transformed into the iron *Great Britain*. She was built in a specially constructed dry dock at Bristol – the dock where she lies today as the long process of restoration continues. The hull design seems to have been a combined effort, involving the traditional skills of the shipbuilder William Patterson and the engineer, Brunel. The keel plates were laid, and it is here that one at once begins to see a new approach, an engineering approach, being brought to ship construction. In the wooden ship, a rigid framework was supplied by the keel, with the ribs and beams set at right angles to it, the whole held together by planking. The *Great Britain* was longer than any previous ship ever built and it was essential to provide longitudinal strength well beyond that provided by the conventional framework. At the base of the ship were ten iron girders that ran from bow to stern, on to which an iron deck was secured. Above that rose five watertight transverse bulkheads and two longitudinal bulkheads creating a series of rigid boxes. This was in no way an adaptation of the old style of construction. Brunel and his partners started from the opposite end: given the need to build a structure in iron, how should it be done? The outer lines of the hull were altogether more traditional, more so in fact than those of the *Great Western*. Where the latter had slab sides, the new ship had a distinct tumblehome – broadening out above the water line, then nipping in towards the upper deck – the shape familiar in the ships of Nelson's navy. Even the iron plating had something of a traditional look to it. One of the problems that early shipbuilders faced when using iron was that, in spite of all the new advances in the industry, the ironworks could still not produce very large plates – in the *Great Britain* they were only 6 ft (1.8m.) long. That meant a great deal of riveting. Brunel used a system where one strake overlapped the one below so that they were riveted together, a great saving. It was not exactly a new idea – to an old shipwright the outer hull was easily described. It was clinker-built.

A great deal of discussion went on over the question of the type of engine to be used, who was to build it and where. Tenders were received from a number of manufacturers, including Maudsley, Sons & Field. Brunel had a long association with the firm, going right back to the days when they had manufactured the block-making machinery designed by his father for Portsmouth dockyard. They were known and trusted – but expensive. A cheaper offer was available from a young man, Francis Humphreys, who had patented a trunk engine, which was manufactured by Halls of Dartford. Essentially this was a space-saving device. Instead of the usual arrangement of piston rod, crankshaft and connecting rod, the

[78]

piston itself was elongated as a hollow cylinder or trunk which was attached directly to the crosshead. There were no obvious advantages for this device in the *Great Britain* other than the fact that it saved money as well as space. Brunel was doubtful. As he well knew, costs for untried designs were rarely accurate. But the Steamship Company opted for Humphreys' design and stayed with it in spite of some ominous signs that soon appeared.

Humphreys' estimate was accepted on the assumption that the engines would be built by Halls, but Halls showed no enthusiasm for the task. They were, they said, wholly unprepared to take on such a large job and were disinclined to order the new machinery that would be necessary. And if they did order new machinery, the entire cost would be set against the *Great Britain* engines. What they were saying, in effect, was that they did not believe that the big iron steamer would be followed by others of similar size, so that any investment in new machines would have to be accounted for on a one-off basis. They suggested that the Great Western Steamship Company might care to undertake the construction of the engines themselves. The directors shrugged off this blatant vote of no confidence and agreed that perhaps that would be the best thing after all. They set up their own engineering works and Humphreys set to work turning his ambitious plans into a reality of hard metal. He had not gone far before the next difficulty materialized.

The engines for the great ship were to power the paddle wheels through an immense crankshaft. At the time, the most powerful forges still relied on trip hammers worked by waterwheels, and none of them was able to take on the task. It seemed as if the whole project was to founder before it had got underway. Humphreys wrote to the manufacturer James Nasmyth explaining his problem. In Nasmyth's own words, the letter 'set me a-thinking'. All existing forges used hammers which were pivoted, so that there was a limit to the height they could rise above the anvil. They were no more than mechanical equivalents of the blacksmith's hammer swung by a strong right arm. But what, reasoned Nasmyth, if one started with a totally different idea, of a heavy weight raised vertically above the anvil and then allowed to fall?

[79]

Following up this idea, I got out my 'Scheme Book', on the pages of which I generally *thought out*, with the aid of pen and pencil, such mechanical adaptations as I had conceived in my mind, and was thereby enabled to render them visible. I then rapidly sketched out my Steam Hammer, having it all clearly before me in my mind's eye. In little more than half an hour, after receiving Mr. Humphries' [sic] letter narrating his unlooked-for difficulty, I had the whole contrivance in all its executant details, before me in a page of my Scheme Book.[10]

It was a simple enough device: the heavy weight was raised by steam power, then released to fall under gravity – a simple device, but one which was to prove of immense value in all kinds of heavy forgings, not least those of the shipyards. It was not, however, destined to play any role whatsoever in the construction of the *Great Britain*.

Humphreys had written to Nasmyth in November 1839, and the results must have convinced him that his troubles were over. What he did not know was that a gentleman by the name of Francis Pettit Smith was at work on another invention at the same time, the screw propeller. One way of looking at the devices used to power ships is to think of them as the reverse of older devices worked by water. Water flowing against a paddle wheel could be used to work the machinery of the water mill: reverse the process, use machinery to turn the wheel and you have the basis for the paddle steamer. Similarly the Archimedean screw had been used since ancient times to lift water as a pump, and it would follow that set on to a floating base it would shift the base instead. Two engineers hit upon the idea of using a version of the Archimedean screw to move a vessel through water. Smith's rival, John Ericsson, was one of those unhappy individuals forever lurking on the fringe of great discoveries, but destined to be forever the stand-in and never the star. As a railway engineer, he was eclipsed by Robert Stephenson and now Smith was about to stride forward to take the applause. Ericsson was to have his moment of glory, but that lay in the future.

Smith was a farmer, and his first experiments began in the unlikely setting of his own duck pond. There he tried a number of different propeller designs, powered by clockwork motors. Chance played a part in his success. He had begun with a propeller incorporating two full spirals, on the not unreasonable surmise that more meant better. It was only when his propeller broke in half that he found that the single turn was far more efficient. In fact, the experiments were so successful that he moved on to a full-scale trial with a launch which he modestly named the *Francis Smith*. The next step was to move to an even grander scale with the three-masted topsail schooner, *Archimedes*. The *Great Britain* triumvirate were as open as ever to innovation. This time it was Guppy who went on the first voyage, and he was so impressed that he was able to persuade the directors of the *Great Britain* scheme to charter the new ship for six months of trials. Brunel – inevitably – found a great deal to criticize in *Archimedes*, but at the end of the period he was wholly convinced that the future lay with the screw steamer. Poor Humphreys! He had just resolved the final obstacle to building his mighty engines for the paddle steamer when the order came through to scrap them and start all over again. Nasmyth described the outcome.

> Mr. Humphries [*sic*] was a man of the most sensitive and sanguine constitution of mind. The labour and the anxiety which he had already undergone, and perhaps the disappointment of his hopes, proved too much for him; and a brain fever carried him off after a few days' illness.[11]

Now all the elements had come together that were to usher in the new age of shipbuilding: the iron hull, the steam engine and the screw propeller. There was still a huge amount of development work that lay ahead. The *Great Britain*'s engines when they were finally built were still cumbersome, low-pressure devices, turning the prop shaft through a clumsy chain drive – but the essentials were all in place. And what was truly significant was the way they had come together by experiment, by technological advance and by utilizing the fruits of the Industrial Revolution.

Rewards, however, do not always – or indeed very often – go to the great innovators. Brunel's ship was built to create a new market for passengers across the Atlantic. It took an entrepreneur to see that a line stood a far better chance of success if it was funded on a guaranteed income, such as that of the mail steamers plying between the British mainland and Ireland. An almost casual note by Robert Napier marks the start of one of the great ventures of maritime history.[12]

Mr Cunard from Halifax [Nova Scotia] came here yesterday afternoon and I have this day contracted with him for three vessels to carry the mails from this country to Halifax. He appears from the little I have seen of him to be a straightforward business man, and from all I can judge I think he has made a very favourable contract.

The contract[13] shows that Cunard was not on the hunt for any innovations, nor was he even interested in trying to develop Brunel's successful design for a transatlantic steamer. He went back to modest vessels, conventionally powered – to be built by a man with a sound reputation. The description is brief, with a great deal left to Napier's commonsense and experience.

Three good and sufficient steam ships, each not less than two hundred feet [60.93m.] long Keel and fore rake not less than thirty two feet [9.77m.] broad between the paddles and not less than twenty one feet six inches [6.55m.] depth of hold from top of timbers to underside of dock amidships properly finished in every respect having boat masts rigging sails anchors cables and whole other usual and necessary appurtenances for the working and sailing of the said vessels with cabins furnished in a neat and comfortable manner for the accommodation of from sixty to seventy passengers or a greater number in case the said Robert Napier shall find that the space will conveniently and commodiously admit thereof each of which vessels shall be fitted and finished with two steam Engines having cylinders seventy inches [178cm.] in diameter and six feet six inches [2m.] length of stroke.

[82]

Brunel had laid the foundations for technical advance: Cunard and Napier together had done the same for the commercial success of the ocean-going steamer.

NEW MEN, NEW WAYS

N OT all the advances came from engineers new to shipbuilding. Scotts of Greenock had begun shipbuilding on the Clyde
at the very beginning of the eighteenth century and in the
middle of the nineteenth century were famous for their very beautiful
clipper ships. At the same time, however, the Scotts worked with
famous James Watt's father on a number of improvement schemes
for Greenock. Scotts saw the development of the steam engine as a
motive force from its infancy, and were among the earliest builders
of steamships. Between 1819 and 1821, they built the three largest
steamships in Britain, including the *Waterloo*, the first steamer to
pass the modest limit of 200 tons. Her lines were those of a clipper,
and the connections with sailing ships are plain to see. The *Waterloo*
was even celebrated in verses which have, if anything, an eighteenth-
century ring to them.[1]

> And now amid the reign of peace,
> Art's guiding stream we ply;
> That makes our wheels, like whistling reels,
> O'er yielding water fly.
> As our heroes drove their foes that strove
> Against the bonnets blue;
> On every side the waves divide
> Before the Waterloo.

The yard was generally considered one of the best of its kind. Weir's *History of Greenock*, published in 1829 – with perhaps a touch of local patriotism – described it as 'one of the most complete in Britain, excepting those of the Crown'. Its structures and buildings were securely walled in, there was a new, large airy dock and, significantly, 'an extensive manufactory of chain cables'. Scotts were, in other words, already no strangers to heavy engineering. However, in the early days, Scotts had all their engines made by outside firms, notably Napier. That changed in 1825. John Scott decided to build his own engines, and bought up a local brass and iron foundry established in 1790. By the time Weir wrote his history, the engine works were employing a work force of 220 men – though they can scarcely have been overpaid since he also estimated that the weekly wage bill was £180. But what is really significant about Scotts was the fact that within a very short time they were building engines for vessels from other yards and for the Royal Navy. The shipbuilding and engine building parts of the firm were obviously connected, but retained a considerable degree of independence. This was one route forward: a traditional shipbuilder reacting quickly and positively to the new technological world. Others came in from the opposite direction.

John Scott Russell[2] was born in 1808, son of a school teacher. He was clearly a remarkably bright boy as he was accepted by Glasgow University at the age of thirteen and at seventeen had his M.A. He set off to follow his father into an academic career, but was soon seduced by the lure of steam. His first interest was not the sea but the land. He designed a road locomotive and set up the Scottish Steam Carriage Company, which ran a regular service between Glasgow and Paisley in 1834. It failed, not because there was anything intrinsically wrong with the design, but because the road authorities were wholly opposed to the idea. Thwarted, he turned to water and his first efforts were experimental iron craft for the Union Canal Company. Like Brunel, he found problems with longitudinal weakness, and designed craft with bulkheads running fore and aft. But he was working, as was almost everybody else at that time, on a try-it-and-see basis. There was quite simply no theoretical basis for ship design. The Glasgow M.A. set out to remedy the defect.

He began, much as any modern researcher would begin, by studying the available literature. Almost the only volume he found that was of any use whatsoever was an obscure eighteenth-century treatise by a Swedish writer. When he looked around the shipyards of Britain, he found the rule of thumb dominant. He managed to acquire practical knowledge from John and Charles Wood of Port Glasgow, builders of the *Comet*, but no one seemed to have attempted to answer even the most fundamental questions. What is the effect of hull shape on speed? How does increased power relate to speed through the water? What shape of hull offers least resistance and so requires the least effort to move it? No one knew the answers, so he had to set out to find them for himself. He used what was at the time an impeccable, indeed daring scientific approach. Earlier experiments had been hit and miss; try different shapes and see which one works best. Scott Russell took a step further back to explore the fundamentals. What happens to the water as a vessel pushes through it?

He began by looking at the nature of the waves themselves. He set up a trough of water, releasing a small amount of water in at one end and found that it moved down the trough as a single, travelling wave. It was, he declared, 'a most beautiful and extraordinary phenomenon: the first day I saw it was the happiest of my life'. He then found by towing a barge down a canal that the bows pushed just such a wave up ahead, and that its shape and speed depended on the depth of water. At times, a point was reached when the wave was slowed to the point where the bows caught up with it and reared up on the swell of water – a maritime equivalent of putting on the brakes. He saw that there was a relationship between hull shape and wave shape, which meant that there must be a design which produced the best balance. He called it a 'wave line hull'. Scott Russell's optimum hull turned out to be very different from the 'cod's head, mackerel tail' of tradition.

Scott Russell was very much one of the new generation of shipbuilders – prepared to learn from tradition, but equally ready to question it. He was also intellectually and professionally equipped to argue with alleged experts, such as Dr Lardner. At that famous meeting where the encyclopaedist had set out to prove that transatlantic travel by steamer was impossible, Scott Russell's voice was heard alongside Brunel's. It was perhaps inevitable that at some time they should work together, and perhaps equally inevitable that they should not always agree. After Scott Russell had taken over Napier's old yard at Millwall, Brunel approached him, suggesting that he tender for mail ships for Australia. Scott Russell responded with two elegant vessels, the *Adelaide* and *Victoria*. They were very successful, and *Victoria* earned a £500 premium for the fastest journey to Australia. But already Brunel was dreaming great dreams. He reasoned that there was already a substantial emigrant trade to America, and that there would soon be an equally busy trade to Australia. To carry this human cargo speedily and profitably called for a steamer: but in order to hold both a large number of emigrants and enough coal for the voyage, it would need to be a big ship — far greater than anything ever attempted before. The *Great Western* had conquered the Atlantic route to America; now a new vessel would be built to dominate the route through the Orient to Australia, the *Great Eastern*. It was to prove a collaboration that was to give little satisfaction to either party. The recriminations have echoed down the years. Two biographies of Brunel have taken dramatically opposite positions. The earlier by L. T. C. Rolt has Brunel as its hero, coping with the prevarications of Scott Russell, a man depicted as eaten away with jealousy at Brunel's fame and fortune. The more recent by Adrian Vaughan takes the contrary view and sees Scott Russell as the plain, 'if plodding, representative of reason and common sense when confronted by the mercurial wayward and generally totally unreasonable shifts and changes of Brunel'.[3] There is a third position, which if less exciting and a good deal less dramatic might well be nearer the truth.

There was undoubtedly a clash of personalities and also a clash of styles. Russell had submitted an estimate based on agreed specifications. He regarded any changes as being a cause for renegotiation. His fees were based on the weight of iron used, and extra was to be paid for above the contract fee.[4]

What I have done has been to go steadily through with the Ship as it was originally, clearly understood and agreed considering that

[87]

as the contract. Everything invented since I have considered as an extra, and I think I am right.

Brunel retaliated immediately.

How the devil can you say you satisfied yourself of the weight of the ship when the figures your clerk gave you are 1000T less than I make it or than you made it a few months ago – *for shame* – if you are satisfied I am sorry to give you trouble but I think you will thank me for it – I wish you *were* my obedient servant, I should begin by a little flogging.

The style of the correspondence speaks for itself, but who was in the right? The question has no rational answer. This was a ship being built to a previously undreamed-of scale. Scott Russell's estimates can have been little more than guesswork. Brunel was, as ever, all for driving forward at maximum speed, whilst at the same time incorporating each and every improvement as it occurred to him. It is all too easy now to talk glibly of keeping costs down, but how many pioneering projects in the entire history of engineering have come in at anything remotely resembling their original estimates? At the time of writing, the US House of Representatives has just cancelled the giant superconducting supercollider, which was to have been used to probe into the fundamental particles that could tell us about the origins of the entire universe we inhabit. The reason? The costs estimated in 1989 at \$5.9 billion had by 1993 risen to \$11 billion. If our age of sophisticated computers can get costs so hopelessly wrong, what can one say about an equally innovative project of 150 years ago? It is against this background that the fiasco of the *Great Eastern* should be seen: it was a project that dealt in imponderables. How to provide power for such a large vessel? How was she to be built to ensure longitudinal strength?

Power was the greatest problem, to which the unsatisfactory answer was a combination of paddle wheels and screw propeller, as it was decided that neither working on its own would be sufficient. In the hull design, Brunel extended the ideas first tried in the *Great*

Britain. There an iron deck had been placed above the hull. Now this was to be extended upwards to create what was in effect an inner hull, rising up above the deep loadline. The inner and outer hulls were joined by a complex of iron work, providing a cell-like structure, that both provided a double protection in the case of an accident and gave great strength without adding a vast amount to the weight of the hull. It was, once again, an innovative design, but ultimately a failure. In spite of the combination of sails, paddle wheels and propeller the great ship was notably underpowered. Her size told against her, as she was too large for many harbours and she had a most unpleasant tendency to roll in even moderate seas. The ill omens began at the launch.

The ship was much too long for a conventional launch into the river, so she was sent down the slips broadside on. The cradles on which the hull rested were controlled by checking chains and winches, or should have been. In the event, the vessel moved in fits and starts and the forward cradle shot forward alarmingly and at the same time the stern appeared to have stuck. The winch that was controlling the cable was set free and whirred round like an out-of-control merry-go-round, hurling off the unfortunate men who were manning it. One died, others were injured. The launch that began on 3 November 1857 was only completed when the great ship slid into the water on 31 January 1858. Of the main participants, Scott Russell was bankrupted and Brunel was to be dead within the year. It can seem at times that the steady advance of the age of iron and steam was one of unfettered progress. The *Great Eastern* stands as a reminder that there is always a price to be paid. John Scott Russell paid with a ruined career, Isambard Kingdom Brunel paid with the ruin of his health. Brunel did more than most to push forward the possibilities of the new technology. In his last ship he pushed a little further than the technology could accommodate.

An interesting little note from Robert Napier to John Scott Russell brings together a number of the themes of the day: the need for a professional body to help shipbuilders keep abreast of the new technology, the need for the new generation of shipbuilders to meet and discuss theories – and a useful reminder to Scott Russell that in the end the most important factor is still the need to satisfy the commercial customer.[5]

> The Society of Naval Architects is likely enough to answer and to become a strong body, and I think it will in the end be a most powerful body for the protection of the true interests of Naval architects that is to Shipbuilders who 'know what they are about' ... I doubt if you are quite right in cutting off your wave line by a tangent. I feel disposed always to have the wave line, but to shorten it where I cant afford length. It makes a somewhat ugly bow, but from all my observations the water seems to like it better than the straight. I am afraid in building vessels to sell, you must a little, consult the taste of the buyer.

One of the few men to attempt to bring scientific ideas and methods to bear on iron ship construction was William Fairbairn who had begun shipbuilding on the Thames in 1836. He came, however, from a very different background. As a structural engineer, he had been responsible for helping to develop the fireproof textile mill, based on an iron framework, and he had written a number of treatises on the subject. He now applied the same principles to building a ship as he had to building a cotton mill, and again set down his ideas in print.[6] He described experiments and measurements and set down the results in a series of mathematical formulae that could be used to calculate stresses and strains. Although the book has a basis in theory, it remains a practical manual to be used by practical men. For example, in the section on riveting, he explains why a punch rather than a drill produces a cleaner hole and a better fit. He recommends a machine that works using punched card, like a Jacquard loom. He is less impressed with the more common practice of using a sledge-hammer 'in the hands of one whose muscular developments are generally in excess of his reflective functions'. The result of bad practice is a hole that has to be packed with a steel pin. He also showed up a common error – that joints were the weak points in the hull. In a series of experiments he showed that the plates themselves were generally the first to give under stress. Experiments such as those lead to practical improvements in construction techniques.

The continuing need for technical improvement was obvious to many shipbuilders. In particular, it was clear that if ships were going to be making longer voyages, the answer to the problem of keeping them fuelled was not going to be the *Great Eastern* solution of making them bigger to hold yet more coal. A far more satisfactory solution would be to make the steam engine more efficient. Robert Napier was not just a sound and very successful engineer in his own right, but he headed a firm where employees were well taught and often went on to build successful careers and companies of their own. One of these was John Elder, who with Charles Randolph set up Randolph, Elder and Co. to build steam engines. Their new generation of engines used a technology that was already half a century old.

Early development of the steam engine was blocked by James Watt's all-embracing patent. Engineers realized that his engine was not very efficient, and nowhere was this more keenly felt than among the mining engineers of Cornwall, working a long way from the nearest coalfield and so forced to pay high fuel costs. It was no great feat of imagination to realize that when steam was exhausted to the condenser it must still be under pressure – and if so it could be fed into a second cylinder before being condensed. The first two-cylinder or compound engine was built by Jonathan Hornblower in 1780, but was soon closed down again by Mr Watt and his lawyer. With the expiry of the Watt patent in 1800, development was started up again by Arthur Woolf and the engines with their small high-pressure cylinders and bigger low-pressure cylinders were soon put to work. At the same time, boiler pressures were being increased, particularly in Cornwall.

Shipbuilders were understandably a mite cautious about having high-pressure boilers in their vessels, and there were unhappy examples of what happened when things went wrong. On the *Great Eastern*'s first voyage, as a result of two cocks being closed which should have been open, pressure built up in the boiler feedwater section, with disastrous results. *The Times* correspondent described the event[7]:

> The forward part of the deck appeared to spring like a mine, blowing the funnel up into the air. There was a confused roar amid which came the awful crash of timber and iron mingled together in frightful uproar and then all was hidden in a rush of steam. Blinded and almost stunned by the overwhelming concussion, those on the bridge stood motionless in the white vapour till they were reminded of the necessity of seeking shelter by the shower of wreck – glass, gilt work, saloon ornaments and pieces of wood which began to fall like rain in all directions.

It was not an isolated incident – and was certainly no encouragement to flirt with high pressure. So the emphasis turned instead to designing compound engines. Randolph, Elder & Co. already had experience in building engines for use in factories but it was not until 1854 that they built their first marine compound for the *Brandon*. Up to that time, the best coal consumption available was 4 to 4½ lbs (1.8 to 2kg.) per unit of horse power per hour. On her maiden voyage, *Brandon*'s fuel consumption dropped to 3¼ lbs (1.46kg.), a decidedly impressive improvement. The point was not lost on companies trading in areas such as South America, where coal was scarce and expensive. The first major line to order compounds was P & O, who also had coaling problems on their long voyages to the Far East. The first of the new steamers, the *Moolta*, was delivered in 1861. The engine was fine, but although they were still working on the comparatively low pressure of around 30 psi there were still problems. The first was not so much with the engines as with the unreliability of the boilers and, from contemporary accounts of life in the P & O engine room, the erratic steam supply affected everything.[8]

> Piston rods and valve spindles as black as coal tar; slide valves chirping like a cageful of canaries; low pressure pistons thumping like big drums, softened occasionally by water through the indicator cocks, to prevent the whole fabric coming down.

[92]

There had been improvements in marine boilers over the years. The fire-tube boiler was another of those devices that came to ship-building from outside the industry, in this case borrowed from the railways. It made its first appearance in Robert Stephenson's famous locomotive, the *Rocket*. It was adapted for use in ships, and eventually developed into the 'Scotch' boiler. Many companies were involved in the business of improving engines and boilers, and one of the most successful was Howden Engineering.[9] James Howden's career was typical of many of his day, beginning with a general background in engineering before deciding to specialize. He was one of those who rose through the apprenticeship system rather than through formal and academic education. He was born in 1832 at Prestonpans, and at the age of fifteen he was apprenticed to James Gray, a manufacturer of steam engines and blowing engines for foundries. His extraordinary talents won him the post of chief draughtsman before he had even finished his apprenticeship. In 1854, still just twenty-two years old, he had the confidence to set up on his own as a consulting engineer. At the time his main interest was in machine tools – his first patent was for an improved way of making rivets and bolts. He soon turned to marine engines, following a correspondence in *The Engineer* begun by Alexander Martin on ideas for improvements. He and Martin took out a joint patent and Howden began designing his first steam units.

Steamers, even those with compound engines, were still working at low pressure – 20 to 25 psi for single cylinder engines and up to around 60 psi for compounds. With his first two steam units for the Anchor Line steamers *Corra Linn* and *Ailsa Craig*, built by Alexander Stephen, he went straight away for a multi-tube boiler delivering steam at 100 psi to a compound engine. It was a bold and enterprising decision. And from the first he was looking at ways of enhancing efficiency. He took out a patent on a method of improving combustion and recovering heat from the condenser: it was not a great success but he was to continue his experiments. But first he was to establish his own works, where he could manufacture engines and boilers to his own design.

He bought an existing factory in Scotland Street, Glasgow and set to work. He was by now an experienced engineer, with a number of patents to his name – and had just celebrated his thirtieth birthday. Tests showed just how rapidly he was moving forward. In 1869, the original engine of the *Xanthe* was removed and replaced by a Howden compound. Both engines had the same nominal horse power. The older one, somewhat coyly referred to as by 'an English firm of note', gave a maximum speed of 6.5 knots at a coal consumption of 14 cwt (711kg.) per hour; the new gave an impressive 10.3 knots and an even more impressive fuel consumption rate of just 5 cwt (254kg.) an hour, going flat out.

Throughout this period his main efforts were concentrated on improving the efficiency of combustion. He also showed an interest in improving the efficiency of his own works. He added new buildings and introduced a system whereby work progressed steadily from one shop to the next – an infant assembly line. His great success came in the 1880s, with his 'forced draught' system, which used a fan to push hot air through the fire. Again the value of the system was shown in a conclusive experiment. The forced draught was introduced into the *City of New York* which left the Clyde on its regular run to Trinidad in 1884. The engine and boiler were unchanged – only the forced draught system had been added: the result was a modest three per cent improvement in horse power, but a very significant drop in fuel consumption from 2.1 lbs (0.95kg.) to 1.36 lbs (0.61kg.) per 1 hp per hour. The figures were impressive. They certainly impressed the engineers of the day: by the end of the century over a thousand steamships were converted to use of the 'Howden System of Forced Draught'.

Howden was by no means the only engineer working at boiler improvement. Samson Fox was a machine toolmaker who spotted a design flaw in existing furnaces that prevented their being used to produce high-pressure steam. The big tubular flues were in danger of collapsing under pressure, and Fox came up with a simple solution, the corrugated flue. In 1874 he built a new works at Leeds, and a year later the flues were in production, finding a ready market, especially among the shipbuilders of the Clyde. It is ironic that having made the breakthrough in design and early development it was a

German firm manufacturing under licence who came up with a really efficient means of manufacture, the corrugated rolling mill. The point was not lost on Fox: 'The foreigner intends to try a thing which my board of directors and my shareholders are frightened to do.'[10] It was not the last occasion on which developments begun in Britain were taken up and enthusiastically developed overseas. But in the meantime there was no respite in research work in Britain.

John Scott of Greenock actually built an experimental iron steamer, the *Thetis*, entirely at his own expense in 1858 to test his own ideas on high-pressure compounds. The engine worked at what was for then the very high pressure of 115 psi and at the very commendable consumption of 1.86 lbs (.84kg.) per 1 hp per hour. The theory was fine, but the boiler design was inadequate and suffered badly from corrosion. It was a reminder that advances depend not just on good ideas and sound design, but also on the right materials being available. The Howden story suggests a seamless picture of steady improvement, the past being discarded at each new advance. Yet when Howden designed his first engine, the builders were Alexander Stephen who were just beginning to question the 'advances' they had already made.[11]

Alexander Stephen had opted for iron ships on a number of grounds: they had a better safety record, since a fire did not necessarily mean the destruction of the whole ship, a fact reflected in better insurance rates at Lloyd's; and the iron frame was better able to withstand the vibrations of the machinery as the paddle wheel gave way to the screw propeller. But they were also still building big sailing ships for the long routes to the southern hemisphere. In 1862 they decided to abandon the iron hull for sailing ships, simply because the problem of fouling with weed seemed insoluble. Alexander Stephen Junior went back to the older system of building composite sailing ships alongside their iron steamers. By the end of 1860 they were averaging two launches a month, peaking at three launches in January 1869. In many ways, Stephen's was typical of this transition period, where ships of every conceivable kind were being built, where the new sat comfortably with the old. The one steady factor was the company's growth. In 1870 they purchased the Linthouse estate on the Clyde, and even here the old and the new were ranged side by side. The new works were a mile from the end of the Glasgow tramway, but the company soon extended the line at their own expense – though it was to remain a horse-drawn tramway until the next century. River crossing was even more archaic, still depending on a rowing-boat ferry until 1891. However, there was nothing archaic about the works themselves. The old Linthouse mansion became offices and new sheds were built, including the massive platers' shed, 500 ft (152.3m.) long by 200 ft (61m.) wide.

> In the centre of the shed was a chimney-stack 100 ft. [30.5m.] in height into which the smoke from the furnaces was condensed by underground flues. Throughout this and the adjoining smiths' shop there were 640 feet [195m.] of iron shafting for driving the machinery, the motive-power being supplied by an engine of 80 horse-power, constructed on the high-pressure condensing system. In the smithy, which opened out of the platers' shed, there were 80 smiths' hearths and three steam hammers.

The building of the new works was a time for reappraisal. The age of the sailing ship was not yet dead. Another branch of the family was still at work in Dundee turning out fast clippers. In 1874 they built the *Lochee*, specifically to fetch jute from Calcutta for the mills of Dundee. She was the latest design in sailing ships, a 1,820-ton (1,849-tonne) vessel, 275 ft (83.8m.) long and with a 30-ft (9.14-m.) beam. Unlike the Glasgow Stephen's, the Dundee family had stayed with iron, not just for the hull, but also for the masts and lower yards. Back in the Clyde, however, it was decided that the time to abandon sail had finally arrived. The first step was to build a brand new engine shop, 200 ft (60.9m.) long and 40 ft (12.2m.) high. A contemporary account shows awestruck delight in the sheer size of everything connected with the new industry. It was, declared the writer

> Designed on the most approved principles, the roof being sup-

[96]

ported on a series of cast-iron columns, each of which measures 3 feet [.91m.] in width by 18 feet [5.48m.] in height. As indicating quantity of iron required for these columns, we may mention that 32 of them weigh 6 tons each, while the other three, to which machines are attached, weigh 9 tons respectively. The roof is divided into three bays and is entirely constructed of glass. On each slope of each bay there are 18 feet [5.48m.] of glass – a fact which will be better understood when we state that there are altogether 26,000 square feet [2415sq.m.] of glass used in the construction of the roof. On the north and south sides of the building there are wings each 18 feet [5.48m.] in height by 60 feet [18.3m.] in width on one side and 30 feet [9.14m.] on the other.

There are two high-pressure engines for driving the machinery . . . which is now in course of being installed, will be entirely new and is supplied by Whitworth, Fairbairn and Halse, in England, by Craig and Donald, of Johnstone, and other well-known makers. Among the mechanical appliances, perhaps, the most notable is a universal drilling machine with a 22-ft [6.7-m.] horizontal and a 15-ft [4.6-m.] vertical stroke. In number and variety the machines will compare with any shop on the Clyde. There are 18 turning lathes, 2 large boring machines, 2 radial drilling machines, 1 slotter and other appliances used for engineers' purposes.

What is very striking is not so much the scale of the works, as the huge increase in powered machinery. It was a story that could be repeated in other big yards around the country.

Lairds of Birkenhead had from the beginning seen that there was an irreversible movement from the wooden ship to the iron though even they might have been surprised at the speed with which things were moving. A magazine article of 1874[12] gave the following figures for shipbuilding tonnages in the UK.

	Timber	Iron	Total
1850	120,895	12,800	133,695
1860	147,269	64,899	212,168
1868	161,472	208,101	369,573

Although tonnage overall had virtually trebled in the period the tonnage of wooden ships had only increased by about a third, while that of iron ships had risen to sixteen times what it was in 1850. Companies, such as Lairds, who had been in at the very beginning of the shipbuilding revolution were ideally placed to take advantage of the new trend. Like Stephen's on the Clyde, Laird had been through a massive modernization and expansion programme. They deserved their success, for they had been resolute supporters of the virtues of the iron ship in the face of a good deal of mainly ill-informed doubting. Paradoxically it was an accident in 1842 that did more than anything else to convince the waverers. The ferry steamer *Nun* was grounded at Birkenhead, her stern stuck on a pier, her bows balanced on a rock while the whole of the midship section was in mid-air carrying the full weight of the engines and boilers. A wooden ship would have broken its back, the *Nun* floated off at the next high tide, undamaged.

By the 1870s, Lairds was a vast complex. There were five docks, of which two were covered, the largest being served by a 50-ton crane. A railway line swept into the yard past the engineers', smiths' and joiners' shops, which stretched for a thousand feet down Church Street. Sidings ran out to the dockside cranes. Inside the workshops was heavy machinery, able to bend metal plates up to six inches thick. Altogether the works spread out over twenty acres of riverside land. It was not merely a vast enterprise in its own right, but was connected with others. Not even Laird could cope with some of the massive crankshafts and sternposts which were forged in Scotland, and metal plate came from a variety of foundries including that of a company in Sheffield, referred to in the 1874 article as Charles Cammell, who was, of course, the Cammell who would later form half of the famous partnership of Cammell Laird. A feature of shipbuilding in those days was the heavy involvement of other engineering companies and foundries. At the end of the century, just before the merger, the supplying of shipyards was only a part, and not necessarily the major part, of the Cammell concern. In four weeks in December 1890, the four furnaces turned out over 14,000 tons (14,224 tonne) of pig iron, but by far the largest part of the business was supplying rails for railways around the world. That same month orders went out to Canada, India and Australia – over 30,000 tons (30,480 tonne) of rail in all.[13] It is a mark of the great and growing importance of shipbuilding at the end of the century that a company as powerful as Cammell should choose to merge with Laird.

It is easy to think of shipbuilding in terms of the great names, but there was a multiplicity of small yards as well, each of which has its own story and often its own special niche in the general scheme. Some inevitably suffered in comparison with their grander neighbours. One of Thomas Royden's[14] main claims to fame was that one of his vessels, the *Buckingham*, was launched by Queen Victoria – when the ship ended up as a hulk in Sydney in 1924, her figurehead was sold off as a royal memento. Alas, all the purchaser really got for his money was a bit of a ship launched by two anonymous ladies from Bolton. Royden was apprenticed to shipbuilding and in 1815 set up a partnership with James Ward on the Liverpool side of the Mersey. It was not a great success. In 1825, fire destroyed the yard and the two ships that were being built there. The greatest problem they found, however, was the unhelpful policy of Liverpool Corporation, who charged high rents in exchange for short tenancies. The truth was that Liverpool in the nineteenth century was looking to a future as a port not as a shipbuilding centre. When plans were laid for the creation of the Albert Dock, Royden was assured that his yard was safe. On that basis he took on a contract for building a ship at low cost, planning to use apprentice labour, at which point he was given notice to quit and move to another yard in six months. He was forced to replace cheap apprentices by experienced journeymen and lost money on the deal. The company struggled on until 1893 and with its closure shipbuilding in Liverpool came to an end. It must have been doubly galling to the Liverpool men as they looked across the river to the steady expansion of Lairds of Birkenhead.

One area of especial importance to the smaller builders was the market for fishing boats. Towards the end of the nineteenth century in particular there were immense fleets of drifters, fishing for herring off the east coast. Ports such as Great Yarmouth could hold up to a thousand vessels, and it was possible to walk across the harbour from deck to deck. In 1876, twenty-four-year-old Samuel Richards[15] decided that he had had enough of working for his father in the north of England and, with twenty-five gold sovereigns in his pocket, he hitched a lift on a herring drifter bound for Lowestoft. He acquired a site on a small creek, and soon had his first boat on the water, a 57-ft (17.4-m.) sailing drifter. He broke with local conventions by building a carvel hull instead of the locally favoured clinker hull, and he added his own distinctive touch – a decorative gilded scroll on the bows. He forced his way into the market on a policy of hard work and low pay – seventy-two hours was a standard week for just twenty-five shillings. But it meant that he could offer a 50-ft (15.2-m.) drifter for £360 and throw in a dinghy for an extra five pounds.

Steam power was only slowly brought to the drifters, at first as a donkey engine for manoeuvring the heavy beam trawls. The first steam drifter was built in Scotland in 1814, and even by the end of the century there were still some 300 sailing drifters in the Lowestoft fleet. But owners did order steam – even if they sometimes left it until the last moment. One fisherman placed his order on 21 August with the stipulation that it had to be ready for sea by 6 October – just forty working days away. Cyril Richards told the story of what happened.

The day the boat was ordered her keel was growing on a tree outside Beccles. The owner's surveyor tried hard to catch us out on the penalty clause and produced a long list of things in the specification that had not been done on the day before she was due to go on her sea trials. My father called everyone together and went through the items one by one, detailing a man or a team of men to deal with each one. We got her finished all right, and she went out on the appointed day and returned with a 100-cran catch.

Richards survived and prospered because he knew the market for his boats and made sure that he remained in touch with new developments. Looking forward into the next century, Richards took a gamble and built Britain's first diesel drifter as a demonstration model.

[100]

For once he had advanced too far ahead of his buyers. The ship was clean, fast and economical, but the conservative fishermen who were loth to change from sail to steam were now equally reluctant to abandon steam.

Not all fishermen were so conservatively minded. The Hain family of St Ives had been deep-sea fishermen for generations, but in the nineteenth century they moved from fishing to trading. But this was not enough for the son of the family, Edward Hain, who declared that he would not enter the business unless they abandoned their fleet of schooners and brigateens. Somehow or other he had heard of the company of John Readhead & Sons of South Shields.[16] He arrived at South Shields unannounced, wandered into the yard and began poking around. James Readhead, John Readhead's son, came out to see who the stranger was – and probably to send him packing. In the event, the two young men got on well – they were then the same age – twenty-six – and as a result Readhead began building the first Hain's ship in 1878. By 1960, the list stretched to eighty-seven vessels. It was a feature of many yards that once a successful relationship was struck up between owner and builder, it could survive down the years to their mutual advantage.

Some shipbuilders were on the look-out for new opportunities. A ship-broker writing in 1884 identified just such a gap in the market, with Americans looking for steamers.

The problem is this, the consumption of bananas, already large, is increasing enormously. At present the bananas are carried by about 300-ft [91.4-m.] fore and aft sailing schooners, but the cargo is so perishable that when the sailing ships get head winds or calms the loss through rotting of fruit is great. The first steamers they intend building will enable them to bring cargoes to market in good condition and with a small percentage of rotten fruit. The sailers will gradually be driven out of the trade and other steamers will be required.

The letter written to a newspaper was carefully filed away by the Scottish shipbuilders, Denny.[17]

[101]

During the course of the nineteenth century, the great shipbuilding centres were supplemented by smaller ventures around the country. They may not have had the glamour of the big names, but many did a tremendous amount of business. Martin Samuelson, for example, had a brief career as a builder on the Humber at Hull, lasting only from 1857 to 1864 when he sold out. But in that short time he built something like a hundred ships, and on one mammoth day, 31 October 1863, he launched four ships: the 1,206-ton (1,225-tonne) *Countess of Ripon* and her sister ship the *Lightning*, the 723-ton (735-tonne) *Earl de Grey and Ripon* and the steam tug *Solferino*: a notable day's work for one small yard.[18]

The nineteenth century was a period of great diversity, in which yards big and small built a bewildering range of craft from the wooden sailing ship to the iron steamer. There were to be two more major advances in the second half of the nineteenth century. One grew specifically out of the needs of the shipping industry for yet more economy and efficiency, the other was part of the general development that still characterized the industrial world as a whole. To a large extent the second provided the means for achieving the first, so that is the obvious starting point.

The eighteenth century had seen enormous increases in the supply and quality of iron from the foundries, but steel production lagged far behind. There was nothing very new about steel – it had been produced since the Middle Ages – but it was only available in very small quantities. Steel could be made for swords but not for battleships. In the middle of the nineteenth century, Britain was turning out 2½ million tons of iron, and a paltry 60,000 tons of steel. There were a number of attempts to improve steel production, notably by William Kelly at his iron works in Kentucky. But the big breakthrough came in 1856, when Henry Bessemer presented a paper 'On the Manufacture of Malleable Iron and Steel without Fuel' to the British Association for the Advancement of Science. It involved blowing air through molten pig iron, and was gradually improved over the years. At the same time, Frederick Siemens produced a variation known as the open-hearth process. The result was an extraordinary increase in steel making: by the end of the century, steel making was at a level fifty times above what it had been in 1870. Shipbuilding benefited directly in the use of steel instead of iron for the basic hull. In 1862, the small steel-hulled paddle steamer *Banshee* slid out into the Mersey. There were impressive signs of the usefulness of steel, when the clipper ship, *Clytemnestra*, with a hull of only ⅜-inch (.95-cm.) thick steel plates, successfully withstood a cyclone off Calcutta.

Bessemer himself became interested in ship design, and a ship bearing his name was launched in 1875. The *Bessemer* was a cross-Channel ferry, and its designer had the commendable aim of saving its passengers from sea-sickness in heavy seas. The hull and machinery were quite normal, but the passenger section was suspended inside it. As the ship rolled over or pitched, so an engineer worked hydraulic gear to ensure that while the whole ship might be swinging like a pendulum, the saloon at the heart of it remained always on an even keel. Sadly, the inventor had not allowed for reaction time: try as he might, the engineer could not keep pace with the motion – instead of counteracting it he simply chased it. Bessemer's place in the history of shipbuilding was not going to rest on the *Bessemer*. The steel process was the thing, not least because of the strength of the new steel boilers; and better boilers meant higher pressure; and higher pressure in turn meant that the already successful compound engine could be transformed into the even more successful triple expansion engine.

The triple expansion engine was a three-cylinder engine, pioneered by John Elder of Glasgow, who fitted out the 1864 steamer *Propontis* with a triple expansion engine in 1880. It was only a partial success, because the old-style boiler failed under the new demands. A year later, however, the Napier-built steamer with steel boilers producing steam at 125 psi proved a triumphant success. In a short period the steamship had been revolutionized. Everything was working better. In the engine, the piston moved faster, turning the propeller even faster and ensuring a better performance, but perhaps the most striking figures – certainly as far as the accountants in a shipping line were concerned – was the way in which with the new boiler materials and the triple expansion engine, the increased steam pressure – which can be roughly translated as more power to drive the ship – was joined to ever lower fuel consumption, and that simply meant lower costs.[19]

	1872	1881	1891	1901
Boiler pressure (psi)	52.4	77.4	158.5	197
Coal consumption (horsepower per hour in lbs)	2.11	1.83	1.52	1.48

The steamer had come of age as a big, fast, efficient vessel. The changes since the beginning of the century had been colossal. Those changes in the ships were matched by equally dramatic changes in the shipyards that built them, and in the lives of the men who worked there.

— ❖ —

THE WORKS AND THE WORKERS

T HE arrival of the iron ship might have been thought to usher in a new age of shipbuilding – out with the old craft and in with the new industry. If only it had been that simple, then many of the problems that beset the new era could have been avoided. It was true that the actual construction of an iron hull involved trades and techniques quite unknown to the shipwrights whose tradition of building in wood stretched back not for centuries but for millennia. But the break with the past was far from complete. How could it be? So many of the elements that went into shipbuilding had a timeless quality. The efficiency of a ship to cut a course through the ocean waves depended on fundamental laws that had little if anything to do with the material from which the hull was built. Old crafts may have been adapted, but not scrapped. And it was here that conflict was bred.

The shipwright was part of a tradition stretching back through the centuries. His status was earned by a long, hard apprenticeship. The early unions were not so much concerned with improving pay and conditions as with preserving the status of the craftsmen – and if that status was preserved, then the other benefits would naturally flow from it. This system worked well enough in the old yards devoted to building wooden sailing ships, largely because the yard owners had generally moved through the same slow, steady educational process of learning the job on the job. It only began to disintegrate when the new men came to dominate, men who arrived in the industry from the tradition of heavy engineering rather than from the old shipyards themselves. They looked on their workforce much as the owners of a textile mill regarded their spinners and weavers. It was expressed in an unusually direct and brutal form in a letter to a newspaper of 1885, when it had been suggested that, in the depths of a depression, the employers owed some sort of responsibility to their old employees, who had helped build their fortunes when times were good. Not so, declared the writer, the iron shipbuilder

> had, between 1880 and 1884, a golden opportunity of laying by an ample provision for a protracted period of dull trade, and that he has thrown away the opportunity in the most reckless manner. Further, he has spent neither the extravagant wage nor the inordinate amount of leisure he was able to obtain in a way beneficial to himself, his family, or the community.

The employer owes him nothing. He

> takes labour as he finds it, pays for it the price he can buy it at, uses it according to his judgment, and has no more reason to be grateful to his workman than to the grocer who sells him half-a-crown's worth of tea for two-and-sixpence.[1]

This was, to say the least, an extreme viewpoint, but it does illustrate the changed attitude which had shifted the shipyard worker from a skilled craftsman to a commodity to be bought up as cheaply as possible. The agony that racked the shipyards of Britain for well over a century stemmed from this appraisal. To an older generation of workers, and those who followed in a direct line of succession, there was a tradition which involved acceptance of a craft status. The men were not commodities. They had served a long and difficult apprenticeship and expected due recognition of their hard-earned skills. They were prepared to defend those rights against all comers – and all comers included the new generation of workers who built the iron ships. But the new men had their own skills which they guarded just as assiduously. Had it been possible for each to act quite independently of the other, then no problem would have arisen. A ship is not that simple. In its complexity, everything became mixed together, and then the troubles began. To understand what to outsiders seemed at best wrong-headed and at worst infantile disputes one has to look at the various stages that went into the construction of a ship.

The building of an iron ship began, just as the building of a wooden ship began, with the designer. The designs were then taken, just as they were for wooden ships, to the mould loft. The plans arrived at the loft where they were converted to full-scale chalk outlines on the loft floor. These were then transferred to the body plan, a series of cross-sections at one frame intervals, which were given a final form by being scrieved, that is, gouged, into wooden boards to fix them permanently. The scrieved boards formed the basis for the templates that would be used to shape the iron framework of the hull. This work was a part of the old tradition and went to the shipwrights. It is a tradition that has lasted right up to the present day. It was intriguing to note that the area where wooden mock-ups of sections of everything from frigates to nuclear submarines are made at the naval dockyards at Devonport is still known as the scrieve board and that tool chests still stand around marked with the owner's name, followed by the proud designation 'shipwright'.

The next stage was described in an article on Lairds' shipyard in the 1870s:

These boards are in their turn taken down to the shop below, where the ship frames are bent, on perforated plates called levelling blocks, each measuring 10 ft. by 3 ft., and weighing several tons. In bending a bar of angle iron for the ship's frame, a small iron mould made from the lines on the large board, taken from the mould-loft, is placed on the blocks, and its outline drawn in chalk. The mould is then removed, and after pegs have been placed at intervals along each chalk line in the holes made for the purpose, the heated bar of iron is swung on to the block by crane power, bent to the pegs, and hammered to the required shape. The mould is then applied to the frame, which, when it is perfectly true, is removed to the punching press, to have the rivet holes made in each arm. The frames are then removed to the building slip, and manipulated into the skeleton of the projected vessel.[2]

This all sounds very simple, and in essentials it is, for the building-up of the frames of an iron ship is not so very different from the old technique of building up the frames of a wooden ship. The first stage was to lay out the berth on which the ship was to be built. The longitudinal slope had to be built up with great accuracy to ensure a smooth launch – the lighter the ship, the greater the slope. Latitudinally, the berth had to be perfectly level. When that was completed, the work began on building up the frame of the ship and the metal-workers stepped in and took over.

As one would expect, iron frames were at first treated just as shipwrights had treated the parts of a wooden frame. They were scarfed together and assembled by appropriate joints to create different angles. It was some time before it was realized that metal was not like wood and that the basic structural member, the angle iron, could be manufactured as a single piece. John Scott Russell described the process of slow change.[3]

It was truly curious to notice the early ship-builder ... most assiduously putting together short pieces of angle iron, and regularly scarfing their ends together, to form from their assemblage a single iron frame, all formed out of little pieces. Happily there came an end of this, for he found it easier, cheaper, and stronger, to have his frame rolled in one piece, or at most in two; and in a short time he found out how, out of an angle iron of moderate dimensions, to bend or weld a complete frame, all in one length. But it was a long time before he could reconcile his mind to this fine simplicity; and even to this day there are rude ways of patching one angle iron on to the back of another, to give something like a rough imitation of the graduation in strength, which used to run from keel to gunwale, in a timber ship.

[108]

The iron plates for hull and decks have to be cleaned and cut to size, punched for riveting, planed, chamfered or rolled, depending on how they are to be put together. In general plates are fastened together in butt laps, when the two plates to be joined overlap, or by strapping, where the two plates abut each other, and a third plate is riveted behind to hold them together. The more sophisticated form of riveting used tapered rivets, in which case the holes had to be countersunk. A plate would be marked CKTS (countersunk this side) on one face, and to make doubly sure, CKO (countersunk over) on the other.[4] The platers then positioned the plates on the frame and made way for the riveters. At first all ships were hand riveted. The rivets were heated on site in a portable stove by a rivet boy – the 'boy' would normally be a youngster who would expect to move on to other jobs, but some 'boys' stayed at the job for most of their working lives. The hot rivet was then thrown to the holder-up who caught it and held it in place with a heavy hammer and two riveters striking alternately hammered over the head to hold the plates together. Speed and accuracy were essential as the whole operation had to be completed while the rivet was still hot. The hand riveter clenched the end of the rivet; the pneumatic riveter squeezed the two ends together. It was hard work and brutally noisy – one shipyard worker described it as walking into a wall of noise. It was particularly hard also in crowded shops, such as the boilermakers'. It was described in the article on Lairds, which also included a description of the new type of hydraulic riveter.

The boiler makers' shop is usually the most noisy part of a ship-building yard; and any one who has passed through that branch of the Birkenhead works, will be likely to pause before he again encounters such a trying ordeal, and one so certain to induce head-ache. The boilers are put together in an extensive shed at the upper end of the yard, where machines for shearing, punching, drilling, and riveting will be found in operation. Formerly, it was usual to rivet by hand, a much more laborious process than that performed by the hydraulic and steam machines. In riveting boiler plates, they are suspended by an overhead crane between two dies, one stationary and another moveable. The rivets, after being placed hot in the holes, are brought one by one between these dies, and the moveable die is pressed forward with a force equal to forty tons, thus fixing the rivet in its place.[5]

The automatic riveter continued in use from its introduction for as long as riveting lasted – at first worked hydraulically and later by compressed air when it was aptly known as the 'windy hammer'. But even in the middle of the nineteenth century it was clear that this was a very laborious process. The weight of rivets add considerably to the weight of the hull and the row upon row of knobbly rivet heads produced a hull that was very far from the perfect smoothness of the ideal. As early as 1855, a Mr Bertram of Woolwich had come up with an alternative.[6]

The plates are scarfed and laid together with sufficient overlap and are then hung in a perpendicular position, and temporarily clamped together in their proper places. Two small forges are slung from the roof or from crossbeams erected for the purpose, one forge being applied to each side of the plates. These act in the manner of a blowpipe, and soon bring the iron to a state of fusion, and when this is accomplished, the fires are smartly slid to one side, and two men hammer at the welding part until it becomes as sound as any portion of the plate. The supply of air for the forges is conveyed from a fan blast through small portable pipes.

It was an ingenious idea, but doomed to failure. Such joints were intrinsically weak. It was only with the advance of the science of metallurgy and the introduction of the electro-arc welder in the twentieth century that welding was able to take over from riveting.

The plates met at seams, running fore and aft, and at butts, running at right angles to them, and both needed to be made watertight by caulking. The process, however, was very different from that used in the old wooden ship. Now the caulker used the caulking tool to cut a groove near the edge of the plate, which created a ridge alongside. He then changed the angle of the tool to hammer the ridge flat over the gap between the plates. This added to the general din of the yard. One can easily imagine the effect on a riveter working on the inside of the hull at an interior member perhaps in a very confined space, while a caulker hammered away at the hull next to him. Deafness was inevitably common among riveters.

The time eventually arrives when a ship must leave the berth on the land where she was built and move into her true element, the water. The launch involves a good deal more than simply releasing the vast hulk of iron or wood and allowing it to slide down to float out into the river while the bands play and the crowds cheer. The initial launch calculations will have been made before any physical work has started. These will have determined the height that the keel will need to stand above the ground and the position on the berth, and only then will the keel blocks be laid out along the centre line. As the launch date grows near, these calculations would have been rechecked so that the weight and centre of gravity of the ship are accurately known. Small changes to details can make an important difference to the overall weight and balance. When everyone is happy with the calculations, the standing ways are built up beneath the hull; then for the structure down which the slip will ultimately slide. These are now heavily greased and running or sliding ways run in above them. Wedges are set in place, which when they are hammered home will allow the weight of the ship to fall on the launchways.

The final preparations are made just hours before the launch. The wedges are driven home and the keel blocks which until then had held the weight of the vessel are knocked out and all the shoring removed. Now the ship has to be held back, and once high tide arrives, the restraints can be removed and gravity will do the rest. In the big shipbuilding centres, launches were so commonplace that they rarely warranted more than a brief statement in the local press. Sometimes the occasion was special, as when the successful builders T. & J. Brocklebank decided to leave Whitehaven for greater opportunities on the Mersey. In April 1865, the last of the Brocklebank clippers, the *Mahanada*, built for the East India trade, was launched. She was, according to the press,[7] a 'remarkably fine ship combining

[111]

great carrying capacity with strength, durability and rapid sailing qualities'. Everything went just as it should.

> Her name was given her, as she moved easily and steadily from the ways, by Miss Robinson, daughter of Mr Jos. H. Robinson. The sunny beauty and genial temperature of the morning, and the interest occasioned by the idea which prevails that the *Mahanada* is, in all probability, the last of the noble fleet of merchantmen built here, and owned, by the Messrs Brocklebank, drew a crowd of spectators to the North Wall and its vicinity larger than we remember to have seen on any similar occasion. Representatives of all ranks and classes of our townsfolk were present, besides numerous visitors from St Bees and other parts.

It was also an occasion to reflect on just what a successful company such as Brocklebanks meant to a town like Whitehaven.

> The superior style, regardless of cost, in which their vessels have been invariably turned off, have conferred on Whitehaven-built ships a reputation all the world over – a source of no little pride to the town. The money which they have thus, during the long series of years in which the firm has been connected with the port, put into circulation amongst us, through carpenters, smiths, sailmakers, ropemakers, and the host of other artificers and tradesmen dependent on such a business, could it be told, would appear almost fabulous. Only a faint idea of its amount may be formed when we state that the *Mahanada* is the *hundred and fifty-third* they have built in the same yard; and that, in the opinion of gentlemen well informed in such matters whom we conversed with during the launch, her value, when she leaves Whitehaven, cannot well be under £25,000, if not indeed over that figure. A business distributing capital like this is not one to be withdrawn from such a town as Whitehaven without being felt, more or less, by all and sundry.

The launch was not always a success. In cold weather the grease on the ways froze and, at the moment of release, nothing whatsoever happened – the ship simply refused to budge. On other occasions the vessel budged a good deal too much. The *De Buffel* was sent on its way in March 1868, slowed down in theory by four anchors and 45 tons of drag chains.[8]

> The anchors did not hold well, the st[d] anchors dragged away from the line of launch, among the poles made for No 140 scaffoldng [the next slip]. The Port Anchors dragged in same way among ships own scaffold poles. The clay soil at the bottom of yard brought them up at last with a tremendous jerk breaking starboard stopper in two and putting heavy strain on chains.

This was an unfortunate accident. Another launch in 1883 was a disaster. Everyone at the Stephen's yard at Linthouse was, like the rest of the Clyde workforce, preparing for the annual Fair Holidays. A small ship, the *Daphne*, was ready for launching, but to speed the process up, the engines had already been put in place, and men were still at work down below as the vessel slid into the water. At first it seemed a perfect launch, but then as she hit the water the ship toppled over on her side and sank. The 124 men on board were drowned, their bodies only recovered three weeks later when the vessel was raised.

At the subsequent commission of enquiry, the company was exonerated on the grounds that 'insufficient was known about the stability of ships'.[9] This was patently true, at least as far as Britain was concerned where practice habitually ran a very long way ahead of theory. The result of the enquiry was a new set of guidelines to ensure that there was no repetition of the tragedy. The long-term issue of establishing a more scientific approach to the problems of shipbuilding was addressed by the setting up of the Department of Naval Architecture at Glasgow University.

The launch did not mark the end of work on a ship, just the end of one part. The vessel was now moved to a fitting-out berth to be completed. This involved everything from setting up the complex network of ropes and blocks that made up the rigging of a sailing ship to panelling the state rooms of a liner. The performance and safety of a ship were the prime concern of everyone from designers to riveters, but to the passengers on prestige liners, their whole view of a voyage might depend on quite different matters: for example, do the lavatories work? James Napier was just one of many ship-builders who were concerned with this problem, which he certainly did not regard as trivial. He corresponded over such minutiae as which disinfectant was most effective – McDougall's seemed to be favourite – to water cistern design.[10]

> The urinals of ships are generally in a very bad state – I am of opinion that they might be kept perfectly pure by the use of the sea water only if properly applied. They never have a proper cistern of water, but depend on the occasional supplies from the stroke of the paddle – if the vessel is a paddle steamer, it would be easy to cause the paddle to fill a cistern by catching the water that is thrown up – the water would be delivered steadily to the water closet or urinal in great abundance & at will, not by unpleasant jerks.

A ship, then, is more than just a hull. It is a complex of machinery. It has different spaces for different functions. Some spaces are avail-able for cargo, some for the fuel that will drive the ship along. Other spaces are for people; luxurious for first-class passengers in ocean-going liners; spartan for ordinary seamen. This complexity was reflected in a multitude of different trades – plumbers, carpenters, joiners, boilermakers and many more. Each trade had its own tra-ditions, its own structure – and each jealously guarded its own inde-pendence and status. Nowhere was the contrast more marked than between the shipwrights, joiners and boilermakers. The former had ruled the dockyard roost for centuries, but increasingly had to watch as new trades assumed ever greater importance and their own hard-earned skills based on the rigours of a long apprenticeship system were, as they saw it, ignored and devalued. The new generation of shipyard workers, who understood metal working and engineering practices, were no less jealous of their own trades. As I have said, had each been able to work in isolation, then there would have been few problems, but a ship cannot be compartmentalized in that way. One part depends on another, all interlock to create a whole. Here was a fruitful source of dissent that was to flourish down the years. It was not the only root from which troubles could grow.

Many industries have been subject to trade cycles, but few have shown a more dramatic picture of boom and bust, growth and decline than the shipbuilding industry. This is not surprising. Ships carried the trade of the world in ever-increasing quantities, and that trade was carried more and more in British ships throughout the nineteenth century – and increasingly that meant in steamships. The growth was phenomenal. In 1831 the world's steamship tonnage was a modest 32,000 tons. It more than trebled over the next decade to over 100,000 tons and just kept on increasing until by 1876 it had topped the 3 million mark.[11]

Alongside the growth went a steady spread of routes to create a world-wide pattern of trade – and world-wide patterns can be affected by changes anywhere in the network, but particularly in the markets of the major trading nations. In 1857, financial disaster hit America, with a bank collapse in New York. In this new age of rapid communication and interdependability, the markets of Europe toppled like dominoes and tumbled across the continent. Britain went first, knocking over Germany, then Scandinavia. South America was the next to feel the slump. As trade stagnated, merchant fleets were laid up and orders for new ships cancelled. Britain bore the brunt of the decline in shipbuilding and as the century wore on, each new crisis had a more profound effect, simply because Britain was becoming ever more dominant. The world slump of 1857 was bad news; the slump of 1873, which this time began in Europe, was a disaster. It was inevitable that Britain should be the worst hit, because Britain was dominating world shipping. By the 1890s, Britain had the biggest steamer fleet in the world and virtually every ship in that fleet had been built in a British yard. And the yards did not just build for home consumption. Overall they had over three-quarters of the world market. In the period 1892–6, British yards launched 1,021,000 tons (1,037,336 tonne) of mercantile craft compared with their nearest rival Germany, with a meagre 87,000 tons (88,392 tonne).[12] So dominant were British shipyards that they were even able to compete with the Germans on their home ground – a third of the German fleet was British built. A slump in world shipping was inevitably a slump in British shipbuilding.

The pattern of alternating slump and boom could be rationalized as a trade cycle by the economists, but for the workers in the industry it meant at best uncertainty and at worst real hardship and misery. A pattern developed whereby owners' associations tried to control wages and employment throughout a whole region, which it is not unfair to say generally meant cuts in pay and employment in the troughs and a reluctance to increase pay during a recovery. On their side, the men attempted to exact as large a wage as they could in the good times to help them survive the bad, while strenuously resisting all wage cuts for as long as they could. Before this could be achieved there was a long fight to establish the legal rights of trade unions, which were banned under various versions of the Combination Acts. The repeal of 1825 still left the unions vulnerable to legal action, and the fight for recognition ran on for another half century. A bill put forward to Parliament by Thomas Hughes and A. J. Mundella received the enthusiastic support of the shipyard workers and their writings have a good deal of the popular socialist rhetoric of the 1860s.[13]

> Petition, petition, must be your cry: your action and unceasing exertions to get the Bill of Mr. Thomas Hughes and Mr. Mundella passed. Neglect this and the doom of your children and your future freedom and happiness is sealed, to give place to your enemies, that they may still augment *the one hundred and fifty millions a year* which they are at present dividing among themselves from the labour of the working classes in the three kingdoms ...
>
> We must have laws that will give us power to deal with our employers, and which will give to us and our families much more of the £15,000,000 a year than we have ever received.

By the second half of the nineteenth century, the pattern of confrontation seemed to be established: on one side the owners, bonded together in associations, on the other the trade unions. Both sides relied on an alliance of interest to maintain a united front, and there are many examples of what this meant in practice.

In 1895, there was a general movement for a wage increase for engineering workers. Rates had been cut in the slump, and it was expected they would rise again with renewed trade. On the Clyde, workers and managers had reached agreement, but there was no settlement across the Irish Sea at Harland and Wolff. The main sticking point was piecemeal rates for riveters. The company had a number of fixed-price contracts in hand based on the old rates and said that a rise would erode their profits; the Belfast riveters claimed their right to the same rates as their opposite numbers enjoyed in other yards. The riveters went on strike, Harland and Wolff locked their gates and 7,000 to 8,000 men were out of work, on strike or locked out. Harland and Wolff's main fear was that their men would take the short trip across the Irish Sea and head for the shipyards of the Clyde, so they wrote to the Clyde shipbuilders asking them to lock out one quarter of their workforce to ensure that no Belfast men signed on. All the big companies, who were in the employers' association, agreed to the request, and as a result thousands of men in Glasgow and Greenock, who had no quarrel with their employers, found themselves out of work. Even *The Engineer*, a journal generally friendly to the employers, saw where such actions could lead.[14]

> If it is contended that the Clyde masters have both right and reason to lock-out their engineers — with whom they have only indirectly cause of quarrel — simply out of sympathy with Belfast, then the federated engineers have a perfect right to bring out their fellow-workers and society brethren on the Tyne, the Thames, the Mersey, or wherever also they may be at work.

Nevertheless, within a month of the start of the dispute, the north-east was asked to join the 'lock-out in sympathy'. To keep work moving, jobs which had been done by the engineers were entrusted to apprentices at which point the union called the whole workforce out. The Belfast dispute had spread turmoil to most of the major shipyards in Britain. Harland and Wolff offered better terms to their men in December, two months into the dispute. The offer, which might well have been accepted before, was rejected. At Christmas, Harland and Wolff opened their gates to all who wanted work and offered them dormitories inside the gates to protect them from attacks by the strikers. There was the inevitable trickle back as families began to suffer and the strike crumbled away.

The ironies of this case multiply the more one looks at it. The sympathy lock-out was a crude bludgeon to enforce Harland and Wolff's local interests – but the whole situation only arose because the Belfast company was suffering from its own inefficiency and secret back-door deals. Outwardly the yard was the model of prosperity. There had been a major redevelopment in the 1880s and even the professionals of the Institute of Mechanical Engineering, when they held their annual meeting in Ireland, were impressed. The magazine *Engineering* gave an account of the scene.[15] After describing the new slips, able to take 'the largest vessels' the article went on to describe the new workshops.

> The machine tools placed in them are of a description that becomes the work turned out in this yard, and are necessarily of great size and power in order to deal with the big work and notably the extra long plates used in the construction of the two big vessels. There are several heavy punching and shearing machines and double punches, the largest capable of punching a 1½ inch [3.8cm.] hole in the middle of a plate 7 feet [2.13m.] broad and 1½ inch [3.8cm.] thick. There are also shearing and punching machines with 3 feet 6 inch [1.06m.] gaps. These tools are by James Bennie & Company of Glasgow. The next machine is a shear punch of the same size, which has attached to it a second punch for making limber holes, or for punching 5 inch [13cm.] squares for centre plates where the frame goes through. There is one of David and Primrose's angle-iron levelling machines placed on rails conveniently between the angle-iron furnaces and the frame bending slabs. Beyond are two large radial drills with jointed

radial arms, which have a range of about 10 feet [3.05m.] radius, and near here is a large plate edge planer by Smith Brothers and Company of Glasgow, which will take a cut of 27 feet [8.23m.], and a still larger machine, a side end planer by Hetherington and Company of Manchester, which will plane 28 feet 6 inch [8.68m.] in the length of the plate and 7 feet [2.13m.] across. The most notable features in this part of the works, however, are the very massive plate rolls by Messrs. T. Shanks and Company of Johnstone.

The prestige ships built for the White Star fleet, *Teutonic* and *Majestic*, positively shouted both their modernity and their splendour. Unlike earlier vessels, the prominent masts now made little or no pretence of being able to carry sail: they were flagpoles. Below decks luxury ruled.[16]

In each ship, the midship-saloon is 60 × 57 feet [18.3 × 17.4m.], the full width of the ship, 10 feet [3.04m.] in height, with a crystal dome in the roof. The decorations in this splendid banqueting hall are in the Renaissance style. Bas-relief figures of tritons and nymphs in gold and ivory gambol around, and the ceiling is decorated in a corresponding style.

It was all very beautiful, and also very expensive. The new yard looked impressive, but the modernization writ did not run throughout the yards. There were still a thousand joiners doing work by hand which in other yards was done on machines. Harland and Wolff were an expensive yard that was keeping customers by offering secret 'favoured client' contracts, which gave the lines privileges including first call on repair and building berths, and contracts were taken at fixed prices which barely covered costs. It is against this background that Harland and Wolff's reluctance to increase wages has to be seen. The other shipbuilders were, in effect, subsidizing inefficiency at Harland and Wolff.

Belfast already had its own unique and uniquely distasteful form of internal conflict within the workforce. Harland and Wolff was

not immune from Ireland's sectarian conflicts. In 1863 a new programme of dock building was put in hand. Most of the navvies were
Catholics and they went off into Belfast for the unveiling of a statue
of the nationalist leader Daniel O'Connell. The Protestant workers
responded by burning an effigy of O'Connell. The result was a week
of rioting during which the shipwrights demanded that all Catholics
should be dismissed. Edward Harland responded by declaring that
if any Catholics were driven away he would close the whole works.
The troubles subsided, but re-emerged every time the Home Rule
movement became active. There was more violence in 1872 and
again Harland stood firm, but his rule did not run outside the dockyard gates and Catholic families were forced to leave the area. In
such an atmosphere it is scarcely surprising that very few Catholics
wanted to work at the yard. In the 1880s the whole issue became
more violent. Harland and Wolff men roamed the city attacking
Catholics with bolts and scrap metal, that came to be known as
'Queen's Island Confetti'. By now there were only 225 Catholics out
of a workforce of 3,000 and 190 of them left, intimidated. It is one
of the darker stories of shipyard history.

The problems facing other yards were very different, but in each
of the major shipbuilding regions owners felt the need to band
together to present a united front. The Wear Shipbuilders Association
was, like many others, formed amidst a fine unfolding of principles.[17]

> At a meeting of shipbuilders held this evening to take into consider-
> ation several regulations respecting the hours of labour, wages and
> other matters it was resolved that 'this meeting is of the opinion
> that the time has arrived, when for the mutual benefit of ship-
> builders of the Port of Sunderland and their men a proper under-
> standing and a feeling of good will should exist between them'.

The new Association was soon setting out a book of rules to govern
wages and conditions. Within a year, however, they were in the
familiar round of wage negotiations. Sometimes the association had
its way, but that very much depended on the unanimity and common
interest of its members. In June 1854, the Committee passed a resol-

ution calling for a reduction of wages. There followed a see-saw of claim and counter-claim, decisive action followed by wavering.[18]

> Resolved that in consideration of the depressed state of the Freight Market, and the want of a demand for new ships, a corresponding reduction of wages should take place, and that the Secretary should give early notice for a general meeting of the members of the Association.

The general meeting two weeks later approved a reduction in shipwrights' wages to five shillings a day and ordered that notice should be given to the men. Matters did not go according to plan. On 20 July there was obvious dissent among the builders.

> Several shipbuilders had not given notice to the men of the contemplated reduction of wages to 5/- a day. Proposed by Mr Laing that the wages remain as they now are the shipbuilders withdrawing their notice if the shipwrights withdraw theirs. (the shipwrights having given a counternotice of an advance to 6/6 per day).

That would seem to have settled matters, but the question rose again in September when a general meeting was called, once again trying to agree a general reduction in wages to 5 shillings. There were arguments but at the end everyone agreed what was to be done and adopted a suitably militant stance. 'Unanimously resolved that should the shipwrights refuse to take the wages offered, and a strike be the consequence, that those present will stand firm until they (the Shipwrights) take the proffered wages.' That was end of September and, predictably, the shipwrights did indeed go on strike. Again the united front of the employers collapsed. On 6 December another general meeting was called

> In consequence of Mr Michael Byers and Mr John Smith having given the shipwrights 6/- per day and started full work. Some of the shipowners have given shipwrights 6/- per day and commenced work. There was a certain amount of dissent but the termination

[121]

of the strike became general, the men resuming work on Saturday the 9th December at 6/- per day.

In 1857 the whole process began again with a reduction this time to four shillings a day.[19] Now it was the strike that collapsed. By April, the yards were offering 4 shillings a day for anyone who would work and there were more than enough hungry takers. For all the grand talk of co-operation, confrontation was the reality. At the end of 1866 shipbuilders and shipwrights met to discuss the sad state of trade and what could be done about it. The meeting only showed the gulf that existed between the two sides.[20]

Mr Laing (Chairman) drew the attention of the Delegates to the fact that great depression existed in the shipbuilding trade in Sunderland especially. Wages also were at many ports lower than here, and the hours of working longer. Sunderland was once the great market both for building and repairing, but in consequence of the rules made by the workmen it was evident that much of the trade was going to other ports. The Chairman also referred to the subject of caulking and remarked that in many ports a much greater number of feet was done by the men for a day's work than here, as to allowance it was suggested to the deputation whether or not it would be advisable to discontinue the present practice of giving ale and for the men to take an allowance of money instead. On the subject of piece work the chairman stated that more contracts could be obtained to build vessels in Sunderland if the men would agree to do the work by the price. After several members of the deputation and various shipbuilders had discussed the several subjects introduced one of the delegates stated that the views of the masters would be laid before the men at their next meeting. They then withdrew.

The reply was sent in the New Year.[21]

Sir, I am instructed to write you that the deputation laid the suggestions that were advanced by the shipbuilders before their members.

[122]

As to the given up [*sic*] the time for allowance during the winter months, the suggestion for to do more caulking at old ships, and also as to contracting for ships, and after discussing the different suggestions in all their bearings, the members could not see where the Shipbuilders were placed at a disadvantage with their neighbours and they considered that they had given way quite sufficient lately and they could not see anything they had got in return, and it was unanimously resolved that the trade regulations remain as they are at present. John Coxon, General Secretary to the Wear Shipwrights.

So the arguments went backward and forward. The shipwrights refused to accept a reduction and the employers responded by large-scale redundancies. The high hopes expressed when the Association was formed came to nothing. This is not surprising, since it soon appeared that in practice co-operation meant that the employers would tell their men what to do, at which point the men were expected to agree with the Association's sound judgement and impeccable logic. There were some who were prepared to take a different view.

William Denny also introduced new rules for his yard in 1886, but these were not rules imposed from above, but agreed by consultation. He was personally enthusiastic about notions such as the Awards Scheme, which paid premiums to workers who came up with new ideas, and applauded the selflessness of the journeymen and craftsmen who were prepared to give up a share of the company doctor's time so that apprentices and labourers could also be treated. At the end of a conference with the unions in 1885, he said:[22]

I think I am right in saying that the step taken by this firm in asking their workmen to join with them in the preparation of the rules of this yard is a new step in the history of labour. I cannot find from anything I have heard or read that any firm previous to my own firm has asked the men in their employ to join with them in the preparation of the rules by which these men were to be governed. I do not know that it would be advisable for every firm to do this; but the men we employ have shown in the past that they are able to take prudent and just views of things, and we wish to give them this mark of our confidence in asking them to confer with us in this matter. We believe the men whom you represent have sufficient experience of the world to know that no business can be carried on without effective rules, that the wise discipline of a business is an essential element in its efficiency, and that the efficiency of this business is the great means by which work is brought into the yard, and you are kept in constant employment.

He was singularly unafflicted by snobbery. There was a custom at many yards to take in the sons of the other shipbuilders as 'gentlemen apprentices' – at a suitably high premium. This was intended to fit the young men for a future role in shipyard management. Denny would have none of it.

With rare exceptions, the class called premium apprentices are what might be called failures. You hardly ever meet a premium apprentice coming to distinguished success. He is a 'petted darling'. He has been paid for by his parents, and his foreman has been instructed not to speak any harsh words to him. He is expected to get longer holidays and greater privileges than his fellow-apprentices. He is a child wrapped in cotton wool.

In Denny's works, preference went to boys and girls whose parents and relations were already in the yard, and after that places were open to all. He was always delighted to see real advancement. In 1881, a young girl was promoted to the tracing room after coming top in an examination. Denny wrote to the examiner.

I have a story about her which will interest you. When she joined us nine months ago, she was an illiterate field-girl, walking up and down to and from the print-works up the river every day of her life. The girls in the office on this account, or rather their foolish mothers, turned up their noses at her, and declared that her character was not what it should be, not fit for their girls to associate with. Two of the girls came with such messages to Miss Smellie, our superintendent, who, to her credit, stood by her charge. I told Miss Smellie to ask the girls to convey the following message to their mothers: that the firm was surprised any mother should send such a message by her daughter and that unless the charges against the girl's character were put in writing and signed no attention would be paid to them. This squashed the mothers, but their daughters formed a cabal of nearly the whole office and sent the poor girl to Coventry. Her reply to this has been such a display of quiet energy, steadiness and pluck as has won her the esteem of all the men in the office, and at last even of some of her female enemies. Your award has been a triumph for the poor thing, and a most healthy admonition to snobbery.

Denny was not the first to promise a better deal to his workforce. As early as 1850, James Napier introduced a scheme of profit-sharing to the workers at Govan.[23]

Believing irrespective of all other considerations that the Maxim of the Bible, which says 'We are to do to others as we would have others do to us' is the best worldly policy, that it is the surest road to happiness I have endeavoured to follow it by giving you now what I think I should like you to give to me were our positions changed namely an interest in the success of the business . . . I have set aside a sum for the profits of the Post vessel we built which shall be divided among you according to the proportion which as nearly as I can judge each of you have had in the making of it. . . . I have entirely excluded those who unfitted themselves for their duty by their drinking habits. I have partially excluded others for similar reasons.

The labourers or helpers & boys are not at the same rate as those who have a charge on their time. . . . I have endeavoured to make the division such that every one will be interested in his neighbour's work, that every one will be interested in preserving in the highest state of efficiency the Tools & machinery about the

[125]

place, in destroying nothing, in wasting nothing, in making the most of everything.

This is the voice of paternalism – kindly paternalism – but behind it lies the belief that the owner can decide what is best – 'what I think I should like you to give to me' – without any need to consult anyone, least of all the recipients of the bounty. The mention of alcohol is a reminder of one of the great problems of the day. An attempt was made to limit opening hours, the Forbes MacKenzie Act of 1863. An enquiry from Joseph Jones MP brought this reply from A. L. Stephen.[24]

In answer to your enquiry as to the result of my experience as an employer of labor regarding the general effect of the 'Forbes Mackenzie Act', I have much pleasure in stating that in my opinion its tendency has been most beneficial, my firm employ upwards of 1000 workmen and the attendance on Monday mornings is much more regular than was formerly the case indeed the attendance on Monday mornings is almost as regular as on other days and previous to the Act referred to coming into operation a very different state of matters existed. The Public houses being shut at 6 o'clock in the morning when the men are proceeding to work removes a temptation from their way, which was often attended by the most injurious consequences. They would step in merely to take a glass, and the consequence not infrequently was that they spent the whole day, or even several days in intemperance.

Denny and Napier stand out as exceptions among owners. There was, however, a spirit of collaboration in the air, especially during the 1870s. Trade unionists felt more comfortable once their position had been recognized, and the Boilermakers even had a song praising the new co-operative spirit.[25]

> Now 'tis true that capital
> All the risk must run,
> Like a ship exposed to all

Winds beneath the sun;
Feels the first trade's ebb and flow,
Must keen competition know.
So 'tis just and meet
Labour should co-operate,
And to help with all their might
Masters to compete.

The optimism was short lived.

In general the philosophy of the shipbuilder was very much that of most Victorian manufacturers. Labour was a product to be bought as cheaply as possible. They were slow to raise standards in good times and quick to cut wages or reduce the workforce in bad. The result was a round of strikes and lock-outs, very similar to those of other industries. In one area, however, the shipyards had a problem that was all their own, and it had its roots in history. The rough amalgamation of old trades and new, ancient crafts and modern practices that had marked the move from wooden sailing ship to iron steamer had produced a workforce of great complexity. Different jobs were allocated to different trades, and each tradesman jealously guarded his own particular area. But although a ship is a complex mechanism, it also has its own unity. One part connects to another and areas of responsibility overlap. The resulting arguments were to become the bane of the British shipyard – the demarcation dispute.

Virtually the only way of settling the demarcation disputes was by arbitration, and most areas had committees to deal with the problem. Reading the decisions of the Tyneside Board for a period covering three years in the 1890s shows a world of Byzantine complexity.[26] Who, for example, should be responsible for the sparring in the Storerooms of No. 625 Ship at Elswick? The rule book had nothing to offer, so it was decided that the work should go to the joiners, unless any spar was greater than 1½ inches (3.8cm.), in which case it would be done by the shipwrights. With solutions such as that there is no need to look for problems. The entire committee sat in solemn session to debate who should put 'a small door about

18 inches square' in a bulkhead. The decision was that it should be done by whoever put up the bulkhead. An admirably rational decision, but one can all too easily imagine the delays and wranglings that preceded the judgement. To an outsider the whole process is totally absurd – but not to the workers concerned. In an age when old skills were being gradually replaced and old hard-won status being steadily eroded, each case mattered very much indeed. It was not just a question of pay, but of pride in skills mastered. Entry into the different unions was strictly controlled. The Boilermakers barred labourers, and anyone proposing anyone for election who was not well known to him personally was liable for a fine of thirty shillings – a full week's wages for men at the time. It is scarcely surprising that those who ventured into this maze of rules and regulations emerged dazed and bewildered.

An umpire appointed to decide on a dispute on Tyneside in 1889 described the problems he faced.[27] The parties involved were the shipwrights and joiners. The arbitrators sent out forms to the different parties, but each side appeared to be doing the same work. Witnesses were interviewed, but still no decisions could be resolved. Eventually they all had to troop off to the yard.

Several days were occupied in the investigation, but the time was well spent. The facts, so far as they were procurable, were thus ascertained. After this sifting process the differences were reduced, but they were still considerable. This extreme difficulty in getting at the facts did not arise in any great degree from any wish to conceal the truth – still less from any intentional misrepresentation. In many classes of work there is really no uniformity. In one yard shipwrights do the work that Joiners do in another; in a second, both are doing precisely the same; while in a third a complete reversal may have taken place within a few years or a few months – the work done at one time by Shipwrights, being done by Joiners, or *vice versa*.

With these conflicting claims, and with no recognised line of demarcation between the respective traders, it is not surprising that disputes occur. The wonder is that they are so few.

[128]

The shipyards were notorious for their complexity, but it is not difficult to see that too often problems festered that could have been prevented from ever arising. In 1877 there was a strike of shipwrights on the Clyde. It followed a familiar pattern. Wages had been cut when times were bad and now when the shipwrights felt that things had improved they wanted to go back to their former rates. The matter was made worse by the fact that rates in Scotland were lower than those in England, and adding insult to injury, the amount cut from the shipwrights' pay had been given to the joiners. The shipwrights were reluctant to strike and offered to go to arbitration. The owners refused, but as the strike ran on for week after week they finally agreed. The arbiters could not agree, and the final decision was taken by the umpire Lord Moncreiff. He found in favour of the owners, and his report is worth quoting for what it shows of attitudes at the time.[28]

He discussed the total failure of communication between the two sides.

I thought the shipbuilders were wrong in not meeting the proposal for arbitration which the shipwrights had made at the time of the strike. Most cordially, I believe, from the tone and temper exhibited by those who represented the workmen, that had they done so the strike itself, and the great loss which it entailed all round, would have been averted. Nor am I without hopes that the discussion which has taken place, and the contact into which both sides have been brought into through this arbitration, may have laid the foundation of a better understanding. Had the shipwrights fully understood, what unfortunately they had no means of knowing with accuracy, the ground on which the shipbuilders proceeded I think it not improbable that they would have acted differently. I am very strongly impressed with the hardships which they have sustained and greatly regret that these were so, as they might have been prevented.

He then moved on to the question of different rates.

The rate of wages at other ports, especially the Tyne, the Wear, and the Tees, did for some time make a considerable impression on my mind. The rate certainly is higher than on the Clyde, and I cannot say that I was altogether satisfied with the explanations which were given of that undoubted fact. If I had found that the available labour in the Clyde had been diminished by drafts made by the Northumberland shipbuilders, that would have been a material element in favour of the workmen, but there was no such proof. The shipwrights on the Clyde seem to stand admittedly at the head of that branch of industry, but their numbers have not been sensibly or in any respect diminished by the slight excess in point of wages which was found to prevail in those establishments.

Or, to put it another way, as men were not being drawn away from the Clyde by higher wages, there was no case for offering any extra money to keep them. On the joiners, he wrote:

It seems that in 1875 while the wages of the shipwrights were lowered, those of the joiners were raised. Generally before that time the wages of the shipwrights were the higher in these two branches of industry. I can quite understand the feeling which this may have engendered; but it was clearly shown to us that there had been a very large increase in the demand for joiner work during these years from causes which are very familiar, and although it seemed hard that the penny or half penny an hour which was taken from the shipwrights should be given to the joiners, that fact so far from aiding is only another obstacle thrown in the way of the demand which is now made.

The money, having been given to the joiners, was not available for the shipwrights. In the end it all came down to whether the increase in trade warranted an increase in pay – and on that Lord Moncreiff made his judgement. Whether the judgement was a fair one we have no means of knowing, as the figures given to the arbiters were confidential. What does seem clear is that industrial relations in the shipbuilding industry on the Clyde at the end of the nineteenth century were conducted in an atmosphere of distrust and mutual hostility. Men had been on strike since April and had suffered great hardship largely because, as Moncreiff makes clear, they were not trusted with the essential information on which to base a rational conclusion. In the end they got nothing. The employers were saved from having to pay a greater wage bill, but no one put a price on low morale, distrust and a deep sense of grievance. The newspaper account declared the masters the winners. In this dispute no one was the winner: certainly not the shipbuilding industry of the Clyde. A small human voice can be heard among the pontifications of the great and the good, a voice that speaks of plain human misery. James Black was charged with breaking a street lamp.[29]

I did it deliberately for the purpose of getting into prison. I am one of the strike men, locked out through the carpenters. I was starving, had neither money nor anything else, and I thought I would be much better in prison.

Assessor – Are you telling a true story – was that your real reason for breaking the lamp?

Prisoner – So help me God it was.

By the end of the nineteenth century the British could proudly boast that their shipbuilders ruled the world.[30]

If British engineers are at times justly reproached for their dogged adherence to old machines and old methods, British shipbuilders are, at any rate, entirely blameless in this respect. They may fairly claim to be the leaders of the world in the development of new systems of ship-building and to be the most open-handed of all nations in the trial of elaborate and costly experiments, and in the construction of expensive tools and apparatus. Of all our great firms there is probably not one which watches more closely the modern development of machinery and the application of it to their own craft than Messrs. Harland and Wolff.

[131]

Their machines may have been magnificent, but not their understanding of the human beings that manned them. Robert Owen had shown as early as 1816 that when he reduced the working hours at the cotton mill at New Lanark, productivity rose. No one followed his example – few believed his evidence. It was well over half a century later that the shipyard owners, Short Brothers, discovered the same thing all over again, when the 54-hour week was introduced.[31]

> The firm have found that instead of the production being less from the apparently shorter hours of work, it has on the contrary gradually increased. . . . The men started at six o'clock and stopped at eight for a half-hour for breakfast, had another interval of an hour at noon and the day's work finished at five. The conditions under which the old system was carried out were such that many workmen were incapable of maintaining the long hours. It was in point of fact quite common for a man with 24s a week to lose on an average three quarters per week simply because he was unable to rise at six o'clock and work full-time. . . . Under the 48-hour system, the men start after breakfast at 7.30 and go on with only one break until 5 o'clock . . . They are able to do more work this way than under the old system and at the same time more work is got out of the machines.

The lesson that co-operation bred efficiency and productivity was learned slowly in Britain – too slowly as it transpired. And in one important branch of shipbuilding, the other vital lesson that growth depended on continuous innovation was learned at a lethargic rate. While the mercantile fleet saw spectacular advances in the first half of the nineteenth century, the navy stagnated.

$$\bullet$$

THE STEAM NAVY

A<small>T</small> the end of the Napoleonic Wars, 'Britannia Rules the Waves' was no more than a statement of fact. Nowhere in the world was there another naval power that could even begin to challenge the supremacy of the Royal Navy — nor did there seem to be the least possibility that one would arise. Whatever challenge might be thrown down, Britain as the leading manufacturing country could be confident of meeting it. The country's ships were not necessarily superior — British commanders in the war were far happier commanding a captured French vessel than one that had been home-built — but with the French now defeated there was no risk to counter. This would remain true for the rest of the nineteenth century. So, for a very long time, the wooden sailing ship firing broadsides remained the stalwart heart of the fleet. Steam power was well established by the early years of the century, but for the navy it had little virtue except as a means of moving warships down rivers and estuaries to the point where sails could be set. The steam tug had its place, but not the steam battleship. True, the tiny paddle steamer, the *Diana*, was commandeered for service in the First Burma War, which broke out in 1823 and lasted until 1826. The vessel was too small to carry guns and was armed with a battery of Congreve rockets. It was more intimidating than effective.

It is easy to depict the Admiralty as being staffed entirely by diehard reactionaries. It might well have been, but there was reason behind their conservatism. There were two powerful arguments against using paddle steamers as warships. The first was vulnerability. It was not simply a matter of the paddle wheels offering themselves as very tempting targets, but the machinery that drove them was even more likely to be hit since much of it rose above the water line. The second argument related to fire power. Wars at sea were still decided by broadsides fired from cannon, and paddle wheels effectively prevented armament being placed in the one spot where it was most needed, amidships. There was one serious attempt to produce a powerful paddle steamer with a full range of armaments. The American, Robert Fulton, designed a vessel with an internal paddle wheel, which he called a steam frigate. Named the *Demologus* it was in fact little more than a floating battery for harbour defence, and was incapable of operating far from home.

During the first decades of the nineteenth century, there was continuous development of the sailing warship. During Sir Robert Seppings' period in office as Surveyor of the Navy, there were big advances in hull design. His introduction of iron strapping meant that the length of hull could be increased by as much as twenty-five per cent; and his introduction of the rounded stern enabled a warship to develop all-round fire power. His successor Dr William Symonds produced a new class of frigates, which although they were notably fast were equally notably unstable, making gunnery more a lottery than a science. In an article of 1846, the *Nautical Magazine* noted that 'for rolling, pitching and lee-lurches, the Symondites beat the lot'. Two advances in technology were, however, to change the whole notion of warship design: the screw propeller and the rifled gun.

The propeller, engines and shaft were not exposed to fire as the machinery had been in the old paddle steamer, and the whole side of the vessel was available for ordnance. In 1845, a famous contest took place to decide the relative merits of screw propeller and paddle wheel. Two sloops of identical tonnage and horse power were fastened together stern to stern. When the order 'Full Steam Ahead' was given the propeller-driven *Rattler* towed the paddle steamer *Alecto* backwards at a speed of about four knots. There could scarcely have been a more convincing demonstration. The screw propeller did have one disadvantage: it did not work well with wooden ships. The vibration tended to shake the hull to pieces, while in turn the movement and flexibility of the wooden hull affected the all-important alignment of the propeller shaft. The obvious answer was an iron hull, but in the new age of rifled guns, the iron hull was quite useless. It was not just that the shell went straight through but it did so to the accompaniment of a high-speed shower of lethal iron fragments. There were experiments with small iron steamers. Lairds built gun boats for the East India Company and one of their small iron paddle steamers, the *Nemesis*, took part in the first Opium War in 1839. It was devastatingly successful, but was faced with nothing more daunting than a fleet of Chinese junks.

In 1847 Parliament decided to look into the future of the navy, and took advice from experts of various kinds.[1] Arthur Anderson, managing director of P & O, was questioned on his ships, twenty-three of which covered 600,000 miles (1,000,000km.) a year between them. Although not armed, their mail-carrying contract required that they should be fitted with four guns of the largest calibre then in use, so that the merchant fleet could quickly become a fleet of warships – not, one would have thought, a very practical alternative to a genuine modern navy. It was, however, contended that the privately built vessels were altogether better, and invariably faster than the navy's own ships. William Pitcher, a shipbuilder, described the P & O vessels as being of immensely strong construction, of English oak with outer planking of teak – the planks themselves up to 70 ft (21.3m.) long. The navy, however, seemed unconvinced. Lt Julius Roberts of the Royal Marine Artillery described the problems and expense of clearing the decks to make space for guns and to give them a field of fire, and he showed the old doubts about the vulnerability of machinery. One of the parliamentary committee put the direct question. 'What do you suppose the effect of shot passing through the boilers would be in the engineroom?' To which he replied with commendable brevity – and accuracy. 'I should not like to be down there.'

There was still no great sense of urgency – the only other major conflict of the age, the Crimean War, used ships simply as floating platforms from which to bombard coastal batteries. The French built a number of 'floating batteries', slow, ponderous, shallow draught gun platforms whose sides were protected by wrought-iron plates backed by timber. They were scarcely ships at all, but can qualify as the first of the ironclads. The French followed this up, at the end of the war, with the first real pioneer of a new generation of genuine armoured warships, designed by Depuy de Lôme. The *Gloire*, launched in 1859, was in essence a wooden frigate with heavy iron plating fastened on the outside. Here was a genuine threat to Britain's by now rather aged fleet, and the response was immediate. It was clear from the start that the race to produce powerful, armoured, steam-powered warships would be won by the world's leading manufacturing nation, Britain.

Eighteen fifty-nine was the watershed year. A new battleship was launched, HMS *Victoria*, a three-masted ship with wooden hull and three rows of cast-iron cannon poking out through the port holes. All that distinguished the vessel from a ship of Nelson's navy were two stubby funnels proclaiming that somewhere below decks was a steam engine. In the same year, Sir John Pakington, First Lord of the Admiralty, commissioned a design for an armoured warship to challenge the *Gloire*. The work went to Isaac Watts, Chief Constructor to the Navy, and John Scott Russell. The design they produced for what was to become HMS *Warrior* was based on the concept of an armoured box, 'the Citadel', which would contain guns, ammunition and the vital machinery to run the ship. Forward of the box was a handsome clipper bow, aft of it a rounded stern and below, the rounded keel beneath the water line. Enemy fire might damage stern or bows but would neither sink the ship nor stop it continuing as a fighting unit. Technically, the vessel was to be a frigate, simply because she was carrying all her guns on one deck, and so the new ship would, in theory, rate a long way below other warships in the fleet. In practice she could demolish every single one of them with impunity.

Once the basic concept had been agreed upon, the new world of technology took over. The basic hull was of wood 2 inches (5cm.) thick, inside which were 4½ inch (11.25cm.)-thick wrought iron plates and beyond these a backing of teak 18 inches (46cm.) thick to complete the sandwich.

At this point work passed from the Admiralty to a private company, as no naval dockyard was equipped for building iron hulls. The yard selected was The Thames Iron Works and Shipbuilding Company at Blackwall. The site has a long history of shipbuilding: repairs during the Second World War unearthed evidence that the Romans had built ships there. Its fame, however, dates back to 1834 when it became the first yard to be entirely devoted to building in iron.[2] T. J. Ditchbourn, who was later to form a partnership with C. J. Mare, had experience of wooden shipbuilding, but with a good deal of foresight saw that the future lay with iron and steam, not wood and sail. The early development centred on building cross-Channel ferries. It is typical of the period that there was great interaction between apparently very different sections of the industrial world. The vessels were built superficially to link rail services between Britain and continental Europe, and the company was soon to have an even closer rail connection. It began with an accident in 1847 when the launch of the iron steamer *Prince of Wales* went badly wrong and the vessel was left stuck at bow and stern, with over a hundred feet of hull suspended in between. The hull suffered no damage, a fact which greatly impressed Robert Stephenson. The ship's hull was acting as a hollow box girder, and this was the design he was to adopt for his two railway bridges at Conwy and across the Menai Straits. Sections of the bridges were to be supplied from Blackwall. It is only a small step from constructing a vast hollow girder inside which trains could run, to building a fortified box for a warship. The company had changed hands, but the tradition continued.

The keel for *Warrior* was laid down on 25 May 1859. She was very long by the standards of other warships at 380 ft (115.8m.), and was designed to work as a steamer or as a sailing ship – and could use steam and sail together. Her trunk engines by John Penn of Greenwich were fed by tubular boilers at a pressure of 20 psi. On her trials she was to achieve speeds of over 14 knots, which was considered highly satisfactory. Success was not so apparent during the actual process of building. Inevitably, with such a pioneering effort, the costs shot far beyond the estimates and there were to be a number of delays. Some were caused by the yard itself, which was seriously short of the capital needed for such a major venture and had to be rescued from bankruptcy. Other delays were caused by doubts about the armament she was to carry.

The traditional armament of warships had changed little for the best part of a century. Production standards survived that were first laid down in 1774, based on the use of cast iron. It became clear during the Crimean War that gunnery needed greater range, great accuracy and a change from ball to explosive shell. A sound method of improving accuracy was 'rifling'. A small projection on the shell engaged with a spiral groove cut inside the barrel which gave the shell spin and greater accuracy. The trouble was that cast-iron barrels could not be rifled as they would crack under the stress of the shell accelerating up the grooves. Steel would have been an ideal material, but was still only available in small quantities. That left wrought iron, which seemed an unlikely material. One practical solution was found by William Armstrong.

Born in 1810 the son of a successful businessman, Armstrong showed an early aptitude for all things mechanical, but was trained not in engineering but for the more 'respectable' profession of the law. Engineering, however, won out and he went into business as a manufacturer of hydraulic machinery. Perhaps it was a good combination, the practical ability allied to the methodical, step-by-step processes of the law. In any case he recognized the significance of a well-known attribute of wrought iron – an attribute well known to every country blacksmith. If you take two pieces of wrought iron, hold them together and bring them to a white heat and hammer them, they will weld into one solid piece. Armstrong's idea was to coil iron bar into a spiral, then heat it and hammer it to form a tube. The tube could then be welded to other similar tubes to create a single tube, the length of a gun barrel. Extra strength was still needed, so a second tube was stuck over the first. This required the two tubes to be machined to fine tolerances. The eventual result was a new type of gun. In 1858 he demonstrated his eighteen pounder, testing it against a conventional cast-iron eighteen pounder. The results were impressive: the Armstrong gun was half the weight of the older cannon, fired its shell twice as far and with considerably more accuracy. There were faults in the Armstrong gun that were to appear in the reality of the smoke and confusion of a gun deck during action, but the fundamentals were sound. It was clear to the Admiralty that a new age of naval gunnery had dawned. Armstrong was knighted, appointed Engineer of Royal Ordnance and by January 1860 was manufacturing guns from a new works at Elswick on the Tyne. Guns were also to be made at the Woolwich Arsenal. His guns were now to be fitted to *Warrior*.

The new battleship was a curious hybrid. Some elements were entirely new: the armour plating, the Armstrong guns. In other ways the ship looked back to an earlier age. The guns were still arranged to fire a broadside, and the steamer could also be worked as a fully rigged three-masted ship. The *Warrior* had not just improved on earlier designs, it had made all earlier designs instantly obsolete. British engineers had moved warship construction into a new age and their success was an instant encouragement for others to take the movement forwards. Some who did so were to concentrate throughout their careers on warships, others were to be led in more peaceful directions.

Two issues were clear following the launch of *Warrior*: guns were becoming ever more powerful and that would create a demand for still more resistant armour plating. The shipbuilders looked to the iron masters to provide larger and thicker iron plate, and one company which responded found itself drawn ever closer to the world of shipbuilding and it was that world that was to make its founder's name famous. That name was John Brown.

John Brown's early life followed a path not dissimilar to that trodden by many another Victorian entrepreneur and manufacturer.[3] He was born in Sheffield in 1816, left school at fourteen and was apprenticed to a staple ware manufacturer, working for no wages at all for the first two years and six shillings a week for the next five. After that his father bought him a new suit, gave him a sovereign and told him he was on his own. In 1837, he was offered a partnership but had not enough money to accept the offer, so he took over the factoring side of the business. With £500 capital, a house, a gig and boxes of samples of files and cutlery he set out to sell his wares. He was successful enough to be able eventually to start up on his own and then turned his ideas to manufacturing. In 1848, he invented and patented the conical spring buffer. He was so proud of this device that in later years, when he was showered with honours, he incorporated it into his coat of arms, no doubt under some suitably heraldic name.

Brown set up the Atlas Steel and Spring Works, where he concentrated on producing iron of a quality that could be used for making steel — up to then it had mostly been supplied from Sweden and Russia. By the late 1850s his dozen puddling furnaces were turning out 100 tons of iron a week, some for steel making, the rest for bridges and boiler plates. The company was an undoubted success, but Brown was always ready to try the new, and he became one of a select number of iron makers to use the Bessemer process for steel making. When the early problems arose, due to the large amount of phosphorous in British ores, Brown allowed his licence to lapse. Then, as the problem was solved and Bessemer became a new neighbour, Brown went back to steel making, paying Bessemer a royalty of £1 per ton. It was a period when innovation was generally, but not always, appreciated. The railways in particular were slow to see the advantages of steel. A delightful story which may be apocryphal but which one hopes is true tells how the Midland Railway was converted. Its lines ran close to Brown's works, and one of the managers, John Devonshire Ellis, sneaked out at night with a gang of plate layers, removed a new iron rail and replaced it with one of their own steel ones. When it came time to replace the iron rails, the steel was unworn, and Ellis admitted his deception.

John Brown first became interested in the idea of armour plating during a visit to France, when he asked to visit the *Gloire*. Permission was refused, but he saw enough of the hull to discover that it was built up of 4½-inch (11.4-cm.) plate, 5 ft (1.52m.) long and 2 ft (0.61m.) wide, which had been made by hammering. He was convinced that larger and better plate could be produced by rolling. The idea was not entirely new. Armour plate had been rolled at Beale's of Rotherham for a floating battery built by Palmer's of Jarrow during the Crimean War. But the end of the war marked the end of Beale's interest in armour plating. Brown seems to have been unaware of the precedent; in any case his move into armour plating was to turn a modest business into an industrial giant. In 1862 rolled plate was sent down to Portsmouth for a series of tests against the older, hammered plate. The new won decisively and Brown's went into production.

In 1857, Brown's had employed some 200 men. Ten years later the workforce was 2,000 and turnover had risen from £3,000 a year to £1 million. The technology showed equally impressive growth, as in the same year the company demonstrated its new powers.[4]

On Friday last one of the finest, thickest and heaviest armour-plates ever rolled in the world was pressed into the very perfection of a manufacturers armour-plate at the great Atlas Ironworks of Sir John Brown & Co, Sheffield. The size of this monstrous slab of iron when in the furnace was a little over 29 foot [8.84m.] long by about 4 ft [1.22m.] broad and 21 inches [0.53m.] thick. Its rough weight was over 21 tons [21.3 tonne]. It was built up in the furnace before being rolled by five mould plates, each 3 inches [7.5cm.] thick, and one solid plate of six inches [15cm.]. This mass when reduced by intense heat to the consistency of dough was withdrawn from the furnace and in the course of less than a quarter of an hour was passed between the rollers many times, was reduced to a compact slab of iron of uniform thickness of 15 inches [38cm.].

The effect the new generation of iron slabs was having on the navy was demonstrated equally dramatically at the same time. The ship of the line, *Colossus*, built in 1848 for £100,000 and still in excellent condition was sold for a niggardly £6,178 10s. 0d.[5]

John Brown himself was proud of the work and the men who did it.[6]

> Mr Brown was constant in his admiration of the 'brave workmen' who had heated 20 tons [20.32 tonne] of iron, dragged it from the furnace, and passed it in an instant through the rolls into an armour plate, 40 feet [12.19m.] in length, 4 feet [1.22m.] in width, and 4½ inches [11.4cm.] in thickness. The like had not been done before, not in England only, but in the world. Twenty tons [20.32 tonne] of iron in a white heat were for the first time ever, fired, and handled as quickly as seen.

John Brown had gone public in 1864, with J. D. Ellis of midnight-rail fame as managing director. Brown himself did not take kindly to power-sharing and set up a rival company, which did not prove to be a great success. Under Ellis's control the original John Brown's continued to develop and prosper, but as old markets withered in the face of foreign competition, the company returned to shipbuilding. They acquired the works of James and George Thomson, and with them a connection that was to ensure their fame and fortune. Thomson's was established as an engine and boiler works on the Clyde in 1847, and began shipbuilding in 1851.

In 1867 the company received its first order from Cunard for a screw steamer, the *Russia*, to be followed by a number of other big steamers, a line that culminated in the *Gallia* of 1879 and the *Servia* of 1881. The latter was the largest vessel of the fleet at 7,392 tons [7,510 tonne] and had what was for the day a monstrously huge compound engine, with a high-pressure cylinder of 72-inch [1.83-m.] diameter and two low-pressure cylinders, each 100 inches [2.5m.] across. The space needed for engine and boilers was so great that there was very little room left for cargo. So Cunard decided to concentrate instead on passenger accommodation. It marked a real change in the company's development, and Thomson and Cunard prospered together. In 1897, Brown's took over the yard, and began perhaps the most famous of all maritime partnerships, John Brown and Cunard, that culminated in the launch of the

[142]

Queen Mary. It had been a long and tortuous path from builders of hydraulic machinery to builder of ships, one which might never have been followed had it not been for the need to develop armour plating.

Returning to the position immediately following the development of *Warrior*, one finds a curious anomaly, a mixture of old ideas and new. The armament was modern, even if the breech-loading mechanism had not been well worked out, but was still arrayed as it would have been a century before. The vessel was unquestionably a steamer, but was fully rigged with sail. The armament question was one that led to much pondering. One of the troubles with the broadside was that, at any one time, half the guns were in use. One system designed to overcome this was by utilizing a complex rail network on the gun deck that enabled guns to be moved as and where required. Not surprisingly, this was not very widely adopted. The other alternatives were in some ways similar. The French 'barbette' was an armoured tower protecting the guns' machinery, with the guns themselves mounted on a turntable above; the alternative, developed simultaneously by Cowper Coles in Britain and John Ericsson in America, was the rotating turret. This latter was given its most famous early outing during the American Civil War. The Confederate ironclad *Virginia*, in fact an old frigate whose armour seemed largely to consist of reused railway track, set off to wreak havoc among the ships of the Federal fleet. Out to give battle came the *Monitor*, a vessel armed with two rotating turrets on a hull with very low freeboard – aptly referred to as 'a cheesebox on a raft'. The duel was indecisive, but the world had witnessed the first war of the ironclads.

The navy experimented with two vessels, *Royal Sovereign* and *Prince Albert* in the 1860s, each of which had four turrets mounted along the centre line of the vessel. They could be called forerunners of the modern navy, but at the time they were largely ignored. The genuine new beginning came with the *Devastation* which carried two turrets, one forward and one aft. It suffered from a problem that beset all early turret craft: the low seaboard, which left the decks awash in anything more than a gentle swell. The problem was finally

[143]

solved with a combination of barbette and turret that marked the arrival of the Dreadnoughts at the end of the century. By now the navy had firmly relinquished sail, though not without a struggle. There was a deep-seated reluctance to accept the idea that expertise existed outside the service. Even Captain Coles, the innovative designer of the turret, tried to take his own ideas into areas where he had no experience. When one of the first vessels to carry the new turrets was launched Coles found much to complain about – although the vessel performed commendably well. He was allowed to design his own vessel, the *Captain*, heavily weighted down and with an exceptionally low freeboard even by the standards of the day. *Captain* capsized in mid Atlantic, taking her designer and most of the crew down with her.

A feature of the age was the intense competition between the navy and the private shipbuilders for the right to build the new ironclads. One feature that struck outside observers, such as P. Barry who toured private and naval dockyards in the 1860s, was the different attitude shown towards the men.[7]

> When in the shipyard of the Messrs Laird, at Birkenhead, I saw provision for the workmen receiving their own cooked meals within the gates, to wean them from the seductive beer-shops, I felt keenly the injustice I had done the ill-paid and ill-used artizans in Chatham dockyard. The artizans whom I had seen searched on leaving work, or standing in the rain outside the gates, until the lords within thought fit to call them, cannot be expected, I will even go so far as to say, cannot be desired to labour as the artizans who are cared for, respected and encouraged not by the Messrs Laird only, but by the other great employers of shipyard labour.

He was equally clear that the new technology and the needs of skilled men were more clearly understood in the private yards. He reported a conversation during a visit to John Brown's Atlas works as Brown showed off his machinery.

Do you see that begrimed mechanic at the steam hammer? What do you imagine we pay him every year? We pay that man £900 per annum! If then, the dockyards were to pay their hammermen £900 a year, what should we have to pay the Admiral Super-intendents?

In part, the reluctance of many naval officials to accept new ideas could be put down to the fact that dockyards such as Devonport were set up entirely to deal with wooden ships. It was difficult for the navy to repair vessels of the size of *Warrior*, let alone build them. There were two not altogether compatible views held by the private builders. The first was that the Admiralty should not be allowed to compete.[8]

It is my strong conviction that unless the Iron Shipbuilders employ some influence to prevent it the whole of the Royal dockyards of England will be converted into Iron Shipbuilding Factories so as to be formidable competitors with the private yards, at enormous cost to the Country.

The other argument was that the Admiralty was too inefficient to be allowed to build ships. This position was still being maintained in 1880 when the inevitable parliamentary committee, this time under Lord Ravensworth, met to look into the matter. The naval architect, Professor Edgar, gave his own uncompromising view of the royal dockyard as 'a relic of the past'.[9]

The traditions of the timber age have been perpetuated in the iron age. Ships are laid down in considerable numbers and a little is done now and a little again, just as though iron became seasoned and improved after being worked into a hull. Then again, the difference . . . is due to the red-tapeism, which accepts the creed that all the available talent of the country is employed at Whitehall in designing ships of war, as well as to the lack of business habits which prevents the specifications from being made as complete as they are made in the case of ships for the merchant marine. Most of all, however, is the difference to be accounted for by the length of time occupied in vessels constructed at the Royal Dockyards. Their practice undoubtedly leads to a waste of money which is little short of a public scandal.

The technical press of the day generally came down on the side of the private yards at the end of the enquiry.[10] They were particularly hard on the British navy's slowness to adopt a scientific approach. Even at that date the standard reference work on stability, first published in France in 1814, had still not been translated into English. The criticism was not altogether fair. The Admiralty had shown a new approach, particularly after the establishment of the School of Naval Architecture at Portsmouth in 1848, and in an area that was to prove vital to the development of ship design, the Admiralty proved to be an understanding and helpful patron.

William Froude's early career had been mainly as a railway engineer, working for Brunel on the Bristol to Exeter line and again on the disastrous atmospheric railway originally intended to carry the line on through Devon. It was Brunel who introduced him to the world of shipbuilding when he asked for his advice on the launch of the *Great Eastern*. If nothing else this was a mark of Froude's standing – it was very rarely that Brunel asked the advice of anyone. In the 1860s he moved to Paignton, where he began a series of tests on model ships in a water tank. The results of his tests were made known to the newly formed Institution of Naval Architects, but there was no great enthusiasm for this form of testing, until Sir Edward Reed, the chief constructor of the navy, came on a visit. He was impressed by what he saw, and suggested that Froude apply to the Admiralty for funding to set up a purpose-built tank and establish a set of experiments on hull design. Froude duly put in his application, stressing the possible savings in running and building costs for ships.[11]

Assuming the enquiry to result in even nothing better than the saving of a permanent expenditure of ten horse power in all, in the annual reduction in the national coal bill even thus would pay

[146]

the interest of the outlay by which the saving had been effected, were it to render unnecessary half a dozen measured mile trials in the course of each year the same result would follow, were it to result in beneficially taking 10 feet off the length of a single iron-clad the whole would probably be recouped at once.

The Admiralty agreed to pay £2,000 towards the test, encouraged by the loss of HMS *Captain*, sunk mainly because of poor design. Tests at the new tank in Torquay proved conclusively that tests on models when scaled up were an accurate reflection of the performance of a real ship in real conditions. Although the work had been initially funded by the Admiralty, it was rapidly taken up in the commercial world. William Denny established a test tank at Dumbarton in 1881, which was to remain in use for just over a century, and still survives today. Froude had spoken of modest savings: in the event every shipbuilding country in the world was to use models as a design test, and the cash savings are literally incalculable.

This was a case of a private individual, albeit an eminent one, receiving public encouragement. It was not typical of the way in which advances were made. They were as likely to come from the slightly eccentric, rather wayward entrepreneur and inventor as they were from the official and all too ponderous establishment. The story of Alfred Fernandez Yarrow[12] is perhaps not typical of anything, apart from the life of the said Alfred Yarrow, but it does show that there was never any obvious route to innovation and success. There was certainly nothing to suggest heredity at work. His father lost a great deal of money by investing in a Cornish copper mine, thanks to his own gullibility. He was given a sample of ore and considering himself a shrewd business man he had it assayed, and received the splendid news that it was a high grade ore. Sadly, he neglected one further precaution. He never checked to see if the ore came from the mine in which he had been invited to sink his capital. It didn't. His son, wisely, decided to build his career on his own tests and discoveries.

Alfred Yarrow was one of three children who could have been taken as models for the old saying: 'the child is father to the man'.

He was inventive from the first, and his inventions had a sound basis in practical common sense and usefulness. Bored by holding skeins of wool for a zealously knitting aunt he invented an automatic wool-winder. Tired of traipsing upstairs to see if his grandmother was ready to put her candle out, he developed his automatic candle-snuffer. As soon as granny's head hit the pillow, she broke a thread and the snuffer descended. Unfortunately he forgot to tell granny who wondered why the second she got into bed she was plunged into gloom. Rather more practically, whilst still a schoolboy, he rigged up a private electric telegraph to a friend's house. As his father's finances tottered, he decided to put his inventiveness into making a profit. With a friend, Hilditch, he designed a steam plough, which was modestly successful, and a steam carriage, which bowled along at a highly respectable 25 mph but fell foul of the new law which decreed that it had to be preceded by a man with a red flag. He raised enough cash from his inventions – the sum of £1,000 – to move into a boat yard on the Isle of Dogs in 1863. He was then twenty-three years old.

The initial idea had been to set up as ship repairers, an area in which his partner Hedley claimed to have good connections. Yarrow went off twice a week touting for business from a little rowing boat, and at the end of the first year he had lost £100. The following year, they greatly increased their workload by cutting costs – and lost £2,000. Yarrow had once worked on a steam launch, and in a last fling he advertised

STEAM LAUNCHES
anyone wanting a steam launch would be well served if
they came to Yarrow and Hedley, Isle of Dogs.

Yarrow acquired one customer, who paid £145 for a launch that cost £200 to build – but at the end of the year Yarrow bought it back for £100, and sold it on again for £200. He had finally made a profit. He stuck up a picture of the launch in pubs up and down the Thames. He got more orders and from 1868 to 1875 the partnership turned out 150 launches. He then split with Hedley and it was

Yarrow who thrived. In 1874 he was able to build a vessel for Lake Nyasa to help in the suppression of the slave trade. It was built in sections, hauled overland and took to the water 1,400 miles (2,254km.) from the coast at an altitude of 1,300 ft (396m.). He went on to build a sectioned launch *Le Stanley* for the famous explorer, H. M. Stanley. It was in nine sections, each one of which had wheels so that it could be used as a cart, and the sections were all bolted together to make the boat. He also built sternwheelers for the ill-starred expedition that hoped to relieve Gordon at Khartoum. He was inventive, successful and doing well, but it was an American invention that was to make his fortune.

During the American Civil War, a Confederate officer, Captain Hunter Davidson, devised a new weapon – an explosive charge placed on the end of a long pole stuck out from the bows of a rowing boat. The idea was to ram the enemy, detonating the charge – and then begin rowing backwards as fast as you could. It seemed to Yarrow that a faster boat might have a better chance of escaping the explosion, and he tried the experiment using a fast 30-ft (9.16-m.) launch carrying its weapon – the spar torpedo. It might have remained of minor importance, if another invention had not appeared in 1877, Robert Whitworth's self-propelling torpedo. A new age in naval warfare had begun and a new age in the history of Yarrow's. He began building torpedo boats for countries from Argentine to Japan.

The British Admiralty were not noticeably quick to join the race. Yarrow had a large order for boats for Russia, which had to be cancelled when war broke out with Turkey, so Yarrow offered them to the Royal Navy. The Admiralty baulked at the price, so they were offered again at the same price as vessels offered by the nearest rival. The Admiralty agreed, but inserted a clause stipulating that the price would be decreased for every knot the vessels dropped below a speed of 18 knots. Yarrow consented – on condition that the same sum be paid to him for every knot above the standard. It seemed a safe bet for the Admiralty, but Yarrow discovered a paradox. Where other designers were striving for greater speed by increasing the size of propeller, he tried the experiment of reducing the size.

[149]

The experiment worked and the vessels reached 21.9 knots, earning a purchase price above the original of the Russian deal.

Yarrow's inventiveness took many forms. With forced draught to the boiler there was always a chance of a blow back, which at best would scald and at worst kill. He solved the problem by a simple one-way flap – a modest device, but one which saved much suffering. On the larger scale, he persuaded the Admiralty that torpedo boats now represented a real threat, which could only be counteracted by building bigger, faster ships to chase and engage them. In 1892 he designed two vessels, *Havock* and *Hornet*, each 180 ft (54.8m.) long and 18-ft (5.5-m.) beam, which raced across the water at over 27 knots. They were the first of a whole new class of warship – the destroyer. Their remarkable speed was due to another of his innovations, which was based on the sound principle that theory alone is useless unless backed by experiment. Boiler designers had assumed that the end of a boiler tube nearest the fire would expand more than the rest of the tube, and built in increasingly complex shapes to compensate. Yarrow found that in practice this was not the case, and designed a new type of boiler which used solid drawn steel tubes in place of the old welded variety – a notion he borrowed from the bicycle frame. The Yarrow boiler was perhaps his greatest success. When war broke out in 1914, he wrote to the Admiralty with characteristic generosity.[13]

> If it be desired that fresh firms be employed in destroyer construction, we should be quite willing to permit any of the firms on the Clyde to inspect the destroyers we are building, and to allow their people to gain whatever information they desire.

The Yarrow story is so interesting because of the way it moves from the little vessels that seem to epitomize Victorian tranquillity, conjuring up scenes at Boulter's lock on a sunny Sunday afternoon, to the epitome of the new age of fast, deadly warships. Accounts such as this suggest a simple path forward blazed by an inventive genius, but Yarrow was never quite alone in his ventures. Others were following a similar route, notably John Isaac Thornycroft.[14]

He was one of the rare individuals who took a formal approach to his profession, even if he started from an unlikely background. His parents were both sculptors – Thomas Thornycroft's best-known work is 'Boadicea' on Thames Embankment. His father also had an interest in engineering and taught his son metal working at his riverside studios at Chiswick. By 1862, the nineteen-year-old John had built his first steam launch – a vessel which was also the first to be able to keep up with the university crews in the Boat Race. He went on to Glasgow University, and a period in John Elder's drawing office and continued his education at the School of Naval Architecture in Kensington. By then his father had already bought riverside land and was able to start him up for launch building at Chiswick in 1866. His scientific training led him to challenge many accepted ideas – including those of his former professor at Glasgow, while he saw the potential in torpedo boats, and gave a dramatic exhibition for French naval dignitaries in 1877, using the *Bayonnaise* as a target.[15]

> The Thornycroft put on a last spurt and struck the *Bayonnaise* with its whole force on the starboard bow. The sea was terribly agitated, a deafening report was heard and the *Bayonnaise*, with a rent as big as a house, sank with wonderful rapidity. As for the Thornycroft, rebounding by the shock about fifteen metres off, even before the explosion occurred, it went round and round for a few minutes and quietly resumed the direction of the squadron.

Like Yarrow he went on to build destroyers, but once having moved to the bigger craft he could no longer stay on a site separated from the sea by an array of low bridges. In 1904 the works was moved to Southampton.

Both Yarrow and Thornycroft were shaped by the times in which they lived. The long peace when the British navy had little to do apart from fly the flag at ceremonials and patrol distant parts of the Empire was ending. The navies of Europe were growing and technology was creating ever more powerful forces. Earlier in the century, it was the development of the mercantile fleet which had forced an often reluctant navy into the slow processes of change.

[151]

Now that had changed. The threat of war was becoming more real, but with it came the demand for technological change which attracted the innovator as much as it did the profiteer. A fast steam launch was fun: a fast torpedo boat was a force in world affairs. Change was accelerating, and there was now a constant interplay between civilian and military needs. The new relationship could be exemplified in the story of Sir Charles Parsons, which shows how developments in one branch of engineering spread to another.[16]

Parsons, son of the Earl of Rosse, was in 1884 the junior partner in the engineering firm, Clarke Chapman & Co. The company was at the forefront of a new technology, building electric generators. A generator needs smooth, high-speed rotation and Parsons found the perfect answer – the turbine. It proved far more successful as a power source than the old reciprocating engines used to move the dynamo. It was clear to Parsons that a high-speed rotating shaft had other uses besides driving generators. The work of men like Yarrow and Thornycroft had demonstrated the need for high-speed warships – and speed in a vessel is directly related to speed of the propeller. In 1893, Parsons began experimenting with boats and in 1894 the Marine Steam Turbine Company was formed. An experimental vessel, the *Turbinia*, was built, lean and sleek, 100 ft (30.4m.) long and just 9 ft (2.74m.) beam, she looked the part of the speedster. But appearances were not matched by performance. The single turbine drove a single propeller, and it seemed likely that voids were being created in the water, what Froude had called the cavitation effect. Parsons again brought new technology to the problem. He set up a test tunnel, a strobe light and a camera: the cavitation effect predicted by theory was revealed by photography.

Parsons at once set about redesigning *Turbinia*, this time with three shafts driven by a compound turbine. It was an immense success. The speed of the vessel rose from a niggardly 20 knots to a dashing 34 knots. Travel aboard was a lively affair. The vessel was almost entirely filled with machinery and as anyone who has visited the engine room can testify, there is scarcely room to move let alone swing a shovel. Above decks was little better. With the fan turning to provide forced draught for the boiler, flames and hot cinders shot from the funnel and an unfortunate photographer on board found that the black cloth covering his head and the camera had caught fire. The most famous high-speed run was the dash across in front of the assembled warships at the Spithead Review of 1897. Popular mythology has it that this was a cheeky interloper that outdistanced the official boats sent to stop it – thus proving its superiority. It was, in fact, a well-staged and dramatic official demonstration of the new machine. No one had seen anything quite like it, as *Turbinia* raced along at the previously undreamed-of speed of 34 knots. But Parsons soon realized that speed was not the only attribute of the turbine. Its smoothness and efficiency were equally valuable, and by the end of the century he had introduced gearing that could reduce the shaft speed. His first attempt, a steam launch, reduced a turbine speed of 20,000 rpm to a shaft speed of 1,400 rpm. Double reduction gearing made even slower shaft speeds possible. The turbine could power the fastest torpedo boat or a majestic ocean liner.

By the outbreak of war in 1914, huge battleships carrying armament vastly more powerful than anything available a century before roamed the seas, and amongst them scuttled the first torpedo boats with their new weapon, the self-propelled torpedo. But they had also been joined by another class of vessel which had been long in development but was now emerging as potentially the deadliest of them all – the submarine. The submarine had its origins in the diving bell, which dates back to the sixteenth century. A Dutchman, Cornelius van Drebbel, had a vessel which could be moved under water by oars by 1620 but no one could find any real practical use for it and the same fate overtook a submarine powered by clockwork devised by the Frenchman, de Son, in 1653. Interest in the submarine died away, until it was realized that what was a toy to civilians could become a powerful weapon of war. In 1776, an American inventor, David Bushell, designed a simple submarine powered by a hand-worked propeller, which he hoped to use to break the British blockade. The little vessel, almost as fragile as the egg it resembled, made its way out to HMS *Eagle*, stationed off New York, carrying army sergeant Ezra Lea and an explosive charge. Unfortunately there was nowhere on the copper-plated hull to fix the charge which floated away. The vessel had worked, but failed for want of a suitable weapon. Bushell's compatriot Robert Fulton took up the notion and offered his designs to Napoleon to see if he could do what the Americans had failed to do in 1776. But when the French showed little interest, he offered his design to the old foe. The Royal Navy showed even less enthusiasm. It was all considered a bit infra-dig, skulking about underneath the waves. Lord St Vincent, the old naval hero, expressed the views of many others. 'Pitt was the greatest fool that ever existed to encourage a mode of warfare, which those who command the sea did not want, and which, if successful, would deprive them of it.'

There were to be other attempts to produce a working submarine, but what was lacking was a suitable source of power, and if that was found there was still the need for a weapon. It was thought at one time that the spar torpedo might be the answer to the second half of the problem, and it did prove its effectiveness during the American Civil War. In 1864 the *H. L. Hunley* sank the steam sloop *Housatonic*. Unfortunately the submarine was powered by oars and sank along with its victim before it could get clear. A decade later, the way ahead started to clear.

Robert Whitehead improved on an idea first put forward by an Austrian, Captain Luppis, and designed a torpedo that was powered by compressed air and was stabilized to maintain its depth and balance. Its success was soon proved in torpedo boats, such as those of Yarrow and Thornycroft, but it was not very long before it was realized that this was the vessel for which the submarine had been waiting. While Whitehead was perfecting the weapon, the next submarine designer appeared in the somewhat unlikely shape of a clergyman, the Reverend George Garrett, whose first vessel was built at Liverpool in 1876. The Admiralty again showed little interest, but it was taken up by the Swedish manufacturer Thomas Nordenfeldt. The first 'commercial' submarines were built at Vickers' yard at Barrow on the Cumbrian coast in 1886, but still the Admiralty stayed away. This is not altogether surprising, as these early submarines were steam powered – a wholly unsuitable system. A number of vessels were sold on to Greece, Russia and Turkey, officially described as 'merchant ships'. The submarine had not yet been perfected, but it was well on its way.

Design work continued, and the breakthrough came when Isaac Peral fitted a submarine with an electric motor in Spain in 1888. It was rapidly developed by the French, and rather less enthusiastically in Britain. J. D. Holland made improvements, sold his patents to Isaac Rice who founded the Electric Boat company, and eventually production got underway at Vickers.[17] The first vessels were tiny craft, a mere 60 ft (18.32m.) long and ill suited to heavy weather. But they contained the essential features that were to characterize submarines for the next half-century. They used electric motors, run by a huge array of lead-acid accumulators underwater and diesel engines on the surface. They could make 8 knots on the surface and around 6 knots submerged. Improvements then rapidly followed. Sir Howard Grubb, an expert on optics, designed the periscope. By 1907, Vickers were turning out vessels 160 ft (48.7m.) long, capable of 14 knots and wholly seaworthy. Submarines were suddenly profitable, and other companies joined in.

By 1912 Armstrong's were getting heavily involved in submarine manufacture at Elswick on the Tyne. Their first thought was to manufacture the engines themselves, and by February 1913 Lieutenant le Mesurier, head of the Diesel Engine Department at Chatham Dockyard, was appointed to supervise the work.[18] Unfortunately the Admiralty had other ideas, and wanted Vickers' engines installed. Right through 1913 and on into the next year, the arguments went on about design details. In July the Admiralty placed a provisional order for two large submarines, but by the end of September Vickers were still refusing to allow Armstrong to build their engines until the financial arrangements had been settled with the Admiralty. It was the middle of October, two months after war had begun, before the whole affair was settled. Paradoxically, that same year Armstrong was busy with a massive order for the Turkish government, worth nearly £4 million and including a battleship, two scouts, four destroyers and two submarines.[19] Clearly the British Admiralty did not take the subject of submarines very seriously. By the end of the war they knew differently. In August 1914 Germany had twenty-nine

U-boats; by the end of the war they had built 390. They had sunk 6,250 ships, damaged more than 7 million tons of shipping and almost destroyed the mercantile fleet that kept Britain supplied.

From a slow, lumbering start at the end of the Napoleonic Wars, the British fleet had been transformed. A whole array of big, commercial companies – Lairds, Harland and Wolff, Armstrong, Vickers and more – depended heavily on naval orders for their profits and even their survival. There was a sense of security in building for the navy. Trade conditions might change, but the island and its sea routes needed to be protected. And with the growing size and complexity of warships each order became more valuable than the last. As the shipbuilding industry looked into the twentieth century, there was scarcely a major yard that was not to a greater or less degree dependent on the trade in warships – not just for Britain, but for overseas powers as well. Britannia, and Britannia's dockyards, did rule the waves.

[8]

——— ❖ ———

A GOLDEN AGE

THE latter part of the nineteenth century and the years leading up to the First World War do appear to represent a Golden Age for British shipbuilders. Everything, it seemed, had come together to ensure prosperity. The British builders had a solid base. They supplied the world's largest merchant fleet and that fleet remained resolutely loyal to British manufacturers. They supplied the world's most powerful navy, which provided quite enough business to keep both the royal dockyards and private companies busy. And beneath these twin supports lay the equally sound foundation of the world's first industrial nation. With such a huge and secure home market, British yards were well placed to compete for orders for overseas business. Even the most modest companies vied in the international market place, companies whose names are now largely forgotten. M. Clover & Son went into business in 1854 on an awkward site, with only a narrow frontage on the Mersey at Liverpool, yet early in their career they were able to acquire an order for modernizing a Turkish frigate. It seems to have been an interesting experience. 'The apprentice shipwrights used to bait the Turks and many exciting chases along yardarms and up rigging were witnessed, knives being freely flourished.'[1] So self-confident was this small company that they could even afford disparaging remarks about their near neighbours across the water, John Laird.

They designed & built some vessels of a new type. A large heavy gun was mounted on a small barge like craft. They were given a trial at the bombardment of Sveaborg in the Gulf of Finland during the Russian war. One shot was fired from the gun & the recoil turned the ship over. Birkenhead did not get Admiralty work for a long time afterwards.

If Clover was so successful and confident, what would one expect of the big names of the big yards? The short answer is 'a great deal'. Technological advances flowed in a steady stream, if not an actual torrent, and the industry seemed set on a path of expansion with no end in view. Contemporaries were impressed. David Pollock, writing in 1884,[2] described the changes brought about in just a few years. The most striking feature was the almost total eclipse of wooden shipbuilding in a spectacularly short time. In 1879 nearly 500,000 tons of iron and steel vessels were launched, against 26,000 tons of timber; just four years later the former figure had more than doubled, while the latter had halved. He noted how the less fortunate foreigners viewed British achievement, quoting an American: 'In the whole world there is no place whatever that can in any degree compare with the Clyde for either extent or quality of steamship building.' He went on to list all the impressive changes that had taken place in recent years, singling out the introduction of the longitudinal cellular bottom combined with water ballast as the major improvement in hull design, but reserving his most fulsome praise for the advances in engine efficiency. The marvel of the age was the *Aberdeen*, the work of A. C. Kirk of Robert Napier, with its splendid triple expansion engine, which took it from Plymouth to Melbourne in a record-breaking forty-two days. To nineteenth-century observers, speed was the thing. It was speed that gave distinction to a line; it was speed that drew the passengers to what were to become known as the 'ocean greyhounds'. And like other racing greyhounds, they were to have their prize trophy, the 'blue riband' for the fastest Atlantic crossing.

If any one yard was associated with the new age of speed in the Atlantic, that yard was Fairfield and the man who came to power

[158]

there in the 1870s, William Pearce. It was he who proposed the notion of a transatlantic race open to all countries, and began it with the *Arizona*, built for the Guion line. In 1879 it crossed the Atlantic in seven days eleven hours, and returned in seven days fourteen hours. It was the first in a line of Fairfield Blue Riband holders, making ever faster runs.[3]

		days	*hours*	*minutes*
1879	Arizona	7	10	53
1882	Alaska	6	23	50
1884	Oregon	6	18	37
1884	Umbria	6	9	42
1885	Etruria	6	6	8
1887	Umbria	6	5	31
1888	Etruria	6	4	42
1893	Campania	5	14	24

Pearce died before he could achieve his ambition of building the 'five day ship', but the plans had already been drawn up.

Pearce was in love with speed. One night at dinner he talked to the directors of the London, Chatham and Dover Railway and declared he could build a ferry that could do the Dover–Calais run in an hour. What was more, he added, he would continue to do the trip as one hour each way for a whole month – and if he failed even once they need not take the ship. The PS *Victoria* went into service in 1886 and for a month the service was maintained, if only just. On one day of bad weather, the times were 59 minutes out and 59½ minutes back. The *Victoria* remained the fastest ship across the Channel until turbines were introduced – and her 1886 times are still better than those of the scheduled service a century later. Pearce had more than a touch of the showman. When he was elected to Parliament as member for Govan in 1865, he steamed up the Thames in his own yacht and dropped anchor outside the Houses of Parliament.

Shipping lines and shipbuilders vied with each other for the Atlantic record. For a time the Blue Riband was held by the White Star

Line, and a series of compound-engined screw steamers built at Harland and Wolff, starting with the *Oceanic* in 1871. The Inman line responded with the *City of Berlin* from Lairds on the Clyde. Eventually it seemed that the battle would be rather like the Putney to Mortlake Boat Race – the same two competitors every time – Inman and Cunard. The complacency of British builders was broken at the end of the century when a new competitor appeared, determined to take the record and the traffic that invariably went with it.

In 1897 the Norddeutscher Lloyd company based in Bremen introduced the *Kaiser Wilhelm der Grosse* to the North Atlantic. It was not just the ship that was big: she was also fitted with the biggest marine engines yet seen, not triple but quadruple expansion, which pushed the great ship along at 22 knots. The company went on to even bigger vessels, culminating in the ship that marks the very end of one line of development. The *Kaiser Wilhelm II* of 1903 actually had two quadruple engines, one to each shaft. This was a very serious challenge to British supremacy as a major carrier, and a shipbuilding nation and, as the government realized, as a naval power. If Germany could build bigger and faster passenger liners than Britain, then they could also build bigger and faster battleships. Something had to be done, and the government entered into a partnership with Cunard to construct two new liners that would win back the Blue Riband. The initiative worked, the partnership was a success. It is tempting to contemplate what the future of the country's shipbuilding industry might have been had the initiative been followed through.

The agreement of 1903 called for two steamships 'capable of maintaining during a voyage across the Atlantic a minimum average speed of from 24 to 25 knots per hour ... in moderate weather'.[4] The important clauses in the agreement were financial not nautical: a loan of £2.6 million was on offer at a very generous 2¾ per cent interest and there was to be an annual subsidy of £150,000 to cover running costs. Originally the work was intended for Swan Hunter on the Tyne and Vickers and Maxim of Barrow, but as the design evolved, the beam and depth were increased to a point where Barrow could no longer take part. Fortunately a major improvement scheme had just taken place on the Clyde, so Swan Hunter took one ship, the *Mauretania*, and John Brown the other, the *Lusitania*.

Design had moved a long way since the early days of iron hulls. Now the scientific tests so notably lacking in earlier days came into their own. The safety standards were exacting. Stress was measured in terms of a wave the length of the ship, with a height from crest to trough equal to $1/20$th of that length – which for the ships meant a wave 760 ft (231.5m.) long and 35 ft (10.6m.) high. Such a monster was unlikely to be met, but a safety factor of 3.5 times that was demanded. There are two stresses, sagging stress when the vessel is in a trough and hogging stress when it rides high on a peak. It was the latter stress that proved the greater, and the midship section was strengthened by high tensile steel, specially produced for the *Mauretania* by John Spencer of Newburn. The new steel enabled a saving of ten per cent in the scantlings over that sanctioned by Lloyd's for mild steel.

There were two years of model tests in the tank and larger-scale tests using an electric launch in a closed dock. Meanwhile Swan Hunter prepared for work. A new covered shed was built, 750 ft (228.5m.) long, 150 ft (45.7m.) high with a 100-ft (30.5-m.) span glass roof. Seven overhead electric cranes were installed. Around the large shed were the workshops for boilermakers, joiners and other trades and the river opposite was specially dredged to prepare for the launch. Everything was on a grand scale and everywhere the latest technology was used. *Mauretania*'s keel was built up from three thicknesses of overlapping plates, hydraulically riveted. A new type of mild steel rivet was used, heated in a specially designed oil furnace. In all 400 million rivets were hammered home – 700 tons of hot metal. The *Kaiser Wilhelm II*'s quadruple expansion pair of engines were more than matched here: four turbines were to drive the ship forward, and two more moved it astern. The newspapers of the day regaled readers with the astounding statistics of the floating giants. There were 560 first-class passengers, 475 in second and 1,300 in third class. There were 70 'sailing crew', 376 purser's staff and 366 more men below decks keeping the engines turning. Parsons supplied four turbo-generators which provided enough power to run a town with a population of 100,000. This was a great improvement

[161]

on the system first installed in the White Star liner *Celtic* in 1873 by Porter and Co. of Lincoln. This was a gas plant, run on vapourized oil, not unlike the system used for lighting railway carriages.

The general effect in the saloon, where there were thirty jets, and in the emigrant accommodation when the whole was lit up, was much admired, being a marked contrast to the candles then customary. Considerable trouble was, however, given by failure of the pipes through the working of the ship at sea, and other causes, allowing leakage, and it was eventually abandoned.[5]

Swan Hunter had comparatively few problems with supply – everything was available locally, with engines only coming up from the Wallsend slipway. Brown's had more of a problem, with the larger castings being sent overland from Sheffield:

It was a curious thing that when the breakdowns of the traction engines took place, which was a fairly frequent occurrence, they nearly always happened within a hundred yards or so of the Snake Inn, or one of the other very isolated places of refreshment on that barren route.[6]

The two vessels entered service in 1907 and after a certain amount of jostling, the *Mauretania* settled down as race leader. She first took the eastbound record in 1907 with an average speed of nearly 24 knots – not quite the minimum average that the government had called for, but enough to hold on to the record for another twenty-two years. The ships were without doubt a triumphant success; and were hailed as a symbol of Britain's continuing role as the leading shipbuilder. The new image was scarcely in place before the picture of success was marred by an ugly stain.

Not every line favoured the pursuit of speed as its main objective. Bruce Ismay of the White Star line put passenger comfort and luxury at the head of his list. He ordered a new liner from Harland and Wolff. The *Olympic* was slightly larger than the two Cunarders and had a number of interesting features. The vessel had triple screws.

The two wing screws were each powered by conventional triple expansion engines, and the exhaust steam was then fed to a Parsons turbine that turned the central screw. One of its most publicized features was the system of fifteen watertight bulkheads that could be controlled electrically from the bridge. The liner, launched in 1910, was a great success. Her sister ship was to become synonymous with maritime disaster, for she was the *Titanic*. When she hit the iceberg, the gash in the hull opened up six of the watertight compartments. The rest were closed off, but they only extended up to D or E Decks and, as the ship's bows went down, the water simply flooded over the top of them. Of the 2,367 crew and passengers on board, 1,630 were drowned, including Thomas Andrews, managing director of Harland and Wolff. The *Titanic* tragedy seemed all the more appalling as the ship was widely advertised as 'unsinkable'. No one had contemplated as many as six compartments being holed in one accident. In the circumstances it is doubtful if anything could have saved the ship, but if the bulkheads had risen the full height of the vessel, she would have remained afloat a good deal longer – long enough to save hundreds of lives. Recriminations have echoed down the years, but as far as the ship itself is concerned it is worth noting that the *Olympic* enjoyed a long and prosperous career in the North Atlantic, and finally went to the breaker's yard in 1935.

The great liners were prestige symbols and, apart from the horror of the *Titanic*, British-built ships could claim to be world leaders. But behind these noble vessels lay a complex system of wheeler-dealing. In 1900, J. Pierpoint Morgan began negotiations to form a new enterprise that would amalgamate US shipping and railroad interests. The idea was that a passenger could buy a ticket in London that would pay for the passage to New York and a journey on by rail to anywhere in America. Harland and Wolff struck a deal. They put up a quarter of the initial capital through their shipping interests, with a guarantee that the German and American fleets involved would bring all their repair work to Belfast. Cunard refused to join in, and the German-US syndicate's challenge was one of the factors that persuaded the British government to back the two new liners for Cunard. Other mergers and price-fixing agreements marked the

early years of the twentieth century. Yet for all their symbolic importance, the great liners represented only a fraction of the shipbuilding
world as a whole. Few yards were able to take on such massive
projects, and even for those who could there was still other profitable
work to be done. For every large passenger ship there were perhaps
a hundred little tramp steamers bustling around, doing the humdrum
work of the world. It was here that Britain's real strength lay, for
ninety per cent of those tramps were British-owned and virtually all
British-built. The position looked solid, and to an extent was solid,
but competitors were starting to appear. Looking at the period from
1892 to 1914 and the outbreak of war reveals an intriguing pattern.[7]
Britain remained the dominant force, building ever greater tonnage
throughout the period, rising from a million tons (1.02 million tonne)
to 1.7 million tons (1.72 million tonne) in the period, an increase of
70 per cent. The competitors, however, grew even faster. Germany
went from 87,000 tons to 328,000, a 377 per cent increase, the USA
from 85,000 tons to 253,000 tons, a 197 per cent increase. Virtually
every shipbuilding nation showed a faster growth rate than Britain.
Even those who had only the most modest of industries – or perhaps
one should say especially those – showed huge increases. And, which
was more worrying from Britain's point of view, these were precisely
the countries with the greatest potential for future expansion. Japan,
for example, was building nineteen times the tonnage in 1914 that
she was in 1852. Not everyone was surprised. The annual review
for 1897 in *The Engineer* put the point plainly enough.[8]

> Japan provided the largest amount of work for our builders, com-
> prising fourteen vessels of 59,420 tons [60,371 tonne], the corre-
> sponding figures for 1896 being seven vessels of 24,620 tons [25,014
> tonne]. Only a few years ago the work for Japan was infinitesimal,
> and this remarkable advance would be much more gratifying were
> it not that Japan will dispense with the services of our builders as
> soon as possible and build her own ships. With this in view, they
> have stipulated for detailed drawings of each ship to be delivered
> with it, and have already been engaged building duplicate vessels in
> home yards from plans furnished by British builders.

There were other, more worrying signs, that Britain's lead might be slipping. The major advances in technology were coming from elsewhere. In 1892, Rudolf Diesel, a German engineer born in Paris, took out a patent for a new kind of engine. It was based on the four-stroke Otto cycle – the familiar cycle of events in everyday use in the modern motorcar engine. In Diesel's engine, air is compressed, resulting in a heating effect, so that when oil is injected in carefully controlled amounts it immediately ignites. In 1898 Burmeister and Wain had built the first experimental engine, and by 1902 it had found its way on to the water. It was a modest affair fitted to a canal boat in Paris. The earliest known diesel ship was, appropriately enough, an oil tanker, built in St Petersburg in 1904. At this time the diesel suffered from one major disadvantage – no one had worked out how to make it go in reverse. That problem was solved by Burmeister and Wain the following year. A Dutch oil-tanker for ocean service appeared under the Danish flag. Winston Churchill, on seeing it, declared: 'Denmark, who has long ago led the way in agriculture, has now disclosed herself as leading on the sea.'[9] Had he seen the Dutch tanker or even the earlier Russian tanker, he might just as easily have applied an accolade to those countries. One thing, however, was still true – whoever deserved the praise for inventing and developing the motorship, it was not Britain.

It is often the fate of pioneers to be overtaken by others. Partly this can be put down to complacency. Having enjoyed an initial monopoly, the innovator often seems to believe that it will last for ever. Partly, too, the drive that came from individual founders of enterprises was not always present in their successors. When one country monopolized a trade, there is no great incentive to push harder to promote new developments nor to expand into new markets. All these problems appeared in different companies at different times, but the trends are seen at their most dramatic when they all seem to converge on one firm at just one time. This seemed to be happening to Armstrong, later Armstrong Whitworth, at the turn of the century.

When the company went into the business of building armoured warships in the 1860s, it seemed as if all they had to do was sit comfortably at home and wait for the orders to come in. And come in they did.

Count Kalinsky presents his compliments to Mr Stuart Rendel and having read in the papers an account of the Gun Boat 'Staunch' constructed upon new principles upon the proposition of Mr S. Rendel he believes that it would be of much interest for the Imperial Admiralty to be furnished with some information of this novel Gunboat. As the armament consists of one of Armstrongs 9″ guns of which Mr Stuart Rendel spoke to Count Kalinsky the other day, this might be a very good opportunity for drawing the attention of the Austrian Admiralty on this gun.[10]

Though, as many an entrepreneur had discovered over the years, acquiring overseas orders could be a good deal easier than acquiring foreign payment. In 1868 Armstrong's provided armament for a Turkish vessel, but got little in return.

As your Excellency is aware the terms of our agreement provide for cash payments & we regret that under existing circumstances we cannot agree to install the armament until payment is made and as it is unprofitable for us to allow the matter to stand over indefinitely it will be necessary for your Excellency to name a day of payment.

Your Excellency must of course understand that should the vessel be despatched without her guns and an arrangement for payment be further postponed we shall not be able any longer to retain these particular guns at the disposal of the Imperial Government.[11]

The industry was in a state of flux, and it was difficult for the manufacturers to keep pace with the rate of change.[12]

The power of artillery has by degrees so increased since iron armour was introduced twenty five years ago, that whereas 4½ inches [11.4cm.] thick were then thought sufficient for the protection of ships of war from the heaviest . . . guns, a thickness of 22 and 24 inches [56 and 61cm.] is now actually employed and can hardly be regarded as impenetrable.

Armour of half this weight cannot practically be applied over the whole surface of a ship of war on account of the excessive weight.

Owing to the long time required to produce ironclads and to the rapid progress of artillery science it has often happened that ironclads have become out of date before they were ready for use.

Armstrong's responded by developing a new class of cruiser that would only have essential areas protected, but relieved of the weight of heavy armour could use speed and manoeuvrability to hunt down and destroy the ponderous battleships. This was positive thinking and ensured that the company's order books were kept full. But in time serious competition appeared and no one seemed prepared to meet it. From a company that was prepared to lay down the law to foreign governments they were reduced to the role of pained complainants to their own government. In 1903 Stuart Rendel wrote to Lord Lansdowne of the Foreign Office complaining that they had been promised an order for a battleship by the Japanese government, but it had gone instead to Vickers, as a result of a direct intervention by the Foreign Office. In reply Lord Lansdowne admitted this was the case, but Vickers had written complaining of lack of government help in obtaining orders and suggesting that more should be done for British yards. The Foreign Office had responded directly, unaware that the competition they were helping to see off came from a rival British yard.[13]

Who was to blame – the Foreign Office for not checking their facts, Vickers for duplicity or Armstrong Whitworth for complacency? Stuart Rendel of Armstrong gave his verdict a few years later. He wrote to John Noble, son of Sir Andrew Noble, the retiring chairman.[14]

I am satisfied that the chief reason why Vickers has come up to, and stepped past us, is that they have worked from London while we remained at Elswick. Your father would not leave Newcastle

and his retirement will enable us to remedy this fatal defect. . . .
That we have lost the first place with our own government is our
own most needless and grievous fault.

It was all part of a greater malaise, where the men at the top split
into factions and bickered amongst themselves. The old autocratic
rule had its faults – there was a touch of the King Lear in Sir Andrew
Noble's rule. A board member, Henry Whitehead, tried to make a
perfectly sensible suggestion about saving money on the saving of
the £30,000 a year on the gas lighting bill.[15]

> During my remarks I was more than once interrupted in the rude
> manner adopted by the Chairman when one of the lesser lights on
> the Board interferes with his monopoly of the conversation. I
> finished by saying that I was only prompted in the remarks I made
> by the interest I took in the Company, upon which the chairman
> said 'I don't think so'. With the remark that I should now have
> to consider my position as a Director, I took a silent part during
> the rest of the meeting.

The decline of the autocrats' power seemed only to bring muddle
and confusion in its place.[16]

> And I see that a new danger is upon us. In truth we are not any
> longer under an autocrat. Sir Andrew has lost teeth and claws. He
> has no real grip and no nerve, he is in fact in the shade of the four
> men. They know it. They are already closely allied in profiting by
> an interregnum and their own practical regency to establish a small
> oligarchy which may well be worse than Sir Andrew's autocracy.

Worse, the new men were incompetent amateurs, attempting to deal
as equals with some of the most powerful men in Britain: Faulkner
of Armstrong's against Rothschild.

> It is singularly characteristic of his utter amateurishness and of
> Saxton's incapacity. . . . Conceive of the childish vanity & incom-

[168]

petency of representatives of Armstrong's! They talk when it is their clear duty to listen. They are selfconfident and preposterous enough in dealing with the most astute & experienced men in London who are openly set upon getting our money out of them, not only to commit themselves on the spur of the moment to draft this gravest business engagements, but to actually yield to the audacious demand of Rothschild to at once put these engagements in writing & signing them, and finally they do not even ask for or take a copy of them.

And these are the men who most deliberately exclude the Board from all confidence, who bind some of them by partial revelations and who, while pretending to resent and disapprove Sir Andrew's methods, are taking advantage of Sir Andrew's failing power to give a new lease of life to his system. It is outHeroding Herod.

From complaints of incompetence it was a short step to accusations of dishonesty. In 1904, an affair blew up which demonstrated how easy it was for a large company to lose its way, in a mass of interdepartmental wranglings and uncertainty over responsibilities. It all began as a normal commercial transaction. The company accepted an old steamer as part payment for a new ship order. The man in charge of the department concerned, Swan, then, rather curiously, bought a second on the dubious grounds that it was easier to sell a pair rather than just one steamer. He soon acquired a potential buyer – and then the troubles began. He was approached by a Canadian consortium of dubious credentials with a proposition. They claimed to have an agreement to set up a mail-carrying company, Transports Canadiens, and they were looking to involve a shipbuilder who, in return for investment, would get contracts to build ships for the new line. The hopeful entrepreneur, Carbonneau, was to get a personal hand-out of £35,000 for setting up the deal. In the words of a confidential report[17]

Upon statements of Carbonneau as to Canadian support, and by the usual puffing and bluffing of the adventurer-promoter order, Swan was led to place great confidence in the 'Transports

[169]

Canadiens' as the scheme or embryo co. was called, upon its merits as well as for the sake of the sale of 2 ships. So much so, that having up to this point revealed nothing to the Board or Managing Committee as to the acquisition of the ships, he now, in March last, informed the Board of it in connection with the 'Transports Canadiens' scheme.

The Board of Armstrong Whitworth refused to sanction the deal, but there were so many ambiguities that Swan felt able to press ahead. It seemed clear to its opponents that the Canadian entrepreneurs were playing off both ends – trying to convince the British builders that they had government backing, while pretending to the Canadian government that they had close ties to a highly respected shipbuilding company. The company seemed, in the person of Swan with the possible backing of Noble, at least to have entered into some sort of agreement to join the consortium – and thus to pay the fees. As board member H. H. Smith Carrington put it

> It is the £35,000 paid to scoundrels that one most objects to . . . after all the whole scheme is to enable us to get rid of a couple of old steamers which we have taken in part payment. . . . Surely we can afford to hold them or sell them at a loss, rather than run the risk of injuring our good name.

In the event, the Canadian government stepped in, saying that Transports Canadiens had no agreement with them, and nothing to sell. Disaster was averted, but there was a clear lesson here that the management of Armstrong Whitworth was, to put it mildly, in a mess. Rendel's conclusions were blunt.

> Mr. Swan is honest and well meaning. But he is not able, and his business is not the least worth our having. In this case he is the dupe of cleverer men, and Sir Andrew's habit of command and 'bossing' has led to the supercession of the Board just when it was absolutely needed.

Official company historians rarely dwell on the sort of muddle and inefficiency that the Rendel papers reveal at Armstrong Whitworth. In part it was the penalty of success: most of the problems occurred at the Low Walker yard, which, following the creation of the new warship yard at Elswick, looked after the merchant shipping side of the business. But it was clear that there were problems at the highest level throughout the company, and problems at such a major concern were bound to have effects elsewhere. One thinks of Cammell of Sheffield as inextricably tied to Lairds of Birkenhead. A simple order in 1897 for 3,000 tons of armour plate was worth £33,000.[18] Fortunately, they had already made provisions for supplying ever larger orders of heavy plating.[19]

The Managing Director submitted information upon the recent developments in the manufacture and treatment of Armour and stated that in order to place the Company in a position to produce the Ingots required for the delivery of solid steel plates with the necessary despatch the putting down of other [sic] three melting furnaces at the Grimesthorpe Works would be necessary.

In spite of showing such foresight in the matter of technological change, they were slow to recognize that they were increasingly competing in an international market. It was not until 1894 that they appointed 'a special Representative to various countries' to try and acquire orders from overseas.[20] Perhaps one should not be too surprised. Britain's manufacturers were at their zenith and could be forgiven a touch of smug complacency. The tragedy was that many never outgrew it. As late as the 1970s, the notion of having representatives trotting around the world was still regarded as somewhat strange. A representative of John Brown's, about to be merged into the UCS grouping, could still boast that the company did not need to go out into the world; the world would come to John Brown's. The order book alone showed this to be blatantly untrue. It was, however, a good deal truer at the beginning of the century. But even the mightiest companies were not infallible, and arrogance and complacency have never been a good basis on which to run a

[171]

company. A case of 1907 shows John Brown's struggling to maintain its own normally high standards.

The vessel in question was the *Duke of Albany*. Brown's received one of those letters that no shipyard wants to receive: blunt and very much – too much, Brown's must have thought – to the point.[21]

The joint Committee of the Lancashire & Yorkshire and London & North Western Railway Companies having received the reports of their Officers as to the performance of the S.S. 'DUKE OF ALBANY' during her speed trials find that the vessel does not comply with the specification as she does not run at 30½ knots per hour.

As the special object of the Joint Committee in ordering this new vessel was to obtain a ship having a higher speed than the rest of their fleet, they regret that they are compelled to reject the vessel.

Will you be good enough to inform me how you wish the vessel to be dealt with as she is now lying at your risk at Fleetwood.

Brown's replied, listing a catalogue of disasters during the trials. On the first run, the stokers were inexperienced. On the second run, the stokers were splendid, but they had the wrong coal: 'it was found that in 12 out of 20 furnaces, the back bars were more or less melted together; this was attributed to the coal being of a fiery nature'. The uninitiated could be forgiven for thinking that a 'fiery nature' was what one expected coal to have. On the next run limestone was put on the bars, but this fluxed, made clinker and choked off the fire. By now, Brown's had stopped blaming the coal and were looking for new answers. They discovered that the air-heating tubes were too narrow, so that hot gas and flames were blowing back, causing the melt downs.

At last they decided that the whole design was wrong and it was time to go back and redesign the furnaces. It was an expensive operation. There was not just the cost of adapting the furnaces, but penalties were added for late delivery. Brown's must have been heartily glad to have seen the stern of the *Duke of Albany* disappearing over the horizon, when she was finally taken over by her new owners.

No doubt, every shipyard everywhere has its disasters, but they were not advertised. The big yards liked to think of themselves as the best of the best, beyond failure. That was the image they presented to the world. In fact, shipbuilding was subject to precisely the same strains in the years leading up to the First World War as it had been when iron ships were introduced. They could be put into three main categories. First, there were the problems faced by yards who were unable, often through no fault of their own, to adapt to the new age. Then there were the problems of demarcation disputes, carried over from the conflict between sail and steam. Finally, there were the trade cycles to which shipbuilding was particularly vulnerable.

The River Thames had been one of the great shipbuilding centres of Britain since at least Roman times, but in the new age of heavy engineering, the river was becoming less and less attractive. The industrial axis had moved north, to areas where iron, steel and coal were plentifully available. The region that had seen the launch of what remained one of the mightiest ships of the nineteenth century, the *Great Eastern*, found its prices increasingly undercut. Some experts blamed high wages. John Glover, in an address to the British Association in 1869, added together the daily wages of twelve crafts-men and arrived at figures of 72 shillings for the Thames, 55s. 8d. for the Wear and 54s. 8d. for the Clyde, and concluded that the blame lay with excessive wages. 'This single factor is an explanation of the decline of shipbuilding in the Thames.'[22] Yet in the same address he acknowledged that all the basic raw material costs were higher in the south-east – with coal, for example, costing the Thames yards three times as much as it did on the Clyde. Even employers were reluctant to lay everything down to high wages, many stating quite firmly that though they paid more they always got good value for money. But in 1866, the great slump brought about by the collapse of the bankers Overend Gumey closed yards up and down the river. A correspondent of the *New York Times* described the scene.[23]

The great works and factories at Millwall, once occupied by Scott Russell, are dismantled and closed, the machinery sold, the factory tenantless, and the building yard – the birthplace of the Great

[173]

Eastern – a grass grown waste. . . . The prosperity of London as a shipbuilding port is at an end, and no one here looks for a revival of business.

Even the few yards that survived, like Thornycroft, were soon to leave the river, driven off only partly by high costs. There were, quite simply, areas where all the conditions were more favourable than on the Thames. The anguish caused by closures was real. Glover wrote, 'like a curse, idleness has settled on the district, with sickness, poverty, bankruptcies and pauperism in its train', but there was an inevitability about the change. It did not represent a cut back in shipbuilding as such, simply a geographical change.

It might have been expected that the steady decline in wooden shipbuilding and the spectacular rise of iron and steel would have led to a decline in wasteful demarcation disputes. If anything they grew worse. The problem lay not with pig-headed stupidity but with attributes that are generally seen as admirable: respect for tradition, pride in work and especially for work based on skills. The unions that had grown out of the old craft guilds developed in the pre-steam age did not disappear. They were carried over, proud histories complete, into the age of iron and steel. There they met another tradition, born in forge and foundry and heavy engineering works, exemplified by the Boilermakers Union, founded in 1834, as the United Society of Boilermakers and Iron Shipbuilders. There were inevitable disagreements, and as each side tried to establish and hold a territory, so the hard divisions were broken down into ever smaller units and each unit was vigorously defended. The Boilermakers Union was set up to represent 'angle iron smiths, platers, riveters, caulkers and holders up'. They might all be in the same union, but each had its own well-defined area of operation that was to be defended at all costs against employers and other trades. Different groups worked in the so-called 'black squads' and to an outside observer there was no sense in the arrangements.[24]

The grouping of the plating squad is about the most archaic thing in shipbuilding. In every job except for frames and beams its price is inclusive of marking, punching, and erecting. Now, why should the plating squad 'erect'. It does not bolt the plate ready for the riveter. It merely hangs it up and secures it with a few bolts, leaving the riveter to 'screw it up'. At first sight no very good reason is apparent why the plating squad should not continue to do what has been indicated.

The system persisted because it paid the workforce well. Rates were tied to the nature of the work, and the heavier the plate the more the workers were paid. This was claimed as a disincentive to employers to modernize. They could put in cranes to carry the load, but still the platers' rates went up. There seemed to be no logic at work. There was a logic – it was the logic of poverty. Had the shipyards offered genuine security there might have been more room for compromise, but they did not. This brings in the third factor – the trade cycle. A drop in trade meant redundancies for many and a drop in wages for the rest. It is little wonder that men fought to hang on to what they had.

Eustace H. W. Tennyson d'Eyncourt was not exactly a horny-handed son of toil. His path into the shipbuilding industry was untroubled. His father spoke to his brother, Admiral d'Eyncourt, who spoke to Sir William White who had him taken on as a gentleman apprentice at Elswick. In 1886, at the age of eighteen, he left Charterhouse and made his way to the Tyne. Many premier apprentices remained aloof, but to his credit d'Eyncourt took a genuine pride in his own work and in his fellow workers.[25]

Conditions of employment undoubtedly needed improving when I was young. It always struck me as particularly hard that such skilled, excellent and honest workmen as those I knew in the shipyards had to live in such a state of uncertainty and insecurity, having a good job at the moment but being entirely and helplessly dependent upon the variable conditions of trade. . . . I realised to the full, when working among them how they all, especially the married men, had their future on their minds the whole time – not, as in my case, as something to look forward to, but with a sense of continued fear. From week to week any or all of them, however skilled, might at a week's notice, or even less, find themselves with only their savings to depend on.

One wonders what savings he was talking about, since he also reported that in most families the men pawned their Sunday suits each Monday to see them through the week to the next pay day. He also found, rather to his surprise, that he could learn a lot from the workmen. They had many sensible ideas for increasing productivity, but were not encouraged to bring them out. If anything they were discouraged from getting above their station.

D'Eyncourt may have felt for the men's position, but to the owners there was a good deal to be said for it. Shipbuilding was a volatile market. It only needed a drop in international freight rates for shipowners to begin laying up vessels and cancelling orders. From the builders' point of view, equipment was a liability. Come the bad time all that equipment represented idle capital which could have been earning interest. The matter was even worse if it had been bought on borrowed money for the company was actually paying out money in interest. A labour-intensive yard had no such problem. Men could be laid off and the wage bill slashed until times improved.

In 1907, one of the worst of the slump years, the Rev. Septimus Pater was vicar of Pallion on the outskirts of Sunderland. The name means 'Pavilion by the River', suggesting a rustic world that had long since disappeared under the yards of Doxfords and Shorts. The vicar recorded the misery and degradation of poverty – and the generosity of communities who were themselves far from wealthy.[26]

On Friday mornings, a band of young men would go out with washing baskets into the colliery districts; on the way they would get the loan of a horse and cart. The pitmen were all working at the time – and, anyhow, they are always generous towards those in need. The lads from Pallion called at every house on their way through Ryhope, Silksworth, Herrington and Penshaw. They were never refused a loaf of bread, and sometimes gives [sic] a pot of jam as well – and occasionally a shank of ham. The journey started about 8-30 a.m. and they would get home about 6 p.m. The lads would get their dinner on the way, either at a miner's house or from the Deaconess at Herrington. The whole huge load would be brought back to the Vicarage and stored in the room nearest the front door, which would be stacked to the ceiling with loaves of bread. This was enough to last for a week; when it got stale, after a few days, Mrs Pater would moisten it and re-bake enough for the next day's use.

At 4 a.m. the caretaker would light the fire which was to boil the water. Enough water was heated to give any child in the parish who came for it, a large mug of piping-hot cocoa. The various helpers cut up the bread and, if there were enough jam, put it on the bread, of which every child was given a good slice. After the helpers had said Matins with the Vicar, the children were given their breakfast in the parish hall; the fact must be stressed that the breakfast was given to any child who was in need, and not specially to the Church children.

The outbreak of war in 1914 which was to bring the almost unimaginable horrors of the Western Front brought, too, a huge surge of demand in the shipbuilding industry. It also brought new problems. As men went off to war, the unemployment of previous years gave way to a shortage of skilled workers. Employers had to fight the demands of the military with the not unreasonable argument that if too many men were taken away there would be nothing for them to fight with. Amid the ardour of popular patriotism it was assumed that everyone on war work would forget old differences and work towards the common good. It was never going to be that straightforward. The personal diary of George Bartram, of Bartram & Sons of Sunderland, for 1916[27] shows a shipyard working much as it would have done before the war, facing the same problems and diffi-culties. The war seems an almost minor intrusion until it strikes nearer home in dramatic fashion. The year began with a report that local shipbuilders were beginning to turn away from naval work to build-ing merchantmen again – a reflection of the growing power of the German U-boat fleet. Soon, however, more familiar preoccupations arose. In February bad weather stopped all outside work, which was bad news for production, and equally bad news for the men.

> Will Sherwood down about helpers who demand a ¼ day pay for the time they worked yesterday afternoon when they were stopped by the weather. Told them we would not pay it & he said he would have to go to arbitration.

The bad weather lasted into March, frequently driving the men off the outside work, though, as Bartram rather sourly noted, they were rather more inclined to stay on when it was a weekend on overtime rates. Then in April the war came nearer. It began on the 1st with a Zeppelin raid up the Wear.

> The air raid lasted about 10 to 15 minutes, and one seemed very helpless during that time, from the noise of the explosions one knew it was quite near but of course we did not know when our turn might come.

The works were not hit, but a plater's daughter died in the raid. Bartram refused to allow the men time off for the funeral, but they went anyway. By this time, the workforce had reduced from 750 to 480, and on 11 April there was a visit from the Minister of Munitions wanting still more men for the army.

> He was doubtful about rivet heaters & thought other boys could be set on: he had no idea that rivet heating required the services of men for much of the work but on hearing from Handford that this morning 2 rivet boys by stopping away from their work had kept 2 squads of riveters idle as others could not be got he did not touch them.

After that it was back to the more familiar pattern of shipyard life. The riveters and platers asked for an increase in piece rates for working on new patrol boats, the management refused and it went to arbitration on 17 April. In the event, a not surprising compromise

[178]

was reached: the men got a rise, but not as much as they had hoped – but to Bartram it was a 'monstrous injustice'.

The arbitrator was a Professor Irvine of Aberdeen, Professor of Law at Aberdeen University. He had not the remote idea of ship-yard work, or terms or any of the usual ways that work is carried on between the men & employers. No doubt he did his best but he took the mens point of view. He refused to admit as evidence the figures put before him by Matthews as to what other yards were paying and seemed to have taken a dislike to Matthews.

At least Bartram did not hold a grudge against the patrol boats – he sent the first one out with a gramophone and twenty-four records. And so the year continued, ending on a note of urgency as they were told to drop all work on 'fancy boats' and concentrate all their efforts on plain unadorned merchantmen as the losses to U-boats mounted at an ever greater rate.

For most of the managers and workers at Bartram and other north-eastern shipyards wartime work was little different from that of peacetime. This was not true for every region: it was particularly not true of the Clyde. Trade unionism had arrived at a comparatively late date on the Clyde, but once it took root it flourished. The Clyde became known for militant unionism, strong leaders like Emmanuel Shinwell and William Gallacher and a powerful left-wing movement that earned the area the name 'Red Clyde'. Many of the Socialist leaders opposed the war, but this did not prevent some 200,000 Glaswegians responding to the prevailing mood of patriotism and joining the army. Among those who stayed, opposition to the war was rising and the rhetoric rose with it – 'The class war is the only war worth waging'. A popular joke in Glasgow was a response to the famous 'What did you do in the Great War, daddy?', which has the landlord replying, 'I did the munitions workers'. Industrial troubles were commonplace in the early war years, with claims of exploitation matched by counter-claims of unpatriotism. Major problems broke out with Lloyd George's Munitions Act of 1915. It banned strikes, imposed compulsory arbitration, put a stop to

[179]

restrictive practices and allowed for men to be moved to where they were most needed. It was anathema to the Clyde militants, and a new body was formed to fight it. The Clyde Trades Vigilance Committee united unions, which had traditionally bickered over demarcation disputes, to oppose the Act. Their biggest battle was against 'dilution', bringing in new workers, especially women, to take over what had previously been regarded as skilled jobs. It was a fight the militants could not win. The women, many of whom were living on a pittance while their husbands went to war, welcomed the chance of paid work and had no interest in battles with employers.

In the event, the government felt their position was strong enough to take on the Clyde leaders in a head-on confrontation. Strike leaders were gaoled and the movement broken. It seemed a great victory for patriotism, the government and the employers. But there was no shortage of sceptics. A popular ditty played on the theme of the Kitchener poster.[28]

> Your King and Country Need You
> Ye hardy sons of toil,
> And will your King and Country need you
> When they're sharing out the spoil?

Dilution was a name that seemed to come with a built-in prejudice – those who were brought into the wartime industry must weaken it. This was considered particularly true of women. Yet in some areas, notably munitions which included the manufacture of naval armament, their role was crucial. By 1918 they had taken over ninety per cent of the work, and had shown themselves to be thoroughly competent. Lady Parsons wrote a vigorous defence of the women workers in an article in *The Engineer* in 1919.[29]

> Some of the more skilled work that women learned to do requires emphasis, because there is a strong tendency among engineers to consider that women are only capable of doing repetition work on foolproof machines. There is no doubt that many women developed great mechanical skill and a real love of their work.

[180]

Quite a large number of girls were able to set and grind their own tools, and a small proportion could set up their jobs from drawings. They could mill all the parts of the breech mechanism of howitzers, screwing the internal thread for the breech block, milling the interrupted screw, and screwing the cone that fits into the breech block; milling fire pins and all the parts of gun sights; in each case setting up their own work.

Her final comment was an all too accurate description of the situation at the end of the war as far as the women were concerned.

It has been a strange perversion of women's sphere – to make them work at producing the implements of war and destruction, and to deny them the privilege of fashioning the munitions of peace. The women who worked so hard to win the freedom of the world may not have freedom at home to engage in an industry where the wages are promising. It is fully acknowledged that men will not go back to pre-war conditions; they must have shorter hours, more leisure, more wages. But as for women, they are merely told to go back to what they were doing before, regardless of the fact that, like men, they now have a higher standard of life, and that they also wish to have their economic independence, and freedom to make their way without any artificial restrictions.

Accurate in regard to women it may have been, but the hopes of better pay and better conditions for the men were to be broken in the grey years of depression that were to come.

—— ❖ ——

DEPRESSION

I N 1918, Britain was set to resume the role it had at the end of
the war, as the greatest shipbuilding nation in the world, building
craft for the world's greatest merchant fleet. If anything, the
position seemed stronger then than it had ever been. The demands
of war had seen an increase in capacity of some forty per cent and
order books were overflowing as the shipping lines rushed to replace
the losses of the war years. Everyone felt optimistic, even the workforce, who had seen wages steadily rise through the war years and
continue to climb immediately afterwards. At John Brown's, for
example,[1] wages of a workforce whose numbers remained fairly
stable at between 9,000 and 10,000 rose from an average of
£1 16s. 8d. per week in 1914 to £4 2s. in 1920. Good times were
back again. There were a few niggling indications that all might not
be quite as it should have been. In 1913, Britain had over sixty per
cent of the world market, and by 1920 this was down to just over
forty per cent, but world markets had never been seen as vital to
British shipbuilders: as long as the red ensign ruled the world, they
had nothing to fear. Trade would grow, the fleet would grow and
prosperity would continue. True, there would be periods of depression – there always had been – but each trough was followed
by an ever higher peak. The yards had their response to the trade
cycle: not to put aside too much capital in expensive improvements
and developments. A machine might do the work of two men, but
come the inevitable bad times, the machine still has to be kept there,

an idle, useless piece of metal, costing money. Better to keep the two men – and lay them off when times got hard. It was a formula that had worked in the past and there seemed to be no good reason why it should not work in the future.

The whole structure was based on one essential feature: a steady and prolonged growth in world trade. No one had a policy that allowed for a trough which was not followed, reasonably quickly, by a rise. Yet this is precisely what happened – and happened as far as Britain was concerned in the worst possible conditions. There was a huge outflow of new ships in the decade following the end of the war – and it was now a worldwide phenomenon. But there was at best a sluggish increase in world trade, a mere eight per cent over the whole period. There were too many ships chasing too few cargoes and inevitably freight rates collapsed. Suddenly, it seemed, the demand for new ships had disappeared. All those optimistic figures that had once made such good reading went into reverse around 1920. Looking again at John Brown's, as good an example as any, 1920 represents the peak with 9,297 men on their books. In 1921 the workforce had been cut to 6,322 and pay to £3 13s. 5d. Next year was worse with manpower almost halved to 3,653 and pay had changed to £2. 14s. Things limped along through the twenties, with pay remaining fairly static but work picking up by degrees – only to crash completely in 1932. Brown's was put on little more than a maintenance basis with a rump of a staff down to 422 men. No one on Clydeside had to ask what people meant when they talked about the 'Great Depression'.

The British merchant fleet of tramp steamers was particularly badly hit by the worldwide recession, and that acted as a discouragement to ordering. The yards' other great customer – the Royal Navy – was equally inactive. This was the time of peace – the 'War to end all Wars' was over and there seemed to be no need to plan for the next. All the emphasis was on the League of Nations and disarmament. The most important conference of all, as far as naval shipping was concerned, took place at Washington between November 1921 and February 1922. The United States proposed that all work on capital ships should be halted and that there should be a ten-year ban on new warship construction. Britain agreed, and as a result the only naval work available was on submarines and fleet auxiliaries. However much sense it might have made in terms of international diplomacy, it was the last news that hard-pressed shipbuilders wanted to hear. The weakest soon began to stumble.

Armstrong's, once the mightiest of arms manufacturers, had suffered a long period of decline – largely, as was indicated in the last chapter, as a result of weak management and poor investment decisions. By the 1920s the company was only surviving thanks to support from the Bank of England. However many problems the company might have it was still considered too important to the national interest to be allowed to slide off into oblivion. On the other hand, the government was not keen on pouring in public funds. The answer was found in amalgamation with Vickers. In part at least it was the vigorous competition of Vickers that had helped bring Armstrong's down. The former company's attitude to the slump was also very different from that of competitors. They saw slack order books as providing a space for fitting in a programme of modernization and improvement, so that when the upswing came, as everyone was sure it would eventually, they would be in the best possible position to take advantage of it. The men at the top, Sir Charles Craven and General Lawrence, were themselves decisive and, unlike others in their position, trusted the men they appointed to run subsidiaries. There is a rather charming anecdote which beautifully illustrates their approach.[2] E.L. Champness of Palmer's, part of the Vickers empire, needed capital for development, and he called to see Craven, his briefcase bulging with documents and statistics.

'Ah, Champness', said Craven, 'and what do *you* want?'

'I want £100,000,' Champness replied, and he reached for his briefcase. But Craven was already on his feet, and had opened a door which revealed Lawrence working at his desk in the adjoining room.

'Champness is here,' Craven announced, 'looking for a hundred thousand.' Lawrence looked up from his papers.

'Are you going to let him have it?' he enquired.

'I think so. He's a sensible fellow.'

One result of Vickers' modernization programme was that they were able to compete for foreign orders, even in a bad economic climate. But matters were not helped by government policy. In his budget speech of April 1925, the new chancellor, Winston Churchill, announced that Britain was returning to the gold standard, putting the pound at the same exchange-rate against the dollar as it had been before the war. This was designed to confirm London as a world financial centre – a place of sound money. It also made it a good deal more difficult for exporters to do business, as the pound was, in effect, valued upwards by around ten per cent. It was, however, generally accepted by economists and financiers that the return to the gold standard was a good thing – with Maynard Keynes as the notable odd voice out. He alone prophesied the effect in depression, wage cuts and industrial unrest – a prophecy which was all too rapidly fulfilled in the general strike of 1926. The crisis hit all of British industry, and the shipbuilders were certainly not exempt. Even the greatest and most powerful shipbuilders in Britain – and indeed in the world – were all but devastated. And that, by general consent, included Harland and Wolff. Although its power base remained in Belfast, it owned subsidiaries on the Clyde and the Mersey and at Southampton. Yet in spite of its immense size, it was still run in the old mogul tradition, with Viscount Pirrie very much the man in charge.[3]

Even before the war ended, Pirrie was planning for the future. The war had given the company certain advantages. In exchange for a promise not to make excess profits, it had secured an agreement with the unions that did away with most of the old restrictive practices. The war also gave it a useful weapon against 'troublemakers'. The company simply told the army that these men were no longer required in their reserved occupations, and off they went to the Western Front, where in all too many cases they were to stay. Harland and Wolff had also begun building a series of basic merchant ships, using standard units and a certain amount of prefabrication. As soon as peace was signed Pirrie began on twenty-one contracts for the new 'standard' ships. He no doubt hoped that the new terms agreed in wartime would be carried over to the peace. He was disappointed. The men made it clear that they wanted to claw back their lost wages and demanded a reduction in the working week. There were strikes all over Belfast and the military were called in. Faced with serious threats, the men agreed a compromise – a forty-seven-hour week, instead of the forty-four hours they demanded.

This was a very dynamic period in Belfast. Having conceded shorter hours, Pirrie set about ordering new machines to increase efficiency and make best use of the shorter working day. He also began exploring new markets, and turned increasingly towards diesel and away from the steam engine. He acquired a contract to fuel the Royal Mail Group's motor ships with oil, and then made a deal with the Mexico Petroleum Company, forming a new consortium, the British Mexico Petroleum Company (BMPC). He had the source of oil, the customer for the oil and it would of course be carried in new tankers built at Harland and Wolff. With so much building work in hand, he ensured his supplies of raw materials by acquiring the Scottish steelmakers, David Colville & Sons. There was a suspicion that Pirrie was also hedging his bets, in case the political situation became impossible, in which case he could have uprooted and left for the mainland. The situation was certainly very bad in the early twenties. The Belfast Protestant Association demanded – and got – all Catholics removed from the industry. Then, very much to everyone's surprise, agreement was reached on the partition of Ireland, and Belfast was left safe at the heart of six Orange counties. It brought a great easing of tension, and, in time, Catholics were slowly allowed back into the workforce. The road to prosperity seemed open again, even if the calamitous fall in freight rates cast a shadow over the future. Then, in 1924, Pirrie died.

It was only now that the apparently solid edifice that was Harland and Wolff was seen to be afloat on a sea of loans. Pirrie had retained an extraordinary degree of personal control over a complex of wheelings and dealings, and now that others had to disentangle the works the full scale of the horror was revealed. If the loans were withdrawn, the whole company would collapse – and there was nothing in the books to encourage anyone to keep their money in Harland and Wolff. An obvious answer was to raise capital by going public, but shipbuilding shares were nobody's first choice in the 1920s. Shares to the value of £400,000 were issued – less than £50,000's worth were taken up. It was a disaster, and a disaster that was getting steadily worse.

Pirrie had taken so much on himself that the rest of the management team had forgotten how to manage. It was the Armstrong story all over again. It turned out that the twelve-ship order for BMPC, which was seen as the great achievement of Pirrie's drive to a prosperous future, had been so badly costed that when all the money came in the company would be faced with a loss on the order of £750,000. Extravagance was seen on every hand. It was all very well building a passenger liner to the highest standards of elegant comfort: that was what the liners and their passengers demanded. A vessel like the *Laurentic* was the pride of the fleet.[4]

> Thus from the Louis Seize dining saloon, which seats 310 passengers, one may pass either to the lounge, a reproduction of Italian Renaissance work . . . or to the Empire drawing room, or the oak panelled smoking room, designed on Jacobean lines.

The trouble was that ordinary merchantmen were being built to the same standards. The owners were happy to accept the luxury – particularly as it was not reflected in the price. It had to stop, and a new board was brought in to introduce economies. They were no more successful than their predecessors, and the debts rolled on. In 1927 losses of £300,000 were reported – but that made no allowance for a bank overdraft of £1.5 million and unpaid bills of around £4.5 million. The company asked for its Treasury loan repayments to be suspended, and the Treasury responded by sending in Sir William McLintock to find out just what was going on. The results of his enquiry did not make happy reading. Liabilities were even greater than anyone had thought, estimated at around £30 million. McLintock identified four main causes: dividends were being paid not out of profits, not even out of liquid assets, but from reserves; huge sums invested in David Colville had brought no returns; the expansion programme had locked up capital; major contracts had lost money. It was enough to have sunk almost any other company in Britain. But this was Northern Ireland, and no one was going to allow Belfast's biggest employer to go down.

Harland and Wolff tottered from crisis to crisis. At one point they had no cash, a £250,000 wage bill and a £45,000 overdraft allowance. In their desperation to get orders they offered cheap loans to owners, even though they had no cash to lend. It could not last. And any hopes there might have been of recovery crumbled as Wall Street crashed in 1929. The entire edifice of world trade was shaken and tottered. In December 1931 work stopped almost completely – and from then until May 1934 not a single ship went down the Belfast slipway. By the end of 1932, two thirds of Belfast shipbuilders were out of work. There was always the hope that a new miracle man would step in and create instant prosperity.

Frederick Rebbeck was a brilliant engineer, but an appalling financier. His attitude was at least simple and straightforward. His staff would work out the cost of a new contract, which was then offered to the customer and if the customer then declared the cost was too high, Rebbeck cut it to a level they would pay. The most startling example of the system at work was the *Sir Hastings Anderson* for the War Office. Harland and Wolff contrived to lose £80,000 on a £34,000 order. Not surprisingly the bank stepped in, and yet more trustees examined the intractable problem. In 1936, McKenna of the long-suffering Midland Bank put the position neatly.[5]

The Northern Ireland government was so obsessed with the idea of providing employment that they were exercising considerable pressure on Harland and Wolff to take ships at any sort of price if only they would provide employment and take the men at Belfast off the dole.

The politicians kept Harland and Wolff going. Others were a good deal less fortunate.

Palmer's of Jarrow had a long and honourable history,[6] even if it was one that showed the familiar pattern of boom and recession. In the 1850s, Palmer's was among the pioneers of small-screw steamers, notably the colliers that plied between the Tyne and London. They began with the *John Bowes* in 1852 and she proved an immediate success.

> On her first voyage the *John Bowes* was laden with 650 tons of coal in four hours. In forty-eight hours she arrived in London. In twenty-four hours she discharged her cargo; and in forty-eight hours more she was again in the Tyne. So that in five days she had performed successfully an amount of work which would have taken two average sized sailing colliers upwards of one month to accomplish.

But if the company prospered, little of it showed at first in the town that grew around the yard.[7]

> There is a prevailing blackness about the neighbourhood. The houses are black, the ships are black, the sky is black, and if you go there for an hour or two, reader, you will be black.

Good times were inexorably followed by bad and in the slump of the 1870s men were laid off and were at the mercy of the Poor Law Guardians, and in return for a pittance they were forced to take the most menial tasks. Skilled craftsmen were lined up like Dartmoor convicts, and set to breaking stones. It moved one middle-class lady to pen this poignant description.[8]

> Whose heart would not ache to see what was seen that winter of sad memory, on a day of intense frost – a man struggling with the miserable task, afraid to stop for an instant, lest the cold should compel him to desist, while on her knees beside him his wife was scratching out the stones for him with her benumbed hands.

It must have seemed that, after the degradation of those times, the twentieth century would offer something better. The recession,

[189]

however, hit Jarrow just as it did every other shipbuilding centre. J.B. Priestley visited the town in 1933 and described the miseries of unemployment.[9]

> Wherever we went there were men hanging about, not scores of them but hundreds and thousands of them.
>
> As the years passed, the unemployed man turned grey. Everyone commented on the greyness of the hard-core unemployed – grey hair, grey stubble, even grey skin. He seemed to be looking at the ground all the time. He wore incongruous clothes, perhaps pin-striped trousers cast off and given to charity by a bank manager. He felt he had no dignity. He knew he had no hope.

But as the recession hit, so the big companies sought to strengthen their own position by eliminating rivals. In 1930 Sir James Lithgow – a man whose philosophy for the poor could be summed up as 'no education, no dole, no social services' – formed National Shipbuilders Security. The aim was to buy up ailing shipyards, by means of a levy paid by their more successful neighbours and rivals. National Shipbuilders Security would then guarantee that no work could be done in that yard for at least forty years. They began with three yards in Scotland and then moved on to the north-east. Eight more yards went. In 1934 it was the turn of Palmer's, and Jarrow's one and only industry was dead. One of the tragic ironies of the situation was that in just a few years' time, war preparation would have brought a rush of work. Troopships were indeed built using Jarrow machinery, but not on the Tyne. It had all been sold at scrap prices to Belgium. Irony, however, meant nothing to Jarrow which sunk into utter degradation. There was, however, one hope that things would one day improve again, as they always had in the past.

In 1936, the men of Jarrow set out on their famous walk to Westminster, a march that came to symbolize all the miseries of the great depression. It aroused immense sympathy, but nothing more. The government made its own attitude quite clear: there was no chance whatsoever that they would do anything to help. Shipbuilding at Jarrow was ended.

Not all yards fared equally badly. The Fairfield yard was among the more progressive, and under Sir James Lithgow, among the most aggressive. They were among the first to move away from steam towards diesel in the 1920s, and they were also among the prime movers who attempted to set up a monopoly on naval work in 1919. Together with John Brown, Cammell Laird and Coventry Ordnance Works they formed the Coventry Syndicate. Their prime target was foreign orders and they listed 'warships of all kinds completed; Parts of warships and their equipment; naval and military armaments and ammunition' and added, as something of an afterthought 'merchant vessels, yachts and private vessels of all kinds for foreign ownership to fly a foreign flag'.[10] The objective was the very sensible one of pooling resources to establish overseas agencies to procure orders. Where necessary, technical experts would also be sent overseas from the group to liaise with customers. It showed a welcome, and rather unusual, awareness that there was more to exporting than sitting in an office in Newcastle or Glasgow, waiting for a knock on the door. Competition was growing all the time.

In the 1920s, Scandinavia joined the list of major shipbuilding centres. Britain was still predominantly a builder of steamers but the Götaverken yard in Sweden rapidly established a reputation as a builder of motor ships. They combined technical expertise with sound economics, devoting resources to assessment of trade cycles and using the knowledge to plan a sensible investment programme. They were able to offer attractive terms to owners, with payments spread over ten years. That, in turn, meant that they were able to organize an efficient flow of materials to the yard. In all this, they were helped by good financial backing from the banks – and a certain amount of government subsidy. This stands in stark contrast to the British experience, where long-term planning was rare, finance difficult if not downright impossible, and government interest virtually nil. The personal notes taken by Sir A.M. Stephen of Stephen's of Linthouse make depressing reading. Here is a typical sample from the twenties and thirties.[11]

On 3 November 1926 he visited nine ship-owners and found all wanting smaller ships and lower prices. Not all owners met with the

Stephen approval. Of one company he noted, 'They are all orientals and not quite best type. Not to be trusted too far.' Shaw Savill were looking for half a dozen ships mostly from Fairfield, who were unlikely to be able to handle all the work – 'I said "Well, we'd be only too glad to take a bit of one or a whole one".' In April 1932, he was busy trying to raise finance, but only one bank showed any interest – the rest refused outright. He noted that even the Italians were now losing money on ships, even though they had government subsidies. His own attempts to deal with the British government, in this case, Admiralty officials, were thwarted. 'They don't seem to arrive back from lunch till nearly half past 3.' All very frustrating. At the beginning of the following year, Stephen's should have been in a better position to compete with European builders as steel prices were now more in line with those of competitors. But the British builders were still handicapped by the subsidies paid to rivals. In Germany, £40,000 was paid towards an order for three tankers, while another single order attracted £50,000. Even successful firms, such as Götaverken, were subsidized. Not surprisingly, Stephen's notes keep recording the same sad tidings – 'nothing doing', 'not thinking of building at present'. Among the last comments before war changed everything was this that followed the Iron and Steel Institute Dinner of February 1939. A small committee of builders had tried to put their case to the owners. 'It seemed to come as a surprise to them that the shipbuilders should think of asking that all British Ships should be built in this country!'

Other companies faced similar difficulties. Yarrow's was one of the more successful companies, but Harold Yarrow had to report at the 1926 AGM:[12]

It was well known that certain foreign Governments contemplated ordering a number of war vessels. Although it was admitted that British warship design was superior, nevertheless certain Continental firms under existing conditions were able to quote lower prices and give other facilities due to the support they received from their Governments.

[192]

King George V with James Readhead on a visit to the shipyard in 1919.

Shipbuilding on the Clyde, c. 1900. The view looks across the Simons Yard to the Lobnitz yard

A boiler being delivered by horse power from Harland and Wolff en route to the yard at Southampton in the early 1900s.

One of the anchors for the *Titanic*, being taken from the forge at Dudley by a team of twenty horses.

The Cunard liner *Aquitania* being prepared for the launch in 1913. The stern is just emerging from its surrounding web of timber stagings.

Women at work on machine tools during the 1914-18 war.

A young rivet heater. He is working the foot bellows and preparing to throw the hot rivet held in the tongs to the catcher.

Men at work on the turbo-steamer *Montrose*, 1919. Rivet heating fires are burning on the keelson.

The vast skeleton of the *Queen Mary* under construction at John Brown's yard on Clydeside.

An aerial view of the Clyde in the 1930s. The picture shows ships still being built out in the open.

A group of British shipbuilders, left to right, John Morton of Lithgow, Wilfred Ayre of Burtisland, V. E. Cole of Richmond and G.H.R. Towers of Readhead, investigating new construction techniques in Canada, 1942.

Stephen's of Linthouse in the 1950s. The most noticeable feature is how little has changed since the

Automation at Readheads in 1963: steel plates being cast.

Standard units being assembled on the berth at Readheads, 1964.

An entire bow unit having been assembled under cover is now being moved out to the assembly berth – Kvaerner Govan in the 1990s.

Workers at Swan Hunter hear news of more redundancies with the company in receivership May 1993.

In 1993 as the last ship left Cammell Laird, the support barge was towed away bearing a simple, sad message – 'The End'

Yet even Yarrow's found themselves taking contracts at cost just to keep the plant busy and they were severely handicapped by unfavourable exchange-rates and the need to offer long-term credit. Every shipbuilder in Britain faced the same dilemma. Bartram of Sunderland welcomed a reduction in steel prices in 1938, but noted sourly:[13]

> While the steel reduction now announced will be helpful in certain cases, its likely benefit on the flow of shipbuilding orders must not be over-estimated, because in recent times the margins by which valuable shipbuilding orders for British owners and for export . . . were lost, have been such that even if the British steel-makers had supplied the steel for nothing, the foreign price differential could not have been bridged in many cases.

There was some government help. In 1935, a 'scrap and build' measure was introduced, whereby owners who scrapped old vessels and bought replacements from British yards were given special loans. Over £3 million was advanced and more than fifty ships were built under the scheme. At the heart of the whole problem, however, still lay the two demons of complacency and conservatism. British builders had become too accustomed to being on top, too used to dictating terms. They declared themselves the best in the world and some undoubtedly were, but too many failed to notice how the world was moving on without them. During the 1930s about half of the ships launched in Britain were motor vessels, while about two thirds of foreign ships were powered by diesel. Similarly Britain still relied on the old tramps, the general purpose carriers, while others were shifting to specialized craft, particularly the all-important tankers. British yards clung to the old ways, and it spread all the way through the industry.

In a survey of shipbuilding published in 1926,[14] there seems to be a quite extraordinary sense of a static industry. Where many were looking forward to the new stage of development and the all-welded ship, here one finds doubts expressed about such 'new' technology as the pneumatic riveter. 'Sections of the pneumatic plant cannot be run at a profit, nor, as compared with hand power, is there an appreciable increase in output.' The system described as offering efficiency equal to that of the machines still involved a gang of five: the boy heating the rivets on a portable stove, the catcher boy and the holder-up and the riveters. And before they could start the work had to be screwed up, so that all the holes were in alignment – and if they were not, then a driller had to be called up to make adjustments and, if necessary, counter-sink all the holes. And this, we are to believe, was an efficient method of building a steel hull. Almost as astonishing is the bland statement, offered without comment, that 'thousands of candles are used for lighting'.

The flow of materials through the yard seemed equally cumbersome, involving different gangs each with its own clearly delineated responsibilities. Steel arrived from the rolling mill, after which it was given a painted identification mark. When needed it was taken from the stack racks to the making gantry, where it was marked up for the next stage, that of punching holes. This required a gang of men – a punching plater and six helpers – who manhandled the steel into position. It was then swung across to the countersinking bed. It now moved across to the 'hanger-up' plater and his squad, who worked the plate-edge planer and the bending rolls which did the shaping. From here it went, via the weigh scale, as a single piece to join others waiting at the erection berth. If the system sounds awkward, then so it was. And if one hears from the men who were out there on the berth, then it all sounds a great deal worse.

Daniel Murray began work as a plater's boy at Greenock in 1928 at the age of fourteen. It was a tough life of hard work in wretched conditions and for poor pay – and if you were very unfortunate, no pay at all.[15]

'Cos I mind I was workin' wi' one chap, he came from Paisley, and I was supposed to get 16 shillings a week for workin' wi' him. And the first week I worked wi' him, I got 12 bob off him or somethin', hadnae made much money. And the next week I got nothin'. He duked. He lifted his books and left me, that was me withoot a penny.

In these difficult times everyone was looking to save money. At Hamilton's yard they hit upon the idea of building a ship using nothing but apprentice labour – at apprentice wages. Murray and the rest of the apprentices went out on strike for two months, and when there was no result in sight, he simply moved on. He never did complete the apprenticeship. When he was once more in work, he took his wage packet home – at which point his out-of-work father promptly lost his dole. So the young lad on £2 18s. was now the sole provider for a family of eight. There was nothing for it but to leave home, so that his father could get his money back. Everyone was watched, so that even going back for a cup of tea with his mother had him listed again as family wage-earner and down went the dole yet again.

At this time Murray was working outside in the shell squad, lifting templates on to the plates for marking. It was all outside work. And if it rained:

Well it was just that if you had a good coat well and good (laughs). You just had to work in it. And if . . . many a time if the plater and the shell squad said 'Oh, its raining', they used to go home, but they were away for a drink. Well the helpers and all them had to go home too but they never got paid anything . . . no money. No they never got paid they were away home. The platers in them days that was in the shell squad they done it, they shelled a boat on a contract so they had their money every week no matter how it went.

There seemed to be more ways of losing money in the industry than there were of earning it. Safety at work was also no one's responsibility.

Oh safety, there was no safety precautions in them days. You just worked, you had on whatever you had, just a cap, that's all you had just a cap on your head. Say in them days if anything struck you on the head your head split open. Many a time we were hurted that way, you know.

[195]

Shoes? You never got anythin', nothin! You'd to buy your own. You never got supplied wi' nothin' in the shipyard. Nothin'. All we wore was a pair o' overalls an' eh, just yer jacket. Maybe a pullover and yer jacket on the top, that was all ye had. You never got any gloves or nothin' in them days to cover your hands or that. A' we had tae dae was we made a pair o' leathers wursel' fur yer hands, ye know. You got a bit o' leather out and you cut, you slit a hole in it and you put yer hand through it an' that gave ye a grip. If you hadn't them when ye were shearin' the plates yer hands used tae be all cuts. A plate's like a razor. See when a plates cut wi' the shears, they were very sharp. They were very sharp. They cut yer hands. Many a time yer hand was a' jaggy and cuts wi' it.

Every job had its share of downright hard physical labour and often its danger. Murray, himself, felt that screwing up was the worst job of all. They often worked with just a couple of short planks to stand on, hung out in space under the curve of bow or stern, screwing the vast and heavy plates into place. But he granted that the riveters, working in the narrow spaces at the bottom of the ship, had their own special miseries to bear.

And in below the bottom o' the ship you got 2 riveters and a holder on and a heater boy. And they worked as a squad. And many a time ye watched the riveters riveting all day just in their, just their trousers, no shirt or nothin' on. The sweat was pourin' out them knockin' in rivets, thousands a day. And they used tae have a big pail beside them wi' water in it and meal. Meal fur tae make a drink, ye know, fur when they were thirsty. A riveter was a hard job, no doubt about it. They were worth a' the money, the riveters.

The gradual change-over to welding brought little improvement. Robert Rorison made the change from riveting to welding.[16] He found nothing in the way of improvement.

You're enclosed in places like this. And the fumes that come up from that welding. You were inhaling it and it wasnae . . . Well first of all, the first inkling I got what like welding was going tae be was, eh, I was sent in along wi' another . . . he was a good welder, he says I wish it was tea time till I got home. He says, 'the wife's got tae have a, a glass of brandy for me and a glass of milk,' to take before his tea. This is to try and break the fumes and everything that he had inhaled during the day. I says, 'Well, if its going tae dae that tae me, I'll pack it up. My health comes first.' And I did pack it up.

There was resistance to change, even when it brought obvious advantages. Why for example was there such opposition to an obviously useful tool, the oxy-acetylene burner?[17]

Well, because it does away with labour. I do not believe any individual is so foolish as to want to spend day after day in a huddled position in some ship's tank or under some ship's bottom cutting away inch or inch-and-quarter counter sunk head rivets. It is hard work and damnedly so. It is not that individuals object to the customs being made easier by the advancement of science. It is the dread of that most dangerous and heinous of all most dreaded happenings – unemployment.

Such stories could be repeated, with few changes, in just about every shipyard in the land. Methods seem scarcely to have changed since the last century. There was still a multiplicity of jobs for a multiplicity of specialists, and inevitably that brought the old bogey back – the demarcation dispute. And the same principles were being argued out in the same terms as they had been for decades. In a typical dispute hatch covers had been ordered from outside the yard, at which point they had been blacked by the Shipwrights' Union, on the grounds that they should have been made by their members. The management declared that materials were not available locally, and then turned to the wider principle.[18]

[197]

Whether, as managers, one should be allowed to order any complete article into the yard without consideration of what trade or Society might be employed in the making of that article. While in this case it may be hard for the shipwrights to lose a certain amount of work which they have always undertaken, we do not think that any Society should have the right to lay down who should do work that is undertaken out of the yard.

That type of argument was to rumble on for another half century.

There were special factors at work in the immediate post-war years. As part of the war reparations programme, Germany handed over a number of merchant ships to Britain. This was, to say the least, a most dubious benefit. The British now had a number of more or less aged vessels on their hands — vessels serviceable enough to deter their owners from ordering new ships. At the same time, the German yards could build replacements for their own fleets. It may have looked a good scheme to the politicians, but was nothing but bad news for British shipbuilders. But even setting these special circumstances aside, it was clear that all was not well in the industry.

One factor stands out from this period: the lack of innovation and change. It was as if all the energy that had made the immense changes that characterized British shipbuilding in the years leading up to the Great War had been used up. There was nothing left any more. It looked like an industry rather wearily making its way along an old and well-worn path. There were moments of grandeur. The *Queen Mary* was recognized as one of the greatest liners ever to travel the oceans of the world, only matched by the *Queen Elizabeth*, launched from John Brown's yard in 1938. But such pinnacles only served to emphasize the drabness of the place from which they rose. It took the threat and then the reality of war to galvanize the British yards back into life.

❖

THE LONG DECLINE

I N many respects, the Second World War and the immediate after-math were a rerun of events surrounding the First World War. Whatever the scale of tragedy that war brought, it also brought back work in abundance to the shipyards of Britain. Taking John Brown's again as an example,[1] the pattern of wages and employment is very similar to those during and immediately after the First World War. From a low in 1932–3, when the yard was on a standby basis, there was a gradual pick up from 3,758 in 1934 to 9,583 at the outbreak of war, and employment levels remained stable during the war years. Afterwards there was a slow but inexorable decline. Average wages, however, rose quite dramatically, from £2 15s. 2d. a week in 1934 to £5 10s. 10d. in 1945, and continued to rise in spite of the decline in employment through the next decade, reaching £10 14s. 3d. in 1955. There were differences between the two wars – there was no anti-war movement comparable to that of the Red Clyde years – but the pattern otherwise remained much the same. Government control was not so much a cause of resentment as exasperation for many private companies, who deplored the red tape that entangled them. One yard even produced its very own 'Collect for the Day' which it recommended as a service suitable for any government department.[2]

O Lord, grant this day we come to no decisions, neither run into any kind of responsibility, and that all our doings may be ordered to establish new departments from day unto day, and that we do always that which will make us sit tight. Grant, we beseech Thee that our duplicates and triplicates multiply fruitfully so that we, being defended from fear of insecurity, may pass our time (and the taxpayers' money) in rest and quietness.

Grant that we may continue in strength to enable us, day by day, to 'pass the buck', and so, Lord, order the hearts and minds of other departments to the end that our requests for 'attention' be often ignored, and that we write again tenfold. That it may please Thee to satisfy the desires of Thy servants, and hasten promotion, that our leave be assured and our pension fail not.

Glory be to my Lords Commissioners, the M.W.T., the I.D.G., the O.B.E., the M.B.E., and the afternoon 3 to 4 cup-of-tea, for ever and ever,

AMEN

The most important wartime changes, however, came across the Atlantic in America where a crash building programme was initiated for the production of very cheap, basic standardized ships. They were built on the assembly line principle, with sections prefabricated as units – at first in modest 10-ton (10.16-tonne) blocks, then eventually rising to 200-ton (203.2-tonne) blocks. These were assembled on the berth. The other great innovation was the abandonment of riveting in favour of electric arc welding. There were obvious advantages – a great reduction in weight, economy and greater freedom of design. A whole process – caulking – was eliminated. There were initial disadvantages. Welding needs to be carefully planned and skilfully executed. The intense heat and rapid cooling can cause distortion, and a badly welded joint is a source of weakness and a potential danger. But the American experience showed that welding was a fast and efficient method of production. In 1942 and 1943, 27 million tons of freighters and tankers were launched and 1,238 Liberty Ships.[3] The T2 tanker proved to be the maritime equivalent of the Model-T Ford – plain, no-nonsense, but robust and efficient.

No one considered that the commercial world of the post-war years would accept those standards, nor that degree of standardiz-

[200]

ation, and some indeed looked at the world with a certain complacency, which suggested that everything would go on much as it had before. It was even felt in some quarters that, in spite of the obvious huge advances in aircraft technology, the Atlantic liner would still hold its own. An American engineer, John E. Slater, identified three groups who would go by sea: those scared of flying, those who found flying too expensive and those who simply enjoyed the relaxation of an ocean voyage. He foresaw a future where the mixed cargo-passenger liner would be a dominant force in world transport.[4] But whatever the ship of the future would be, there was very little likelihood that it would be built by the old methods. There was a widespread realization that the future lay with prefabrication and welding. It was now a question of how quickly the new methods would be introduced and with how much enthusiasm.

In spite of its obvious advantages, there was some reluctance to accept welding. Some owners considered it unsafe – there were a number of well-publicized accidents involving the break-up of welded ships. In the early years in America, problems were often caused by what can only be described as criminal practices. Some welders on piece work filled the space to be welded with unused electrodes and then welded a thin layer over the top. Nothing was obviously wrong as far as simple inspection was concerned – the problem only revealed itself when the ship began to fall to pieces. Better controls solved that problem. A more serious concern was 'brittle fracture', when a metal plate would suddenly and inexplicably shatter. Perhaps the most dramatic case occurred during a minor repair to the tanker *Ponagansett* in Boston. A small clip was being welded to the deck, when the whole ship split apart, bow and stern collapsing away. An investigation by the US National Bureau of Standards identified stress patterns, and set out new regulations designed to prevent such a catastrophic spread of a small crack ever occurring again. The problem was solved.

Even though it was shown that difficulties were either the result of bad workmanship or design faults which had now been overcome, there was still a feeling that the good old, solid riveted hull was a better bet. There was also a certain amount of opposition from the workforce, particularly in the early days when the men had no sort of protective clothing, other than what they provided for themselves. Mr G. McLellan was a fitter at Hastie, who made and installed steering gear and he described the work of a welder.[5]

Aye it was the fumes off the welding, I don't know if you've ever seen a welder working it's just a blue smoke comes off it. But it's alright if you're in a big place. But if you're in a wee confined compartment it just gathers and gathers and you just can't see from the one side to the other. And the spray paint, it was bad too. The fumes . . . the fumes in the confined spaces, it was terrible. You got nothing at all and your eyes, they just watered. The best thing to do was to drink a pint of milk but if you wanted a pint of milk you had to go and buy it yourself. And if you were off on the sick you lost the day off your work but you never got paid for it.

The introduction of new methods and new materials was not always easy in Britain. A survey of 1947 reported an experiment in timing the movement of a steel plate from arriving at the yard to being set in place in the ship. Of 436 minutes, 200 were spent on actual operations – cleaning, cutting, punching and so on – and the rest of the time, 236 minutes was spent in simply moving the plate around from one location to another. In part this was due to a fundamental problem affecting British yards. In America, space was at less of a premium than in Britain. It was easy for yards to be built outwards from the river bank or shore-line, whereas in Britain expansion was almost invariably along the river frontage. This made it far more difficult to organize a rational flow of material through the works, as the diagram makes clear.[6]

The American system has a nice logical sequence: the British system inevitably involves a good deal of hopping around from one area to another and back again. There was little the British builders could do about this – almost without exception, the arrangements were dictated by the shape of the available site. Other obstacles

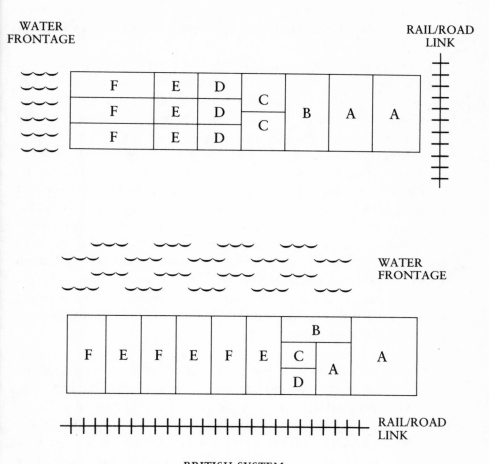

AMERICAN SYSTEM

WATER
FRONTAGE

RAIL/ROAD
LINK

WATER
FRONTAGE

RAIL/ROAD
LINK

BRITISH SYSTEM

A = Material storage
B = Steel fabrication shop
C = Fabricated store
D = Sub-assembly area
E = Pre-erection storage
F = Erection

[203]

towards the establishment of new methods were all too predictable and, too often, just as difficult to overcome.

Once any new method or even new type of material was introduced into the programme, it had to be allocated to one or another group, represented by one or another union. To the outsider, some disputes seemed petty to the point of rank stupidity.

In 1953 Cammell Laird had an order for a refrigerated fruit carrier, the *Calamares*. In 1955, the management realized that there was going to be a problem over who fitted the aluminium sheets to the wooden frameworks of the holds. Both the sheet metal workers and the joiners claimed the job, and after a good deal of wrangling a compromise was agreed. The metal workers were to mark and cut the sheets to size; the joiners to fit them in place. That seemed fine – until the whole question erupted again over the item no one had thought of: who was to drill the holes? Eventually the whole work-force was held up by strikes. Among the casualties was an ore-carrier for the Pan-Ore Steamship Company of America. The president declared that this was the last ship he would place with Cammell Laird. 'No one is concerned in Britain,' he said.[7] Eventually, the question was settled by arbitration. But as Arthur Williams of the Ship Constructors and Shipwrights' Association pointed out, by then the harm had been done.[8]

> This dispute could have been resolved under the same procedure more than six months ago and would have obviated the bitterness and hardship which was engendered by the stoppage of work.

If this Cammell Laird strike could be said to epitomize everything that was trivial and short-sighted about demarcation issues, then the strike at Stephen's of Linthouse of 1957 showed how deep old antagonisms still ran and how difficult they were to eradicate. It arose out of a modernization programme, which substituted the new system of prefabrication of units in covered bays for the old system of gradually building up a ship piecemeal on the berth. The new methods were not covered by the old rule books, those Byzantine documents that laid out in detail such matters as who might pick up a hammer to hit a nail and who could hold the nail. With no precedents to follow, the arguments divided the old antagonists, the boilermakers and the shipwrights. What was so particularly frustrating for the management was that they seemed powerless to affect the issue. It could have been settled by arbitration but arbitration was steadfastly refused. The dispute raged on from June to September. J. G. Stephen gave his view of the action in a speech beginning with an example of current practice.[9]

> The clearest example perhaps is that of the Tack Welder who stands and watches a Plater position a bar. When it is in its place the Tack Welder then tacks it and the Plater stands and watches him, whereas the Plater, or his Helper, could perfectly well do the tack welding. If the Platers and the Shipwrights were allowed to do their own tack welding our firm could dispense with 65 men the next day and probably increase the output as well.
>
> The same thing can be said for burning, spot welding, drilling and the use of the shipping hammer. These tools could all be used by every trade with advantage.

He then continued that it was his belief that Britain was the only country in the world which had restrictions on what tools a craftsman might use, what materials they could work on and what operations they could perform.

> It is these restrictions which are the roots of all demarcation troubles. Every new tool that is introduced into the industry, and every new form of material, makes our handicap greater and the risk of strikes greater. No wonder that in the last two or three years our competitors in other countries have been able to increase their output with new methods very much faster than we have. We *must* put this matter right ourselves. No one else will do it for us.

He received support from Edward Denny, who wrote to him on 20 September.

It is difficult to find adequate words in which to express how much we at Dumbarton sympathise with you and your firm in the position in which you find yourselves.

There is no doubt that the present position in which Clyde ship-builders in particular, and the Industry in general, find themselves is much less the fault of the Unions in pressing continually for unwarranted improvements in their conditions than it is the fault of the employers in failing to present a united front to them. Sympathy, however, is useless without action and I am glad, not only for your own sake, but for the sake of the Industry as a whole that the Association has decided to support Stephen to the maximum extent.

By the end of September, the situation was desperate. Stephen sent out a notice to the workforce.

Owing to the previous and the present stoppages of work by the Shipwrights all other departments are a long way ahead of the steel erection, throwing our whole organisation completely out of balance, and the position is daily getting worse.

The Firm has therefore very reluctantly decided to cease all work in the shipyard other than for apprentices and certain maintenance men, as from stopping time on Friday, September 27th.

And, which must have been even more galling to him, he was forced to write to the owners.

This lamentable step has been forced on us by a recurrence of a stoppage arising out of a demarcation dispute between 2 trade unions – the shipwrights and the boilermakers. The stoppage began in mid June and lasted for 8 weeks until the 2 unions agreed a temporary settlement late in August. This temporary settlement has now been repudiated. As soon as the two unions reach a settlement our yard will be re-opened and we will assess the effect of the stoppage on our programme and inform you of the position.

We deeply regret this, but are confident that the action we have been forced to take is in the long-term interest of all concerned.

The crisis was averted in the 59th minute of the 11th hour when the TUC stepped in to knock heads together. The shut-down was cancelled as the officials took it upon themselves to decide the matter. They produced their report in October.

The Disputes Committee, having considered all the relevant information submitted to them by the ship constructors and Shipwrights Association and the United Society of Boilermakers, Shipbuilders and Structure Workers at a morning and afternoon hearing on October 14 1957, have reached the unanimous conclusion that the present deployment of labour in the shipyard of Messrs Alexander Stephens & Son, Linthouse, is a natural development of the agreement arrived at on the Clyde at the tripartite meetings held in 1948 between the parties concerned and the shipbuilders, and that the stoppage of work by the shipwrights was in conflict with that agreement.

So the dispute was settled, but only at a heavy cost in lost production and an incalculable cost in lost confidence amongst customers. In the event it turned out to be a truce, not a peace. In February 1959, the Shipwrights again came out on strike over the question of the numbers of their members employed in the new fabrication berths. It was difficult for outsiders to see what the fuss was about, and Stephen decided that one way to swing public opinion behind him was to show the world just how important and sweeping the changes were; just how great was the advance in technology that was on view. A reporter was taken around to see the wonders of the new-style shipbuilder and was all but overwhelmed by the novelty and ingenuity of it all.[10]

In quick succession we whisked past a profile cutting machine which can carve out port and starboard plates simultaneously, a giant flanging machine, recently installed, which is used for corrugating bulkheads, and a piece of equipment which cuts all four sides of a plate at the same time. The idea for this was suggested to the manufacturing company by the firm.

Moving across the platers' shed, we came to yet another Stephen's invention – a 16-headed power-operated plane, which shaves ¼-inch strips of steel from the edge of a plate with considerably more ease than the average handyman planes a piece of soft wood. . . .

A complete steel deck house – its weight marked on the outside – stood in one of the prefabrication sheds, ready to be moved out to the building berths. 'Here we can build almost half a deck at a time,' I was told. 'Then we cut it into sections weighing up to 45 tons, which can be carried out to the berths.'

Mechanical marvel followed mechanical marvel, but at the end there was still a human problem to be solved. As the reporter left the works he saw two messages painted on the wall. One read 'Vive les shipwrights', the other 'Up the platers'.

On 12 February, the unions agreed a compromise after twelve hours of solid bargaining – only to have it rejected by the men. There was a reluctant return to work to allow more negotiation. It was not until April that final agreement was reached that there should be a ratio of 3 shipwrights to 2 platers on the building berths. The result for Stephen's was a disaster. It was estimated that the company lost half a million pounds and were forced to call a halt to the modernization and improvement programme. The implications were widespread.[11]

We had reckoned, before the dispute occurred, that we would have been able over these two years to have employed some 700 more men of various trades than we did in fact employ and that they would have earned something approaching a million pounds in wages, that we should have been able to use some 15,000 tons [15,240 tonne] of steel more than we did use and that we should have been able to buy from sub-contractors and other providers of material, including steel, some £2,000,000 worth of materials more than we did. This in turn would have given employment in many other industries.

What the report does not show is the effect of confidence not just on Stephen's customers, but on all potential customers for British yards. It is easy to exaggerate the overall importance of demarcation disputes in terms of lost production, but there is no doubt at all that they were immensely harmful to the industry as a whole. Whatever the reality behind such disagreements, the public image was of squabbling factions, who put their own grievances before the needs of the customers who ultimately paid their wages. The demarcation dispute did immense damage to the reputation of the industry, but there were other factors which ultimately were to prove more important in the long decline of British shipbuilding.

Restrictive practices were not limited to unions. Employers tried to make their own cosy arrangements as they had before the war. In 1948, there were indications of a return to these old ways.[12]

It is suspected that shipbuilders are still guided by secret arrangements regarding price as was the case before the war when it was frequently settled in private conference which firms would get the contracts and at what prices. The shipbuilders reduced productive capacity before the war which endangered national defence when the war began, and must not be allowed to continue restrictive practices which would hinder the winning of peace.

Contracts were still being offered on the old 'time and lime' basis – the customer got a bill consisting of all the costs plus the builder's profit. This gave little incentive to the builder to reduce his costs, since they were to be paid for anyway. But customers were increasingly looking for fixed-price contracts, and Britain's competitors were willing to oblige. And the competition was increasing all the time. Germany had been barred from building merchant ships as well as warships in the immediate post-war years, but the United States were anxious to see the country back on its feet and Britain's objections could not stand out against the stronger forces. The industry in Germany had been devastated by the war, and this now proved a blessing. Where Britain had old but still serviceable yards, Germany had to build anew – and in doing so they could take advantage of all the latest ideas and the latest techniques. And what was true of Germany also became true of Japan. Around the world, shipbuilding practices were being revolutionized. And many of these countries were not dragging behind them the lumber of the centuries. Japan, for example, did not have the same long history of a gradual development from iron to steel, from sail to steam to motor: they came on to the scene as new players.

A mythology grew up in Britain about the Japanese industry. They borrowed other people's ideas, built cheap, used sweated labour and shoddy materials, and used subsidies to create low prices. Such notions were a great comfort to British builders, who could look on work lost to Japan as being entirely due to unfair competition. In 1959 a British consulting surveyor who had spent the last four years working in Japan wrote a memorandum which was circulated among British shipbuilders. It laid most of the old mythology low.[13] There was a certain amount of truth in the suggestion that low prices were initially helped by huge subsidies, the so-called 'sugar compensation', which also allowed for deferred payments spread over seven years. There was a clamour from the other shipbuilding nations, and the subsidy was dropped, resulting in a price leap from 34,200 yen per deadweight ton (dwt) to 79,920 per dwt. But even without the subsidy, Japan was soon very competitive and rapidly earned a reputation for speedy work, delivering ships well within the contract date.

One key to Japanese success was innovation. The old generation of senior men was all but wiped out during the war, and their replacements were young, vigorous and full of ideas. They were, above all, highly trained. A typical training would consist of a university course in marine engineering or naval architecture, a three- or four-year 'apprenticeship' in a working yard and, in many cases, a prolonged period overseas, studying new ideas and methods. After that, they were ready to take on executive responsibilities, and did so at a far younger age than their European counterparts. Many engineers are fired with enthusiasm for new ideas, but have to wait until they are grey-haired and a touch weary before they reach a position where they can put them into practice. Not so the Japanese. They ensured that capital was available for modernization and development. They were not afraid of what were literally big concepts, and the size of vessels rose spectacularly. Where once 12–15,000 dwt vessels was the norm, the Japanese turned out 45,000 dwt and soon passed the 100,000 dwt mark. This in turn meant building ever more powerful engines – gas turbines and diesels of over 20,000 hp.

The workforce was poorly paid by British standards. In 1959 the average pay for skilled men was £6 3s. a week, roughly half that of their British equivalents. But they had a number of benefits, such as cheap travel, company medical care, free or very cheap meals and, in many cases, very low-cost company housing. They also enjoyed such unheard-of luxuries as hot baths at the end of the working day. In return they put in seven hours' work a day for six days a week. Industrial relations were, on the whole, good – not that strikes were unknown, but they were infrequent and were quickly settled. The familiar Japanese pattern of a hard-working labour force tied to a paternalistic management was rapidly established in the shipyards.

The real secret of Japanese success seemed to be meticulous planning. Every detail was worked out in advance from hull performance, established by exhaustive model tests, to the choice of material for the knob on a wardrobe door. This, in turn, meant accurate costings which could be translated into firm contract prices. The care that went into planning continued throughout construction, with twice-daily checks on alignments and regular X-ray examination of welds. Owners were not, as happened in many British yards, regarded as nuisances best kept at arm's length until they were ready to take over their new ship and pay the bill. The yard was always open to them, and suggestions for improvement actively encouraged. The result was a well-built ship, unlikely to need much in the way of repairs other than regular maintenance, which was exactly suited to the owner's needs – and which was delivered in time at contract price. Japan was able to finance seventy per cent of the cost of a ship over seven years at five per cent interest, compared with Britain only able to give fifty per cent at bank rate plus one per cent. That helps to explain why, in 1958, Japan was building eighty-six per cent for the export market, compared with ten per cent in Britain. Only one country had a better record, West Germany at eighty-nine per cent.[14]

West Germany, like Japan, started from a position of war devastation, so that, in effect, they could build a new industry from scratch rather than try to patch up and improve an old one. Some British yards at least took an interest in the German phenomenon, including Alexander Stephen, whose attempts to modernize on similar lines came so sadly unstuck. But as early as 1954, their workforce had been given the opportunity to read for themselves about the German success story in the company magazine.[15] The yard described was Deutsche Werft on the Elbe. The writer seems positively awe-struck by what he saw.

> Once every three weeks a new 18,000-ton tanker slides into the grey waters of the Elbe from the Deutsche Werft yard the traditional home of the German mercantile marine. . . .
> The speed of production from this world-famous yard is staggering to British eyes accustomed to regard the building of a ship as a lengthy, almost leisurely, process, except in wartime.

The main reason for the speed was not difficult to discover: prefabrication.

> The system of building the double bottom of tankers in sections enables 16 ships to be under construction simultaneously although there are only four slipways. As one ship is being completed to launching stage on a slipway three more are being made in parts elsewhere in the yard.

Another factor that gave the yard its competitive edge was the three-shift system of working, which kept the berths busy twenty-four hours a day − and, where necessary, seven days a week. This was the competition the British yards faced or, one should say, failed to face.

[212]

Before I left England I asked the manager of a well-known North-West ship-repairing firm what he thought of the seriousness of German competition. 'It is just about the most serious thing we have ever faced,' he said. 'A job was recently offered in England for the conversion of a ship from coal to oil burning. The best time any British firm could quote was 10 to 12 weeks. The Germans said they could do it in six without even looking at it. They got the contract and did the job inside their quoted time.

To be fair to British shipbuilders, they faced a number of problems in the post-war years, which were by no means all within their control. At first, they were so busy with new orders that they had little time to look at anything beyond the work in hand. Modernization took second place to a busy construction programme, replacing the shipping lost in war time. They were also faced with a serious shortage of steel, which badly hampered the work, while inflation made the task of estimating future costs into something of a lottery. In the heady days of full order books, owners had to leap in quickly to place a ship and secure a building berth – even if they were not sure what they were getting, when they would get it or at what price. A ship-broker acting for a client in San Francisco spelled out some of the problems.[16]

I fully realise . . . that they are still unable to buy steel in advance; also, that the labour is subject to increases. On labour they mention in their quotation that their item would be varied up or down by ⅔ of 1% for every shilling per 44 hour week increase or decrease. Naturally, we are unable to figure this out as it is too complicated.

The builders were not much better placed to make sense of what was going on than were the owners. Bartram's wrote to Roeburn and Verel in 1956, explaining that since work had begun on their ship in 1955, they had paid out two wage increases of between twelve-and-a-half and fifteen per cent. Now they were being asked to quote for work that would not be completed until 1960.[17]

[213]

To attempt to visualise what this price might be is much more in the fashion of 'crystal gazing' than the foregoing calculations. However, the starting point would be the estimated final price of 361 Ship and there would then be three years for which allowance would have to be made. The pattern over the last two years would suggest an addition of about 22½% by the time this ship was completed, but we must reemphasise that there are so many 'unknowns' that this could conceivably be either over or under estimated. No one, not even the Government, appears to know whether inflation will be halted, slowed down or allowed to continue.

Employers were becoming decidedly chary about giving wage increases with promises of improved productivity that failed to materialize.[18]

There was a very strong feeling that no advance should be granted unless some worthwhile concession was obtained in return, and particular reference was made to the means of getting rid of stoppages and other difficulties which give rise to undesirable publicity. It was appreciated that promises which had been given by the Unions on previous occasions had produced nothing at all.

Figures produced by the Wear Shipbuilders Association certainly showed an unpromising situation. Between the years 1950 and 1959, they calculated productivity first in terms of gross tonnage per man, which showed a 39.5 per cent increase, steel tonnage per man which showed a 37.4 per cent increase and wages which showed an 82.8 per cent rise.[19] And these figures had to be seen against a background of falling orders. In 1957, Britain had built 350 ships, but by 1958 the numbers had fallen to 167 and cancellations were outrunning new orders. The familiar arguments were rehearsed. Britain was still looking primarily at a home market, while there was an increasingly aggressive war over freight prices, led by the United States, and a new player in the field, Greece. These owners had no interest in the UK system of cost plus contracts – the old 'time and lime' system.

They wanted fixed prices and they struck hard bargains. The British were alarmed at their competitors' willingness to go to any lengths to secure orders and spoke of Japan in particular doing work at 'suicidal' prices. But Britain was not able to compete even against the rest of Europe. In 1958 tenders were invited for a 10,000-ton (10,160-tonne) insulated cargo liner for the Argentine. British firms put in bids ranging from £1,795,141 to £2,374,508. Taking the lowest of the British bids, they were undercut by yards in Denmark, Sweden, France, Germany, Italy and Holland while Yugoslavia had the lowest bid of the lot at £1,284,680.[20] It was not just the Japanese who had to hack away at prices. A. M. Stephen described the sort of hard bargaining that went on.[21]

Had a long talk with Hull of Ellerman's when I started by offering him something like £40,000 off, then I went up to £50,000 and finding that that didn't quite meet the bill I ended up offering £58,000 on which he settled. He was very nice and very pleased with the ship and said they would of course have another to build but were not ready to do so yet. I mentioned that we had kept a reserved berth for him about 1963 but didn't seem to register.

There was only one way forward and that was through modernization – modernization of plant, which was always possible as long as the builders were prepared to put up the capital, and modernization of working practices – which was a good deal more difficult to achieve. One reason why the latter problem proved so intractable was that for too many owners the problem was seen purely in terms of the workforce out on the berth. The need to modernize management methods was scarcely considered at all. Many of the big companies did move towards large-scale reorganization. Fairfield, for example, installed a system of prefabricating sections under cover. They reduced the number of berths from six to five, to allow broader-beamed vessels to be built, and also allowing space for travelling cranes to be installed, lifting up to 80 tons (81 tonne). A splendid new fabrication shop, 1,000 ft (304.6m.) long and 90 ft (27.4m.)

high was completed, and by 1960 they had spent £3 million on the works.[22]

Most of the big yards had extensive modernization programmes. At Cammell Laird, half a million tons of rock and earth were excavated to create a new graving dock. Its, literally, outstanding feature was the 100-ton (101.6-tonne) gantry crane, as tall as the famous Liver Building across the Mersey, and wide enough for two double-decker buses to drive side by side underneath it. Less immediately impressive, but immensely important, were the new loft techniques. Out went the old system where drawings were used to produce wooden templates, which in turn were set down to allow the steel to be cut to shape. In its place came the Monopol system, where drawings were reduced to 1/100th the scale on film, which was then used to guide the cutters. Such new devices were, however, still regarded with a certain amount of suspicion.[23]

It for instance there is a line too many on the negative, the machine will follow it. If there is a speck of dirt, it will go to immense pains to cut round. The truth is that it has no powers of discrimination.

By 1962, they had rationalized all their operations. They now offered customers a choice based on six standard designs: three sizes of dry cargo vessel, two bulk carriers and a tanker, at sizes ranging from 3,150 (3,200) to 57,400 tons (58,318 tonne). Plans were available for inspection, specifications were clearly laid out and firm contract prices offered all but instantaneously.[24]

The need for modernization became ever greater with the rapidly increasing size of ships, particularly the larger tankers. By the 1960s the age of the super-tanker had arrived, and a major barrier was broken in 1962 when the *Nissho Mare* loaded up with over 100,000 tons of crude oil at Kuwait. Here was a desperate challenge for British yards. It was not simply a question of having facilities to build to such a scale, there was also the problem of location. The traditional riverside sites were useless – vessels of such a size simply could not be launched into the comparatively narrow and shallow rivers. Britain's competitive position was being steadily eroded, and

[216]

most worrying of all the share of the UK's own market was slipping. Where in the immediate post-war years, eighty per cent and more of the British fleet was supplied by British yards, by the early 1960s it had dropped to sixty per cent and was still falling.

No one had any doubt in the 1960s that British shipbuilding was in deep crisis. The industry had been slow to modernize in comparison with rivals. Management and workforce were still locked into attitudes that belonged in the nineteenth century. There was a lack of long-term thinking, which showed itself in low investment in research and development, and even if the cash had been found there was a woeful shortage of skilled, scientific staff. Where graduates in marine sciences flooded from Japanese universities, they appeared in a derisive trickle from Britain's academic institutions. And there were ominous signs for the future. Worst of all, the old reliable bed rock on which prosperity had been built for centuries was also beginning to crumble. The heyday of the British merchant fleet was over, as more and more owners turned to 'flags of convenience' that promised cheap labour and a minimum of rules and regulations. Even that other stalwart customer for British ships, the Royal Navy, was loath to rush into any major building programme once the war was over. Worries were not limited to the owners. The workforce, too, looked to a grim future, and came up with their own suggestions.

As early as 1949, the unions had their solution: nationalization. E.J. Hill of the Boilermakers set out his views, starting from what he saw as the disastrous work of National Shipbuilders Security in the 1930s, when one third of berths were lost. This was followed in 1938 by subsidies to restrengthen the weakened industry. To Hill, it was madness to leave the industry in the hands of men who would cut it to a point where it was no longer viable, and then take public money to build it up again. His gloomy view of the way things were going was remarkable for its accuracy, and his evidence of overseas industries being heavily subsidised by their own governments irrefutable.[25]

The Shipbuilding Industry is so vital to our national economy both in commerce and defence to leave in private hands, especially when

[217]

monopolistic tendencies are evident. There is every indication that high costs and falling orders will shortly face the industry; orders from overseas may be cancelled; competition from overseas shipyards may increase; therefore, time is short in which to re-organise the industry. British shipbuilding production as a proportion of world production is approximately 45 per cent but our record will not be so favourable in 1949 on account of the re-entry of America into the shipbuilding field after a lapse since the end of the war. Her output next year is expected to be second to that of Great Britain. The main reason for this is the fact that American Shipbuilding is being heavily subsidised. The National Maritime Commission has had about 178 million dollars allocated by Congress to spend in assisting American shipowners to build new tonnage and on this basis American Export lines have placed contracts for new Transatlantic Liners and combination passenger and cargo vessels. Meanwhile, the shipyards of Japan and Germany are being rapidly brought back into production for export at real wage rates substantially lower than those prevailing in this country, and whilst representations have been made to the British Government on this matter, it is nevertheless a real menace to British Shipbuilding.

Government help was not forthcoming on a scale to match that of the competitors, and as the gloom mounted, so increasingly desperate measures were proposed. In 1958 the union imposed a ban on apprenticeships to preserve adult jobs. Whatever the short-term value of such a scheme, it hardly showed much confidence in the future. In 1959 Vickers Armstrong welders put forward a suggestion that the men should work a 4-day week to prevent redundancies: the management refused. On 14 January, 226 workers stayed off work and when they returned the following day they were sacked. The dispute went to arbitration. The Union agreed to give up the notion of a four-day week, but proposed a double day shift as a means of increasing productivity while relieving unemployment. The employers, for their part, refused to consider any measures whose only aim was to give employment. Gradually, everything drifted back into the old ways.[26]

It is difficult not to see the industry as floundering, with little sense of direction. The old ways of thinking and acting had finally stumbled to a halt. It was obvious to many that if there was to be any hope of saving the industry from near extinction, there had to be a new appraisal. And that new appraisal had to lead to a fresh start.

[11]

—— ❖ ——

THE LAST CHANCE

I N the 1970s, the small firm of Richards of Lowestoft, which had developed its own niche in the market, originally based on building fishing boats, celebrated its centenary – if celebrate is the word. The chairman was brutally frank:[1]

I am not going to be a death's head at the feast but it would be entirely inappropriate if I did not mention the grisly climate in which both shipowners and shipbuilders are trying to exist today. Too many ships chasing too few freights has dragged the freightmarket down, resulting in a lay-up of ships.

The tanker market now has 46 million tons [46,736,000 tonne] laid up and new ships that could not be cancelled are going straight into lay-up after they are completed at the builders' yards. If that is bad for the shipowner, it is bad for the shipbuilder.

We at Richards reckon that we build for four distinct and separate markets – trawlers for the fishing industry, oil rig supply vessels for offshore oil, tugs for harbour service and vessels such as the *Skeldergate* for short sea trade, but even with this diversity of spread at the present moment we do not have one firm inquiry on our books from a British owner.

This is not to say we have not got inquiries but they are all for overseas work, and to coin a phrase, our present motto now has to be 'Need work – will travel'. Joe Bell is spending a lot of his time in aeroplanes moving round the world as we will go anywhere

where work is offering. So far, Iran, Nigeria, Pakistan – shortly South Africa, Egypt, etc.

In these markets we are up against the full onslaught of international competition and, although we at Richards are reasonably confident that we can meet people on equal terms, we have strong reservations about the Japanese with their apparent policy, probably supported by their government, of taking work at even a throw-away price so as to keep their yards in full employment.

We would certainly love to be talking seriously with a British shipowner now because it is especially galling for us to have to give very keen, fixed-price terms to some foreign owner for whom we will probably never build again, whereas if we had done the same for a British owner we might at least have stored up some goodwill for the future.

The same speech could have been made at any time in the sixties or seventies by any chairman of any shipbuilding company. It was against this background that the government set up an enquiry in 1965 into the state of the industry under the chairmanship of J. M. Geddes.[2] The Geddes Report was notable for two things: its analysis of what had gone wrong in the past and its recommendations on what needed to be done in the future. Much of what was said was not new, but here it was laid out plainly, in no-nonsense terms and with the weight of government behind it. Few would disagree with the analysis of past failings – though there was far from the same unanimity when it came to accepting the proposed remedy.

The Report began with a summary of the current position. Britain had then sixty-two yards, but of these only twenty-seven were big enough to construct ships over 5,000 tons (5,080 tonne), and it was on these that the Report concentrated. One problem soon became clear – the tendency of the shipbuilding industry to regard itself as in some way unique.

There seems to us to remain not far below the surface, some conflict between shipbuilding as a craft and as an industry. Both inside and outside the industry there are many who feel that a ship has

[221]

a value and romantic interest in itself. The pride in the craft displayed at all levels in the industry brings an economic as well as a social benefit. But it has slowed down adaptation to modern industrial conditions.

Geddes was having none of that.

The shipbuilding industry is on the whole an assembly industry and has much in common with the building industries: it involves the prefabrication, erection and fitting out of large individually designed structures. On the other hand, much shipyard work is similar to that in general engineering establishments.

The industry was small in national terms, but vital to certain regions. It was unlike most other industries in having to compete in an international market with no tariff protection and enjoyed only the minimum of protection in the home market. It was, in a word, vulnerable.

There had been various improvements made in the 1960s. Research and development were given a higher priority, but still fell a long way short of competitors. The traditional UK approach was based on the experience of individual shipowners. There was very little interest in basic science or in a systematic development of analysis. A typical example of the British approach could be seen in the development of the turbine. After the innovative work of Parsons, development followed in a wholly pragmatic way, with no attempt to understand, for example, the fundamental physics and mathematics of blade design. New development was left to other countries, notably Japan, the Netherlands, Sweden and Germany. British builders wanted to see how the new ideas worked before introducing them to their own yards. In 1958, R and D was running at a pathetic one per cent of net turnover, and the only real attempt to address the problem came with the establishment of the British Ship Research Association in the 1960s, a rare example of co-operation between the industry and government.

Industrial relations had been rationalized to some extent. The old rivalries between shipwrights and boilermakers had been buried, and a new union formed, the Amalgamated Society of Boilermakers, Ship-wrights, Blacksmiths and Structural Workers. The new unions now represented a third of all workers, but the rest were still divided up mainly between fourteen other unions. Things were far from happy in the yards, and the age-old practice of lay-offs when times were bad had left their mark.

The past is very much alive in the minds of the workers in the industry and coupled with a general lack of confidence in the future of the industry, it has bred a deep feeling of insecurity which is at the root of most of the demarcation disputes and the practices in the industry which are commonly known as 'restrictive' but which the workers regard and describe as 'protective'.

But even when making allowances for the natural fears of the men, there was still a dismal record of strikes and absenteeism: absentee-ism was in fact worse than in any other industry in Britain, more than three times the rate of engineering in general. At the root of the problem lay the bad relationship between management and men.

One of the recurring issues in the British industry was the inability to offer potential customers an attractive financial package. This was partly solved in the sixties when the government stepped in to offer 80 per cent mortgages payable over ten years at rates ranging from 4½ to 5⅜ per cent. The amount on offer went up from an initial £30 million in 1963 to £75 million. This led to a burst of new orders, but sadly inflation saw final costs rising above the contract price in all too many cases. In any event, Britain was only competitive in the limited field of the cargo-liner, while the all important orders for tankers and dry-bulk carriers were going overseas. Customers were demanding a high degree of technical excellence, and whatever an individual company might think of R and D, the customer saw it as a prerequisite in the building of new, advanced ship types. As a general conclusion, the Report indicated that Britain had few prob-lems with good design or with the use of good materials. The problem lay with the way in which they were made. Overseas, the workforce had few of the problems affecting British yards. 'The activities of the labour force appear to be well planned and a full day's productive work from each operative at a steady level of application to be willingly given.' There was not the same multiplicity of unions and, in consequence, the infamous demarcation dispute was almost unknown. But nor did other countries have the same multiplicity of yards, nor did their managers have the same sense of being in some way isolated from the rest of the industrial world. 'There is less tendency for management to consider shipbuilding as a special art divorced from the general run of engineering and management development.' And there was one area where Britain notably failed – marketing and selling. Again, it grew out of a long history of customers beating a path to the British door, and a failure to realize that in the second half of the twentieth century there were fewer and fewer footsteps echoing along that particular path.

Analysing what was wrong in the industry was only a part of the Report. The other part consisted of suggestions on what should be done to put it right. Some were obvious. There should be more emphasis on market research to find out what customers actually wanted. Design must be given a central role, and that meant better training for a new generation of designers who could plan for the future and make full use of the new technology. Production and financial control should be tightened, with the help of the new computer technology. All this was admirable, but Geddes felt that it could not be initiated without a radical shake-up of the whole fabric of the industry. There were simply too many yards chasing too few customers – Geddes estimated that there were at most 600–700 customers for new ships at any one time spread across the entire world. Small companies did not command the resources that were needed to establish the new marketing, sales and research departments that were essential if British yards were to become competitive. New groupings would have to be made, with an ideal of between 8,000 and 10,000 employees turning out at least 400,000 gross tons per year. The industry could not reorganize on its own. Government would have to offer financial help with cheap loans and special allowances – and would have to do their share in helping with forward planning by offering a realistic long-term view of navy contracts.

Geddes saw the new groups as offering a fresh start – an opportunity to bring in modern management techniques and throw out the old union rule books. The next few years were to see the big players in the league trying to restructure their own businesses, and one major attempt to form a massive group out of a number of old yards along the Clyde.

The old, well-established companies seemed set in their old ways, struggling along from crisis to crisis. In 1962, Frederick Rebbeck resigned from Harland and Wolff after twenty-nine years as chairman and a new management moved in with new ideas.[3] Cutbacks were the order of the day as the company withdrew all its operations back to Belfast, where a modernization programme was put in hand with the help of government grants. In 1967, the yard launched Britain's first very large crude carrier (VLCC), the *Myrine*, at 190,000 dwt. It was a false dawn and they were soon in deep trouble, looking for a rescue either by a take-over by Onassis or a merger, with David Brown as the likeliest of contenders. In the event, they played the Northern Ireland card again and secured a government loan, but one with conditions attached. They had to accept a new financial director, J. F. Mallabar, who came with a reputation as a successful company doctor. He found a situation where productivity was low and financial control bordering on the farcical, with debts at the bank of £3.5 million and another £2.5 million of bills waiting to be paid. Faced with the crisis, Mallabar insisted on being given full control as company chairman, so that he could pursue a policy he described as 'energy, ruthlessness and even violence'.

There were good signs. There was a new source of income in building deep-sea oil rigs, and Esso were interested in more VLCCs. Mallabar felt sufficiently confident to put forward a building programme centred on a new dock which would allow for the most modern construction methods to be used. He approached the government for £13.5 million, but that was too much even to support Northern Ireland: he got a £5.5 million grant, which left £8 million still to be raised. The deal went through, but work was slow and the bill soon rose to £16 million. Work on the Esso tankers slowed, the renewed outbreak of sectarian violence lowered morale and productivity actually went down. But there was not too much concern, since of one thing at least everyone was convinced – no one at Westminster could allow Harland and Wolff to go under. And everyone was right.

In 1970, in spite of the chaos, Mallabar announced he had done all he could and resigned. Edward Heath was now prime minister and there was a new hard-line view of industry, expressed by Nicholas Ridley who announced that the government had no intention of propping up British shipbuilding, but when presented with the alternative of a take-over by a foreign concern, the support was put back. Shipbuilding on Clyde, Mersey, Tyne and Wear might collapse, but Belfast was still secure. There was now a head-hunt for a new chairman, the post going to the Dane Iver Hoppe. He too looked to modernization as a way forward, even though he arrived in the middle of a steel strike, which had virtually brought everything to a standstill. Once again government funding was expected to pick up the ailing yard and turn it into a highly efficient unit that would face the future fearlessly, without having to keep turning back to the government for help. The times were not propitious. Sir Monty Finniston was reorganizing British Steel, which meant that Harland and Wolff had to buy in expensive supplies from Japan and Sweden. Productivity had gone up, and the workers were expecting to see their efforts rewarded – but they were caught in a wage freeze, which not only saw them without any real reward for their better work, but actually slipping behind other yards on the mainland.

The company tottered along. Hoppe had not delivered the miracle – largely because he was not allowed to do so – and Hoppe went. Governments changed. Labour followed Tory, then the Tories returned with the Thatcher administration that regarded heavy industry with all the enthusiasm that a dowager duchess showed for bad drains at the manor house. Yet through it all, Harland and Wolff survived. It is impossible not to believe that, had their base been in Newcastle or Glasgow instead of Northern Ireland, they would have been closed down.

Whether reluctantly or enthusiastically, the government kept Harland and Wolff going. Private companies showed, if not enthusiasm, then an unseemly haste in closing things down. On 15 October 1965, at 4.15 p.m. on a Friday, the management of Fairfield's called the shop stewards together and announced they were closing the yard.[4] It was too late to pass on the message, and the first that most of the workers knew about it was an announcement on the six o'clock news. It was terrible news for the Clyde where jobs were already disappearing. At a meeting on the Monday the unions decided to fight closure. It seemed madness to shut down a business which had just been through an expensive modernization programme and had £32 millions' worth of orders on the books. The intermediary with the government was the Member of Parliament for Govan, John Robin, a man loathed by Clydeside owners who consistently refused to allow him on to their premises, even though he had been the local member for twenty years. Fairfield's was the one exception. Robin went to the prime minister Harold Wilson and asked for a stay of execution, at least until the Geddes Report was published with its promise of new plans for the industry. Wilson offered a short-term advance of £1 million to buy time for a new deal to be put together.

Robin wanted a new sort of company in which not just government representatives but also workers would have a place on the board. He went to see the industrialist Iain Stewart, a dedicated advocate of co-operation. Stewart claimed that he stood outside politics, and quoted the men he dealt with. George Brown, the minister responsible for shipbuilding, called him 'that bloody Tory' and the Tories called him 'that bloody Communist', so he felt he had probably got the balance about right. Stewart enthusiastically took up the notion of a tripartite management – government, workers and private capital – but saw that there had to be drastic changes from the start. The first aim was to reduce costs, and that principally meant improved working practices. Already a car ferry for New Zealand had incurred £600,000 in penalties for late delivery. The new key word was 'interchangeability' – an end to demarcation, everyone free to do any job of which they were capable. Stewart went to see Alex Jamieson, the secretary of the Shop Stewards Committee, with the proposal that the only way forward was for the unions to tear up the rule books. The response was, to say the least, less than encouraging: 'Who do you think you are? Jesus Christ? I'm not fucking tearing them up for no one.'

Stewart fought on. Not even the Labour party was united over the idea of saving Fairfield's, but the company had a doughty champion in the combative George Brown – even if the new chairman was 'a bloody Tory'. Fairfield's had become an industrial laboratory, a place where new ideas were to be tested. Co-operation was to replace confrontation, and the new plans had one important supporter, Harry Gallagher of the Confederation of Shipbuilding and Engineering Unions. He put the choice bluntly to the men: it was interchangeability or the dole. There was still the question of finance to be settled, but after a good deal of argument – involving numerous explosions of anger from George Brown – money was put up by Lord Thomson of Fleet and Hugh Stenhouse, and the tripartite management was agreed with Stewart at its head. The package was presented to the House of Commons in December 1965. Now all that Stewart and the new team had to do was keep their promise – to make Fairfield profitable within five years.

Some changes might have seemed purely symbolic, but they were none-the-less important for that. In the old yards there was a clear division between the men and the bowler-hatted foremen. Now everyone got hard hats which were colour-coded, earning their wearers the nickname, 'The Smarties'. It was a small thing but it helped to break down the 'them and us' mentality. One thing soon became clear: there were a great many wasteful practices that were carried on simply because things had always been done that way. The new men looked with new eyes and began to ask the obvious question 'why?'. Draughtsmen had scrupulously drawn everything on the ship – but was it really necessary to draw all 740 identical stools in the cocktail bar of a liner? More seriously, why were ships being built starting at the bows? The answer was that ships always had been built that way on the Clyde. But in the modern cargo ship, machinery and living quarters are set in the stern, so that it clearly makes sense to get that part of the hull ready first for fitting out. There were problems with a ready solution: others involving working practices and malpractices were more intractable.

The bottom line was that in Britain it took eighty-seven man-hours to work up a ton of steel; it took twenty-nine in Japan. Partly the answer lay in poor training. Plates were often taken down and put up again as many as eight times, simply because the welders were not up to the work. It was soon found that a little time spent on training saved an enormous amount of time on the job. Absenteeism was a real problem, and in part it was down to insecurity and that old imperative to make as much out of a job as possible because there might be nothing once the job was over. So men stayed away at the beginning of the week and made the work up at overtime rates at the weekend. And as a ship neared completion everything slowed down to put off redundancy if nothing else came in. The Fairfield doctrine was that if men were kept informed of what was happening and saw their own well-being as tied to the future of the company, then such practices would wither and die. Other problems were simply caused by sloppy thinking. Theft was a major and expensive problem. Gates were manned, the walls topped with barbed wire, while the river frontage was completely open. Anyone with a boat could come in when the yard was shut and help themselves. Once this problem was recognized and dealt with theft virtually disappeared – and it was said that two local scrap merchants promptly went out of business. It was not just a matter of changing attitudes that would convince the men that the actual situation had really changed – the new attitudes had to be seen in practice. And they were. Managers were now on site at least as early as the men – and seen to be there. Training no longer meant 'learning on the job' which too often meant little more than fetching and carrying and making the tea. Training was real and meaningful, with qualified instructors to do the teaching. Most importantly, old divisions were breaking down. There were genuine routes opened for men to move from construction out on the berth and into management. Shop stewards were sent on work study courses to ensure that they and the management both clearly understood how systems worked and why changes were sometimes needed.

Outsiders were brought in to look at ways of improving productivity. Professor Alexander of Strathclyde University sent in a small army of stop-watch toting engineers to do time and motion studies. It worked at Fairfield's because there was a genuine will to move to a new age of prosperity based on co-operation. It has to be said that it did not work everywhere. When looking at the Fairfield success story one has to be aware that other companies were trying similar schemes elsewhere. A former Cammell Laird worker interviewed by the author described the experience with the new regime. The stop-watch men came in, but few of them seemed to have practical experience of the processes they were studying. They did little more than time individual segments of work and extrapolate their figures to set standards to which everyone was expected to adhere. In this particular worker's case, the operatives were given an hour to set up the machine each day, after which they were expected to carry out one operation per minute. He spent two hours carefully setting up the work, and got the time down to 15 seconds. In other words in his six hours of operation in an eight-hour day, he could perform 1,440 tasks against 360 in the seven hours on the old system. He was sent home on full pay for overstepping the set-up time and not keeping to standards. He was later promoted to a supervisory grade and again found absurdities. The works were regularly closed down for stocktaking. He found men scrupulously counting, for example, every single washer of a certain size – as they were all standard fittings all they needed to do was weigh the whole lot. He saw the situation as a failure in management and a failure in communication – he left. This digression does show why Fairfield's succeeded where others failed. Changing attitudes on all sides really was as important as changing practices.

Everything at Fairfield's was examined and changes were widespread – not least in planning. Rigorous controls were applied, for example, to component supplies: it is just as bad to have material delivered early so that it creates clutter and ties up capital, as it is to have it arrive late. Men worked in groups under a system of productivity bonuses, which were applied to the whole group no matter what trade or union the individuals belonged to. The results were spectacular. In two years, productivity improvement was ten times the national average. Of the three ships built under the Stewart regime, all were completed on time and two were early – resulting in new orders. Stewart had promised to turn a loss into a profit in five years. In 1967 the company showed a modest gain of £10,000: he and the workforce had done it in two.

How the Fairfield story would have developed had the company followed the path on which it had started will never be known. But Fairfield's did not fit into the new post-Geddes orthodoxy: it was considered too small to survive by itself. As soon as the Geddes Report was published plans were laid for the industry to be rationalized into five major units: two on the Clyde, two in the north-east and one in Northern Ireland. The Minister of Technology, Tony Benn, was dangling a large and tempting carrot: £200 million available as credit to ship-owners placing orders with a new, big grouping and £20 million available as a grant to ease the way to merger and modernization, organized by a new body the Shipbuilding Industry Board (SIB). A striking feature of the new board was that none of the top men had any experience of the industry: they were William Swallow of Vauxhall Motors, Anthony Hopper of the Tilling Group which had just completed a successful reorganization of Pretty Polly, the hosiery manufacturers, and Joe Gormley of the miners' union. Iain Stewart had shown that it was possible for an outsider to shed a fresh light on an old industry, but it does seem a touch perverse to have three outsiders heading the new board.

In 1966 three yards on the Upper Clyde were enthusiastically discussing a merger – Yarrow, Connell and Stephen – and two others were brought into the debate with rather less eagerness. John Brown's had once been the pride of the Clyde but had fallen on hard times and no one was especially keen to welcome the debt-ridden old giant into the new group. Fairfield's was distrusted – bold experiment was considered somehow rather socialistic by the conservative standards of other yards. Fairfield's themselves were also more than happy to go their own increasingly profitable way. But the pressure to combine was all but irresistible. The government help being offered to the new conglomerates made it very difficult for those left on the outside to compete. If there was little enthusiasm for joining the group, there was even less for staying outside in the cold. The inevitable result was the foundation of Upper Clyde Shipbuilders (UCS) with Hopper as its head. Forced marriages are seldom happy marriages, and this was no exception. Although the five yards involved were supposed to be joining one big family, there was bickering from the start. Who was to get the best cash settlement from the deal? Each company put in its own exaggerated – if not downright dishonest – claim, based on current assets and future orders. The assets were over-valued, the orders could be most charitably described as optimistic. UCS began its working life saddled with old debts. Nevertheless, the new infant swaggered out, ready to take its place on the world stage.

The first priority was, just as it had been for Fairfield's, to build up a new, co-operative relationship between management and men. Hopper was soon to discover, just as Stewart had before him, that rational argument would not necessarily win the day against old prejudices. The core of Geddes' recommendations was that antagon-isms should be forgotten and a new age of co-operation would emerge. Hopper went to one of those meetings intended to usher in the new age. It began with the simplest item on the agenda – were the minutes of the last meeting an accurate record? Management arms shot up in agreement, union arms remained resolutely folded.[5]

> I asked them all if the minutes were correct and approved. I looked down the table and they all looked back silently. I tried again, but still there was no answer from the trade union people. Eventually I said 'Well, either they are correct or they are not. For goodness sake tell me one way or the other'. A voice at my side said 'those buggers don't get a copy of the minutes, just us'.

It was not a good omen – and the new company was desperate for good news, for the future was far from promising. Rational analysis could only lead to one conclusion: there were more building berths on the Upper Clyde than could possibly be filled – and although modernization would increase the opportunities to bid successfully for new orders, it would also inevitably decrease the number of berths needed. It was all clearly spelled out at a joint union–management meeting in 1968.[6]

In any case, UCS was not in a position to tender for all new ships: the Clyde was too constricted to go for the supertanker market. They would have to limit their options to bulk carriers, cargo liners, ferries and dredgers. Even those limited objectives could only be reached because a new charter, establishing a basis for good industrial relations had been agreed. After long negotiations terms were set out.[7]

It was very much based on the Fairfield formula. Flexibility was built into the new structure: men must be able to shift from one craft to another as circumstance demanded, and a training programme was set up to help make it possible. It left, however, a lot of questions unresolved and directives were couched in the vaguest of terms. 'The wages structure will not be disturbed by the introduction of new methods, equipment or working practices, but the resulting increases in productivity may be the subject of a review of overall wage scales.' Promises by management were equally loosely phrased. 'The Company undertakes to keep the men well informed about the Company, its prospects, trading conditions and policies.' This fell a long way short of the regular consultations set up at Fairfield's. Something like a quarter of the charter was concerned with the mechanisms for dealing with demarcation disputes, and one cannot help sensing a negative attitude. The emphasis was not on avoiding such disputes, there was a tacit understanding that they would occur. It was, at best, a damage limitation exercise.

From the start, there was a failure to grasp the difficult issues. It was quite clear that the Linthouse yard was losing money at an alarming rate of around £1 million a year and nothing could save it. Hopper failed to consult the unions and simply put off the inevitable. When confrontation came, Hopper tried to buy peace by agreeing to a modest redundancy programme, in which just 300 jobs would be lost, and a guarantee of employment for the rest of the group – a promise he must have realized he would be unable to keep. To the unions, the lack of consultation marked a return to old attitudes. McGarvey of the Boilermakers walked out of wage negotiations, convinced that the new complex system would only mean his members losing out to other unions. It was all very unsatisfactory. And on the building side things were not going well. The old story of late deliveries was being repeated, and the ultimate ignominy came when Cunard rejected their new prestige liner, the *QE2*. The fault was not all with the builders. Cunard kept changing their minds over specifications, but no one could deny that when she set out on her maiden voyage the ship was far from ready. There was fitting-out work still needed in the cabins, but more seriously the turbines were damaged. The *QE2* was to reflect the image of a new, vibrant industry – but the image was tragically tarnished.

In May 1962, Hopper applied for a further £12 million of aid. Tony Benn was unconvinced: the promises of improved industrial relations had not been fulfilled, management was still complacently running on its old tracks, while owners were repeating the all too familiar complaints of late deliveries. Benn was furious and told Hopper that the best he could offer was funding on a day-by-day basis to keep UCS alive until new plans that might actually work were agreed. The management response was a demand to the unions that they accept 5,000 redundancies, no pay rise that was not accompanied by better productivity and a reduction in absenteeism, and a comprehensive no-strike agreement. There were to be no changes in the management structure. Not surprisingly the unions refused. It was a three-way showdown: Benn would do no more for UCS without a new corporate plan, UCS management had nothing to offer and the unions were on a hiding to nothing: they had to accept worse terms or see the whole edifice collapse with the loss of thousands of jobs. There was no choice: the unions gave in, and agreed to 2,600 redundancies. No one came out a winner. The new management team were discredited. Whatever the faults of the old-style bowler-hat brigade, at least they knew the industry. The new men, for all their fine talk of cash-flow plans and economic forecasts, seemed lost. They saw the problems and broadcast them to the world, but a management that constantly talks down its own company does nothing for confidence either inside or outside the concern. Gradually the new men slipped away to less troublesome sections of British industry, and a new chief executive came in, Ken Dayton from the Sunderland builders, Austin and Pickersgill. At first, the new team seemed to offer a way forward, but there was unease within the alliance. In particular, Sir Eric Yarrow was regretting joining the big UCS group and started negotiating for the removal of his company. He found an enthusiastic response in the ranks of the Conservative party. Nicholas Ridley set out in the bluntest possible terms exactly what his party would do if they returned to power.[8]

I believe that we should do the following on assuming office:-

(a) Give no more public money to U.C.S.

(b) Let Yarrow leave U.C.S. if they still want to, and facilitate their joining Lower Clyde if they still wish to do so.

(c) This would lead to the bankruptcy of U.C.S.

We could accept this, in which case Lower Clyde would take over one or two of the yards. The employment result would be:-

	1970	Then	(men)
Yarrows		4,000	
U.C.S.	7,500		
Lower Clyde	7,000	9,000	
	14,500	13,000	

i.e. 1,500 men would be redeployed to other works and would be rapidly re-employed.

We could put in a Government 'Butcher' to cut up U.C.S. and to sell (cheaply) to Lower Clyde, and others, the assets of U.C.S., minimise upheaval and dislocation. I am having further views on the practicality of such an operation, which I will report.

(d) After liquidation or reconstruction as above, we should sell the Government holding in U.C.S., even for a pittance.

At this stage we should confine ourselves to saying absolutely firmly that there will be no more money from the Tory government.

In June 1970, the Conservatives were back in power, and it was soon clear that Ridley had not been indulging in mere polemic. At the party conference, a keynote speech by John Davies announced that the government was no longer prepared to support lame ducks – it was soon clear that UCS were numbered among that unhappy bunch of fowl. A committee of 'four wise men' – A. Forbes McDonald of Distillers, David MacDonald of Hill Samuel, Alexander Glen of the travel firm Clarkson and Lord Robens, former chairman of the Coal Board – was appointed to look at UCS. Their views were unambiguous: 'any continuation of Upper Clyde Shipbuilders in its present form would be wholly unjustified'. The government withdrew support, UCS went into liquidation and arrangements began for all work to go to the yards in the Lower Clyde. On 30 July 1971, the day after the government announced the death sentence on UCS, the workforce decided to take matters into their own hands. They began a work-in. The shop stewards' argument was that it was they, not the management, who had argued for modernization and understood the problems facing the industry. Joe Black of the CSEU was scathing.[9]

They didn't understand these problems and consequently wouldn't apply the solution. We were talking to the Clyde shipbuilders about critical path analysis and they thought we were talking about a Greek tanker owner.

It was a valiant, but doomed attempt to save a dying industry. Perhaps it needed an outsider to see just how hopeless it was, how a lack of investment stretching back over the years had left much of the Upper Clyde dependent on outdated machinery, badly maintained, and incompetent planning. Wayne Harkin of Marathon Manufacturing of Houston, Texas spelled it out:[10]

I found among these men a real pride in their accomplishments and indeed they have a right to be proud. Skilled craftsmen are in evidence all over the place. What amazed me was the fact that they had been able to turn out the quality of work with the facilities.

[236]

UCS was sold to Marathon in October 1972 for oil-rig construction. The work-in was ended, thousands were out of work and UCS was no more. There had been a real sense of pride and defiance among the men of the work-in, expressed by one of the unlikely heroes of the hour, James Reid:[11] 'We have told the Government that if they want us out of the yards then let the Prime Minister and Davies come and try to do it. We don't only build boats on the Clyde, we build men.'

In the end the fine words counted for nothing. The UCS experiment had ended in failure before it had had time to show whether or not it could succeed. The company died because a new government saw no reason why it should be kept alive.

The one firm to survive from the wreckage was Yarrow's. They began an ambitious modernization programme. In 1971 they were being described as 'the most modern shipyard in Europe'.[12] A million pound programme had culminated in the opening of new covered berths, which would allow two destroyers to be built simultaneously, while preparation and prefabrication of a third would continue between the two berths. The argument for covered berths had always been there: in an average winter three days' work out of ten were lost through bad weather. In 1974, the company moved on again, taking over land and dock facilities at Elderslie from Barclay Curle. A spokesman spelled out just what it meant both for employees and future development.[13]

We are particularly pleased to be able to offer the Elderslie dock-yard employees — about 900 of them — employment in the most appropriate job category. . . .

In addition [said the spokesman], the company will now have scope to extend its operations into other activities, including work connected with North Sea oil developments, should this be in the best interests of the company and its employees in future years.

In all, Yarrow's were planning to put a further £3 million into development — which represented roughly the company profits from the previous year. Few British yards were in that happy position.

[237]

In the post-Geddes years, there was a rush towards finding new agreements to remove restrictive practices. Mick McGarvey put the Union's position simply and honestly.[14]

> Although most Trade Union leaders – and he, Mr McGarvey was no exception – had an inbuilt defence mechanism when talking with Employers, it was time to abandon this attitude. . . . 'They were prepared to declare here and now that there would be no stoppage of work while any demarcation issues were under discussion'.

There was, he said, no point in fighting over a bone, if at the end there was going to be no bone to fight over. Other companies came up with agreements that seemed positively Utopian.[15]

> Steelwork operations (i.e. preparation, assembly, erection and fairing, including production welding, caulking and burning) will be undertaken by platers, shipwrights, welders and caulker-burners, and all members of the Amalgamated Society will as required undertake service operations incidental to the progress of their main job. . . . Minor work could be taken on by anyone. In exchange the companies offered at least 9 months security of employment.

Fine sentiments were not always translated into fine deeds. At Austin and Pickersgill, a strike by shipwrights resulted in tack welders being laid off with no pay, and they were refused unemployment benefit on the grounds that everyone was now in the same union. There was, however, a guarded optimism, and a Report, produced by the Shipbuilders and Repairers National Association in 1973, told a story of past successes and looked forward to a healthier future.[16] In fact, the statistics showed violent fluctuations in the market. From a dismal low in 1962 when production stood at less than 2 million g.r.t. it rose to 3.5 million in 1965, dropped in 1967 and apart from a blip in 1972 rose steadily again to stand at an impressive 7 million in 1973. The figures reflected a long overdue programme of modernization and automation, including the use of computer-controlled cutters, the spread of covered docks and a revolutionary new technique applied on the Clyde, where ships were being built in two halves and welded together. The optimism that marked 1973 turned to ashes in 1974.

Disaster began even before 1973 was ended when OPEC, representing the world's major oil-producing nations, announced a massive seventy per cent rise in oil prices combined with a cutback in production. Add to this a high rate of inflation and it seemed that, almost in an instant, the oil trade had collapsed and with it the all-important demand for new tankers. This was not the end of the calamities. Maritime Fruit Carriers failed, who were customers for almost a third of all the tonnage on order from British yards. There were various estimates of the business lost to British builders, but it was certainly not less than £120 million and could have been as high as £150 million. It was a calamity with little hope of salvation without considerable government aid. The disaster coincided with a change of government, and the incoming Labour administration under Harold Wilson was certainly more favourably disposed to preserving heavy industry than the Conservatives had been. The question was just how much could be saved. By 1976 it was clear that many firms were gone beyond recall. Even the best-managed, most up-to-date shipbuilders barely showed a profit. All but nine yards had empty order books.

The government was prepared to support the industry, but at a price. If it was to be propped up by public money then it would have to go into public ownership. The move was resisted by the builders, but it is difficult to see how many could have survived without government help. However much they might complain, it was clear just who was the paymaster. In 1977 British Shipbuilders, the new nationalized industry, was born. In the first phase, British Shipbuilders acquired thirty-two yards, six marine engine works and six general engineering works. The principal outsider was, as ever, Harland and Wolff, publicly owned but separately run. There were 87,000 employees in the new conglomerate. The industry was reorganized into five specialist groups: merchant shipping, naval ships, engineering, ship repair and off-shore work. A huge amount of money was pumped into the system, but in the first five years 25,000 jobs went and the losses mounted as world demand for shipping stagnated. In spite of the capital investment of over £80 million, the builders still complained it was not enough.[17]

> Unless the government allows British Shipbuilders better credit facilities, then it will be making a mockery of its stated policies of allowing for competition and would in fact be handicapping British Shipbuilders in competition with overseas yards, whose governments subsidise them in credit facilities.

Others spelt it out in more detail.[18]

> The shrinking of the market has changed things drastically. The rules on fair competition within the EEC have been bent and twisted out of all recognition. Countries such as Brazil and Korea have erected, or started to erect, barriers against the importation of marine equipment which can be produced within their borders. That great protagonist of free trade – Norway – is now subsidising not only its shipbuilding industry, but also its marine equipment industry . . . we cannot go on playing cricket while our competitors indulge in less gentlemanly games.

Yet, in some ways, the yards still acted as if they were back in the Golden Age. In July 1978, Cammell Laird celebrated 150 years of shipbuilding and a major and very expensive refit by inviting Princess Anne to launch the Type 42 destroyer, HMS *Liverpool*. The workforce heard of the extensive junketings at about the same time as many got their redundancy notices. They put out a pamphlet:[19] 'We are disgusted at the £1200 to be paid for the champagne dinner for 70 management guests who have been invited to meet the woman from the stables.' The money was nothing in terms of the overall budget of a major yard but what the little pamphlet shows is how quickly the new mood of co-operation, that followed immediately after Geddes, had evaporated.

Arguments in favour of more help were now falling on increasingly deaf ears. In 1979 Labour lost the election and Margaret Thatcher came to power. Industrial policy went into reverse. Nationalization was out, privatization was in. Heavy industry had had its day, the future lay with service industries. Market forces would control the economy. The workforce soon found out just what a return to 'Victorian values' meant in practice. Costs were the all-important factor, whether applied to the ships being built or the men who were building them. The labour force was casualized and men described by the old workers as 'cowboys' were taken on in preference to skilled men. An account of what it meant to one company, Austin and Pickersgill of Sunderland, let the workers largely describe the situation as they saw it.[20] A plumber demonstrated how he could bend a pipe into a perfect curve, but the new men were content to use an elbow-joint: easier, cheaper but intrinsically weaker. Increasingly, work was contracted out – again cheap, but not up to the old standards. But what was to be done? Who, under the new regime, could afford to complain? A man from the smith's shop spoke despairingly of work as he saw it.

Casualisation means . . . if you are casual, then you don't complain about the job, you don't complain about the safety, cause there is always a chance that you'll get kept on, your short-term contract will be extended, and extended. So you tend not to complain and do everything the gaffer tells you, cut corners, do owt, to stop gannin' back on the stones again . . . it reverts you to the market system where – like we used to be – we'd have a hundred and odd people standing of a morning and the gaffer would come and pick who is going to start. Any troublemakers wouldn't get a look in, no chance, no chance.

Everywhere the move to casualization went on. It had great advantages in a shrinking industry, for casual workers had no claim to redundancy payments. And closures were becoming a reality, as the merchant shipping work slipped away almost to vanishing point. Even those who had at first welcomed privatization as a means of regaining local control of a local industry began to suffer.

[241]

In 1986, four directors acquired Swan Hunter at the knockdown price of £5 million. From the start, however, they tied themselves completely to government, signing an agreement that designated them as wholly devoted to warship construction. This not only kept them dependent on defence orders, it also cut them off from various European Community funds available for merchant work. They did their best to show that they had the hard attitudes demanded by the new government. When a dispute looked like holding up the launch of the frigate HMS *Coventry*, the management team came back to the yard at night and launched it themselves. But they did not get the order they really wanted, the £120 million Auxiliary Oil Replenishment vessel – that went to Harland and Wolff. This was at the time when the government was trying to persuade the province to accept the Anglo-Irish agreement. Not for the first time, the Belfast firm was on the receiving end of a political handout. As a direct result over 800 jobs were lost at Swan Hunter.

In the next few days, the company found out just what it meant to be so closely tied to defence orders. Plans could all be overthrown by a change in political direction, in moves in the international scene. There was also keen competition for every order – from Yarrow and more especially from the Vickers group, VSEL. Attempts to break out into the merchant ship market were at best partially successful. They acquired a £30 million order for an Antarctic Survey vessel for James Ross in 1989, but it was technically complex and although it provided much needed work, it was built at a loss. There was a respite that year with an order for three frigates, but the next three went to Yarrow. Now everything depended on one massive order for a new helicopter carrier for the Royal Navy. It was soon clear that it would be a straight fight between Swan Hunter and VSEL.

VSEL was already well established as Britain's builder of nuclear submarines. No one doubts that it is among the most modern shipyards in the world. At its heart is the Devonshire Dock Hall, a covered construction area, 51 metres high, with a floor area of 25,000 square metres. It is so big that over 3,000 men can work there at any one time. As one would expect, all the latest machinery is on hand from radio-controlled 150-tonne cranes to an array of powered bogies used to move modules on to the final construction areas. Swan Hunter's hopes rested to an extent on the notion that because VSEL had control of the submarine programme, they would be given the lifeline of the carrier. They were to be disappointed. In May 1993 it was announced that the ship was to be built at Barrow. Swan Hunter went into receivership.

In July 1992, the National Audit Office admitted that there had been serious errors when the Auxiliary Oil vessel had gone to Harland and Wolff. Rumours soon spread that all was not as it seemed with the new order either. A government spokesman claimed that the decision had been entirely commercial. 'They were not thrown to the wolves. There is a limited market and, due to the competitive nature of the bidding, the government is required to get the best value for every pound. VSEL's bid was way below Swan Hunter's.'[21]

But the arguments were not over. Papers were produced to suggest that VSEL was using profits from its Trident programme to subsidize the carrier tender. At a hearing of the Commons Public Accounts Committee, Alan Williams MP also claimed that a sub-contractor, Kvaerner Govan, had allowed for a loss of £6 million on the work.[22] The object of the exercise was, it was said, to destroy Swan Hunter and leave VSEL with a virtual monopoly of major contracts. Whether that was the intention it certainly seemed to be the result. In December 1993, Kvaerner Govan was able to send out good news to its workforce and shareholders. The company which had been bought up as an almost bankrupt concern by a Norwegian multi-national in 1988 had full order books up until 1996, and had negotiated a two-year pay deal with its workforce. Britain's last commercial shipyard looked set for a profitable future. But that same month, irony was heaped on irony. The seventeen members of the European Union voted in favour of a subsidy to Swan Hunter: the men of Brussels were prepared to do what the men of Westminster were not, save a workforce of over 1,000 men employed directly by the yard, and save the jobs of the many more who depended on it. The grant was made in order to help Swan Hunter turn from a dependence on military commissions to compete in the commercial marketplace. As the year ended, it looked very much as if Kvaerner Govan would lose its position as the last builder of merchant ships in Britain.

The year did not bring everyone the same good cheer. One of the great names of British shipbuilding joined so many more in the slide off into history. Cammell Laird launched its last vessel: not a great liner, nor a mighty warship, but a one-ton cabin cruiser. Then the yard closed.

It is difficult to put figures on what a yard closure means for an area. It is not simply a matter of the workforce employed there, but also all the others who supplied them with everything from steel plates to washbasins. At the beginning of the century Britain had stood proud among the maritime nations of the world, with the biggest merchant fleet and the biggest shipbuilding industry. As the century reaches its end, Britain is reduced to a merchant fleet that stands at number 38 in the world listings. In 1975, there were 1,614 ships flying the red ensign: in 1993 there were 272. The flag of convenience rules. Inspection standards are often low: Cyprus, for example, has 1,350 registered ships and nine surveyors. There is a new tendency to keep vessels at sea long after their useful life should be ended. The country had almost abandoned attempts to compete for new orders for merchant shipping. It had been a precipitous fall, which could not be attributed to any one factor. Everyone had a part to play in the sorry saga: financiers who failed to invest, complacent owners, conservative managers and obstinate workers. The yards have gone quiet on Thames, Tees, Wear, Tyne and Mersey and something special here has been lost. One has only to look back at the great ships of the past to see that their magnificence carried a special aura. It was something that touched everyone who worked in the industry. Perhaps the last word should go to an ordinary workman, a fitter, Graeme Myers, in one of the smaller yards, Smith's of Tees-side.[23]

I think a ship is probably the best thing you could build as far as job satisfaction goes. You build a ship and it actually moves. You go on trials with them and then they sail out at the end, you think you've done something towards that. The job I've got now I'm going to be building transformers for microwave ovens but there's no way on this earth that I'm going to walk into a shop that sells microwave ovens and say 'Oh I helped to build them'. It is just not the same, it's a job, it pays your wages and that's it. Whereas this, you could bring the wife or the girlfriend or your mother or somebody down to the shipyard and say 'Look this is what we do' and actually get a feeling of pride. I would never take somebody round a factory and show them transformers, because it's nothing.

In that loss of pride and achievement lies the greatest tragedy of all.

SOURCES AND REFERENCES

ABBREVIATIONS

BRL   Birkenhead Reference Library
BRCGUA   Business Record Centre, Glasgow University Archives
GMTA   Glasgow Museum of Transport Archives
GUA   Glasgow University Archives
MMM   Merseyside Maritime Museum
TWAS   Tyne and Wear Archives Service

Chapter 1: Rule Britannia

1. Quoted in Colin M. Castle, *Better By Yards*, 1988.
2. The Oral History Project, McLean Museum and Art Gallery, Greenock.
3. Letter to Sir Percy Bates, BRCGUA.
4. Letter dated 28 May 1931, BRCGUA.
5. Letter from Sir Thomas Bell, 12 February 1931, BRCGUA.
6. Letter from Sir Thomas Bell, 7 April, 1931, BRCGUA.
7. James Quiggins & Co. Specification Book, 1855–65. MMM.
8. Laird Brothers Contract Books, 1854–7. BRL.

Chapter 2: The Wooden Ship

1. The North Ferriby, Sutton Hoo and Graveney Boats are described in National Maritime Museum Monograph No 6, 1972.
2. Quoted in Sir Westcott Abell, *The Shipwright's Trade*, 1948.
3. Parliamentary Papers Relating to Ships and Shipbuilding, 1814.
4. *Ibid.*
5. *The Cumberland Pacquet*, 4 June 1833.
6. *The Cumberland Pacquet*, 26 April 1842.
7. R.T. Paige, *The Tamar Valley at Work*, 1978.
8. Frank Booker, *The Industrial Archaeology of the Tamar Valley*, 1967.
9. R.C. Riley, *The Evolution of the Docks and Industrial Buildings in Portsmouth's Royal Dockyard, 1698–1914*, 1985.
10. Figures quoted in Ralph Davis, *The Rise of the English Shipping Industry*, 1962.
11. Quoted in Philip MacDougall, *Royal Dockyards*, 1982.
12. Quoted in Abell, *op. cit.*
13. W.G. Perrin (ed.), *The Autobiography of Phineas Pett*, 1918.
14. Quoted in Anon, *A Shipbuilding History, 1750–1932*, 1932.
15. Quoted in S. Pollard, 'Laissez-Faire and Shipbuilding', *Economic History Review*, 1952–3.
16. Pepys' *Diary*, 19 May 1666.
17. *Ibid.*, 22 April 1669.
18. *Ibid.*, 20 May 1668.
19. Daniel Defoe, *A Tour Through the Whole Island of Great Britain*, 1724–6.

Chapter 3: Trade, Industry and Science

1. Basil Harley, 'The Society of Arts' Model Ship Trials', *Transactions of the Newcomen Society*, 1991–2.
2. Abraham Rees, *The Cyclopaedia*, 1819–20, The section Rees's Naval Architecture reprinted 1970.
3. Anon, *Two Hundred and Fifty Years of Shipbuilding by the Scotts at Greenock*, 1961 (4th edition).
4. R.C. Riley, *The Evolution of the Docks and Industrial Buildings in Portsmouth Dockyard*, 1698–1914, 1985.
5. Letter quoted in L.T.C. Rolt, *Isambard Kingdom Brunel*, 1957.
6. E.P. Brenton, *Life and Correspondence of the Earl of St. Vincent*, 1838.
7. National Maritime Museum documents.
8. Quoted in George Dicker, *A Short History of Devonport Royal Dockyard*, 1969.
9. Anon, *A Shipbuilding History, 1750–1932*, 1932.
10. Dicker, *op. cit.*
11. S. Pollard, 'The Decline of Shipbuilding on the Thames', *Economic History Review*, 1950.
12. Appendix to the House of Commons Report on the Laws Respecting Friendly Societies, 1825.
13. *Ibid.*
14. Anon, *A Shipbuilding History, 1750–1932*, 1932.
15. House of Commons Committee, *op. cit.*
16. *Ibid.*
17. Anon, *A Few Remarks on the State of the Laws at Present in Existence for regulating Masters and Workpeople*, 1823.
18. *The Cumberland Pacquet*, 25 October 1825.
19. *Ibid.*, 1 November 1825.
20. *Ibid.*, 28 February 1826.

Chapter 4: The Steam Age

1. Quoted in George S. Emmerson, *John Scott Russell*, 1977.
2. *Memoirs of David Napier*, Handwritten notes by Napier, GMTA.
3. Newspaper cutting undated, Napier papers, GMTA.
4. 'The Story of Tod and McGregor of the Clyde', *Shipbuilding and Shipping Record*, 22 May 1947.
5. Laird Brothers Contract Books 1854–7, BRL.
6. Joule to Napier, 16 November 1860, Napier correspondence, GMTA.
7. Quoted in Ewan Corlett, *The Iron Ship*, 1975.
8. Quoted in Charles Hadfield, *British Canals*, 1984 (7th edition).
9. I.K. Brunel, *Report to the Directors of the Great Western Steamship Company on Screw Propellers*, 1840.
10. Samuel Smiles (ed.), *James Nasmyth, An Autobiography*, 1883.
11. *Ibid.*
12. Letter dated 12 March 1839, Napier papers, GMTA.
13. Contract dated 18 March 1939, Napier papers, GMTA.

Chapter 5: New Men, New Ways

1. Anon, *Two Hundred & Fifty Years of Shipbuilding by the Scotts at Greenock*, 1961.
2. George S. Emmerson, *John Scott Russell*, 1977.
3. L.T.C. Rolt, *Isambard Kingdom Brunel*, 1957 and Adrian Vaughan, *Brunel*, 1991.
4. Quoted in Emmerson, *op. cit.*
5. Letter dated 31 January 1860, Napier papers, GMTA.
6. William Fairbairn, *Iron Ship Building*, 1865.
7. Quoted in Rolt, *op. cit.*
8. John Key, 'Some personal experience of marine boilers', 1886, quoted in Robin Craig, *Steam Tramps and Cargo Liners*, 1980.

9. Crawford W. Hume, *A Hundred Years of Howden Engineering*, 1954.
10. Newby, George A. 'Behind The Fire Doors', *Transactions of the Newcomen Society*, 1992–3.
11. Anon, *A Shipbuilding History, 1750–1932*, 1932.
12. 'The Practical Magazine', June 1874.
13. Charles Cammell and Co. Board Minute Books, 28 January 1891, BRL.
14. Ernest B. Royden, *Thomas Royden & Sons, Shipbuilders, Liverpool 1818–1893*, 1953.
15. Charles Goodey, *The First Hundred Years, the Story of Richards Shipbuilders*, 1936.
16. Anon, *John Readhead & Sons Ltd, South Shields, 1865–1965*, 1965.
17. Letter dated 10 December 1884, William Denny press cuttings book, BRCGUA.
18. Arthur G. Credland, *Earles of Hull 1853–1932*, 1982.
19. J.P. McKechnie, 'Review of Marine Engineering', *Proceedings of the Institute of Mechanical Engineers*, 1901.

Chapter 6: The Works and the Workers

1. *North British Daily Mail*, 19 December 1885.
2. 'The Birkenhead Iron Works', *The Practical Magazine*, June 1874.
3. John Scott Russell, *The Modern System of Naval Architecture*, 1865.
4. A.C. Hardy, *From Ship to Sea*, 1926.
5. 'The Birkenhead Iron Works', *op. cit.*
6. *The Greenock Advertiser*, 27 November 1855.
7. *The Cumberland Pacquet*, April 1865.
8. Robert Napier, Vessel Memorandum Book, 10 March 1868, GMTA.
9. Quoted in *Glasgow Chamber of Commerce Journal*, June 1971.

10. R. Angus Smith to James Napier, 19 May 1863, GMTA.
11. Statistics from E.J. Hobsbawm, *The Age of Capital*, 1975.
12. Sidney Pollard, 'British and World Shipbuilding 1890–1914', *Journal of Economic History*, 1957.
13. The Boiler Makers' and Iron Ship Builders' Society Monthly Report, April 1869.
14. Weekly accounts in *The Engineer*, between 11 October and 27 December 1895.
15. Quoted in Michael Moss and John R. Hume, *Shipbuilders to the World, 125 Years of Harland and Wolff*, 1986.
16. Henry Fry, *The History of North Atlantic Steam Navigation*, 1896.
17. Wear Shipbuilders Association Minutes 25 January, 1853 TWAS.
18. *Ibid.*, Minutes of 29 June–13 November 1854.
19. *Ibid.*, 4 December 1857.
20. *Ibid.*, 20 December 1866.
21. *Ibid.*, 9 January 1867.
22. Alexander Balmain Bruce, *The Life of William Denny Shipbuilder*, 1888.
23. James Napier to Govan workers, 14 July 1850, GMTA.
24. Letter dated 13 May 1863, GUA.
25. Quoted in E.J. Hobsbawm, *Labouring Men*, 1964.
26. Shipwrights, Joiners and Employers' Standing Committee on Demarcation of Work, January 1895 to December 1898.
27. Royal Commission on Labour, 1893–4.
28. Report from *Greenock Advertiser*, 9 November 1877.
29. *Greenock Advertiser*, 15 August 1877.
30. *The Engineer*, 28 January 1898.
31. *The Times*, 13 September 1896.

Chapter 7: The Steam Navy

1. Report from the Select Committee on the Steam Navy, 1847.
2. John Crighton, *The Famous Orchard Dockyard*, 1949.
3. Sir Allan Grant, *Steel and Ships, The History of John Brown's*, 1950.
4. *The Times*, 11 September 1867.
5. *The Times*, 1 October 1867.
6. P. Barry, *The Dockyards and the Private Shipyards of the Kingdom*, 1863.
7. Barry, *op. cit.*
8. John Scott Russell to Robert Napier, 13 March 1863, GMTA.
9. Quoted in the *Glasgow Herald* 1884, William Denny press cuttings, GUA.
10. *Fairplay*, 9 May 1885.
11. Froude to Sir Edward Reed, December 1868, quoted in A.T. Crichton, 'William and Robert Edward Froude and the Evolution of the Ship-model experimental Tank', *Transactions of the Newcomen Society*, 1989–90.
12. Alistair Borthwick, *Yarrow*, 1977.
13. *Ibid.*
14. K.C. Barnaby, *100 Years of Specialised Shipbuilding and Engineering*, 1964.
15. The *Times*, 13 March 1877.
16. 'Sir Charles Parsons: A Symposium', *Transactions of the Newcomen Society*, 1984–5.
17. J.D. Scott, *Vickers, A History*, 1962.
18. Armstrong Minute Books, 27 February 1913, TWAS.
19. *Ibid.*, 6 May 1914.

Chapter 8: A Golden Age

1. Handwritten notes by Thomas H. Pemberton, Chief Draughts-man, Clover Docks, 1943, MMM.
2. David Pollock, *Modern Shipbuilding and the Men Engaged In It*, 1884.
3. Anon, *Fairfield 1860–1960*, 1961.
4. Anon, *Launching Ways*, 1953.
5. Arthur G. Maginnis, *The Atlantic Ferry*, 1900.
6. Sir Allan Grant, *Steel and Ships, The History of John Brown*, 1950.
7. Sidney Pollard, 'British and World Shipbuilding 1890–1914', *Journal of Economic History*, 1957.
8. *The Engineer*, 18 February 1898.
9. Fred M. Walker and Anthony Slaven (ed.), *European Shipbuilding*, 1983.
10. Count Kalinsky to Stuart Rendel, 27 March 1868, TWAS.
11. Stuart Rendel to the Turkish Ambassador, 15 June 1868, TWAS.
12. Armstrong memo, 21 April 1881, TWAS.
13. Letters 12 to 17 December 1903, TWAS.
14. Letter dated 13 November 1911, TWAS.
15. Whitehead to Rendel, 30 September 1903, TWAS.
16. Stuart Rendel, 9 October 1908, TWAS.
17. Report, Lord Rendel, 28 June 1904, TWAS.
18. Cammell Board Minute Books, 30 June 1897, BRL.
19. *Ibid.*, 28 December 1892.
20. *Ibid.*, 20 September 1894.
21. Letter dated 2 October 1907, GUA.
22. Quoted in S. Pollard, 'The Decline of Shipbuilding on the Thames', *Economic History Review*, 1950.
23. *Ibid.*
24. *Glasgow Herald*, 29 December 1906.
25. Sir Eustace H.W. Tennyson d'Eyncourt, *A Shipbuilder's Yarn*, 1949.

26. C.H.G. Hopkins, *Pallion*, 1954.
27. Bartram's Diary, TWAS.
28. Quoted in Norman Longmate, *Milestones in Working Class History*, 1975.
29. Quoted in Tyne and Wear Archive Service *Wor Lass*, 1988.

Chapter 9: Depression

1. John Brown Company, Pay Bill Book 1914–25, BRCGUA.
2. J.D. Scott, *Vickers, A History*, 1962.
3. Michael Moss & John R. Hume, *Shipbuilders to the World, 125 Years of Harland and Wolff*, 1986.
4. *Ibid.*
5. *Ibid.*
6. Ellen Wilkinson, *The Town That Was Murdered*, 1939.
7. The *Newcastle Chronicle*, June 1858.
8. Ellen Wilkinson, *op. cit.*
9. J.B. Priestley, *English Journey*, 1934.
10. 'Draft Scheme for the Coventry Syndicate', 12 March 1919.
11. Sir A.M. Stephen's London Notes, BRCGUA.
12. *Glasgow Herald*, 3 December 1926.
13. Bartram notes on Shipbuilders Conference, 9 December 1938, TWAS.
14. J. Mitchell, *Shipbuilding and the Shipbuilding Industry*, 1926.
15. Transcripts from the Oral History Project, McLean Museum, Greenock.
16. *Ibid.*
17. *The Camel*, March 1920 [Cammell Laird magazine].
18. Bartram's to the Shipbuilding Employers Federation, 8 June 1937, TWAS.

Chapter 10: The Long Decline

1. John Brown's Pay Bill Book, BRL.
2. Palmers Hebburn Co. Ltd., *Six Years' Hard Labour*, 1946.
3. Figures from Trevor I. Williams (ed.), *A History of Technology, Vol. VII*, 1978.
4. *Shipbuilding and Shipping Record*, 21 January 1946.
5. Transcripts from the Oral History Project, McLean Museum, Greenock.
6. From *Shipbuilding and Shipping Record*, 21 August 1947.
7. *Shipbuilding and Shipping Record*, 5 April 1956.
8. *Ibid.*, 7 June 1956.
9. All quotations are from a collection of documents covering the dispute in Upper Clyde Shipbuilders file, BRCGUA.
10. *The Scotsman*, 11 February 1959.
11. Chairman's Statement, Alexander Stephen & Sons Ltd., 18 September 1959, BRCGUA.
12. *The Govan Press*, 10 December 1948.
13. Memorandum circulated by The Shipbuilding Conference, March 1959, TWAS.
14. Statistics from Shipbuilding Conference papers, 12 November 1958.
15. *Linthouse News*, February 1954.
16. Letter to Bartram & Son, 9 December 1954, TWAS.
17. Letter dated 8 October 1956, TWAS.
18. Wear Shipbuilders Association meeting, 29 December 1960, TWAS.
19. *Ibid.*
20. Figures quoted to the Shipbuilding Conference, 12 November 1958.
21. Sir A.M. Stephen's London notes, 10 March 1960, BRCGUA.
22. Anon, *Fairfield 1860–1960*, 1961.
23. Cammell Laird Magazine, March 1960.
24. Cammell Laird Magazine, December 1962.

25. Boilermakers & Iron & Steel Shipbuilders' Society, Monthly Report, January 1949.
26. Wear Shipbuilders Association Report, 20 January 1959, TWAS.

Chapter 11: The Last Chance

1. Charles Goodey, *The First Hundred Years, The Story of Richards Shipbuilders*, 1976.
2. *Shipbuilding Inquiry Committee Report*, Cmnd 2937, 1965–6.
3. Michael Moss and John R. Hume, *Shipbuilders to the World, 125 Years of Harland and Wolff*, 1986.
4. Sydney Paulden and Bill Hawkins, *Whatever Happened at Fairfields?*, 1969.
5. Quoted in Jack McGill, *Crisis on the Clyde*, 1973.
6. UCS Charter Liaison Committee Meeting, 21 March 1968, BRCGUA.
7. UCS Employment Charter, November 1967, BRCGUA.
8. Confidential Memo from Nicholas Ridley to UCS Ltd., December 1969, BRCGUA.
9. Quoted in Alastair Buchan, *The Right to Work*, 1972.
10. Quoted in Jack McGill, *Crisis on the Clyde*, 1973.
11. Glasgow Scrapbook No. 26, Mitchell Library, Glasgow.
12. *Glasgow Chamber of Commerce Journal*, June 1971.
13. *Ibid.*, June 1974.
14. National Joint Committee Conference, York, 12 May 1966, TWAS.
15. Agreement between the Boilermakers and the Scottish East Coast Shipbuilders' Association, July 1966, TWAS.
16. *British Shipbuilding: An Industry Well On Course*, 1973.
17. Ian Davidson, *Govan Press*, 30 November 1979.
18. Chairman of British Marine Equipment Council, *Lloyd's List*, 22 March 1978.
19. *The Guardian*, 6 July 1978.

20. Tom Pickard, *We Make Ships*, 1989.
21. *The Guardian*, 15 May 1993.
22. *Ibid.*, 23 November 1993.
23. Ian Macdonald and Len Tabner, *Smith's Dock*, 1986.

BIBLIOGRAPHY

Archives: For a comprehensive list of business papers, correspondence and other original material relating to shipbuilding, see: Ritchie, L.A. (ed.), *The Shipbuilding Industry; A Guide to Historical Records*, 1992.

ABELL, SIR W.S., *The Shipwright's Trade*, 1948

ALEXANDER, KENNETH J.W., and JENKINS, CARSON L., *Fairfields: A Study of Industrial Change*, 1970

ANON, *The Development of Shipbuilding on the Upper Reaches of the Clyde: Messrs Barclay Curle & Co. Ltd.*, 1911

ANON, *Ships and Shipbuilding, Barclay Curle & Co. Ltd. 1818–1932*, 1932

ANON, *Bartram & Sons, Centenary Souvenir of the Company's History*, 1938

ANON, *Builders of Great Ships* (Cammell Laird), 1959

ANON, *Denny, Dumbarton, 1844–1950*, 1950

ANON, *Dickenson & Co. Ltd., One Hundred Years of Progress*, 1947

ANON, *William Doxford & Company*, 1921

ANON, *Richard Dunston Limited*, 1953

ANON, *The Fairfield Shipbuilding and Engineering Works: History of the Company, Review of Its Production and Description of the Works*, 1909

ANON, *Fairfield, 1860–1960*, 1960

ANON, *The Grangemouth Dockyard Co. Ltd.*, 1951

ANON, *A Hundred Years of Howden Engineering, 1854–1954*, 1954

ANON, *Kincaids, 1868–1968*, 1968

ANON, *Launching Ways* (Barclay Curle), 1953

ANON, *Lobnitz in War*, 1945

ANON, *Six Years Hard Labour, Palmers Hebburn Co. Ltd., 1939–1945*, 1946

ANON, *Philip & Son Ltd., A Century of Progress 1858–1958*, 1958

ANON, *John Readhead & Sons, A Hundred Years of Shipbuilding at South Shields*, 1965

ANON. *The Launching Years, 1904–1954* (Rowhedge Ironworks Co. Ltd.), 1954

ANON, *Mowbray Quay to Pallion Yard, 1850–1950* (Short Bros. Ltd.), 1950

ANON, *A Century of Shipbuilding, 1810–1910*, William Simons & Co. Ltd., 1910

ANON, *Two Hundred and Fifty Years of Shipbuilding by the Scotts at Greenock*, 1961

ANON, *A Shipbuilding History, 1750–1932*, Alexander Stephen & Sons Ltd., 1932

ANON, *Swan Hunter and Wigham Richardson, Engineers and Shipbuilders*, 1906

ANON, *Shipbuilding – From Smack to Frigate From Cutter to Destroyer* (J. Samuel White & Co. Ltd.), 1928

ANON, *Whites of Cowes, Shipbuilders*, 1950

ANON, *Half a Century of Shipbuilding Mercantile and Naval with a Description of the Clydebank Works of James and George Thomson*, 1896

ANON, *Half a Century of Thornycroft Progress*, 1919

ANON, *Shipbuilding at Belfast, 1880–1933*, (Workman Clark), 1935

ANON, *Yarrow & Company Ltd., 1865–1977*, 1977

APPLEYARD, ROLLO, *Charles Parsons, His Life and Work*, 1933

BAKER, W.A., *From Paddle Steamer to Nuclear Ship*, 1965

BANBURY, PHILIP, *Shipbuilders of the Thames and Medway*, 1971

BARNABY, K.C., *One Hundred Years of Specialised Shipbuilding and Engineering* (John I. Thornycroft & Co. Ltd.), 1964

BARNABY, N., *Naval Development in the Nineteenth Century*, 1902

BARRY, P., *The Dockyards and the Private Shipyards of the U.K.*, 1863
— *Dockyard and Naval Power*, 1863
BILES, SIR J.W., *The Design and Construction of Ships*, 1908
BLAKE, G., *Down to the Sea, The Clyde, Its Ships and Shipbuilders*, 1937
— *Scottish Enterprise: Shipbuilding*, 1947
— *British Ships and Shipbuilding*, 1946
BORTHWICK, ALASTAIR, *Yarrow and Company Ltd: The First One Hundred Years, 1865–1965*, 1965
BOYD, WILLIAM, *The Story of the Wallsend Slipway and Engineering Co. Ltd., 1871–1897*, 1911
BROOKS, C., *Grayson's of Liverpool, A History of Grayson, Rollo and Clover Docks Ltd.*, 1956
BROWNE, B.C., *The History of the New* (R & W Hawthorn), 1914
BRUCE, ALEXANDER BALMAIN, *The Life of William Denny, Shipbuilder, Dumbarton*, 1888
BUCHAN, ALASTAIR, *The Right to Work – The Story of the Upper Clyde Confrontation*, 1972
BULLOCH, S.F., *'A Titanic Hero' Thomas Andrews Shipbuilder*, 1912
CAROZZI, J.L. (ed.), *British Shipbuilding*, 1919
CARVEL, JOHN L., *Stephen of Linthouse. A Record of Two Hundred Years of Shipbuilding, 1750–1950*, 1951
CASTLE, COLIN M., *Better By Yards*, 1988
CAUGHEY, J., *Seize Then The Hour, A History of James P. Corry & Co. Ltd. and of the Corry Family, 1123–1974*, 1979
CLARK, TOM, *A Century of Shipbuilding*, 1971
CLARKE, J.F., *The Changeover from Wood to Iron Shipbuilding*, 1986
— *Power on Land and Sea: A History of R. & W. Hawthorn Leslie and Co. Ltd.*, 1979
CLOWES, G.S. LAIRD, *Sailing Ships their History and Development*, 1932
COCHRANE, ALFRED, *The Early History of Elswick*, 1909
CRAIG, ROBIN, *The Ship: Steam Tramps and Cargo Liners*, 1980
CREDLAND, A.G., *Earle's of Hull, 1853–1932*, 1982

CRIGHTON, JOHN, *The Famous Orchard Dockyard Past and Present*, n.d.

DAVIDSON, JOHN R.. *From Collier to Battleships: Palmers of Jarrow, 1852–1933*, 1946

DAVIES, MICHAEL, *Belief in the Sea: State Encouragement of Merchant Shipping and Shipbuilding*, 1992

DAVIS, RALPH, *The Rise of the English Shipping Industry*, 1962

DICKER, GEORGE, *Devonport Royal Dockyard*, 1979

DILLON, MALCOLM, *Some Account of the Works of Palmers Shipbuilding & Iron Co. Ltd.*, 1900

DOUGAN, DAVID, *The Shipwrights*, 1975

— *The Great Gunmaker*, 1971

— *The History of North-East Shipbuilding*, 1968

EMMERSON, G.S., *John Scott Russell*, 1977

D'EYNCOURT, SIR E.H.W.T., *A Shipbuilder's Yarn*, 1928

FAIRBAIRN, W., *Treatise on Iron Shipbuilding, Its History and Progress*, 1865

FINCHAM, J., *A History of Naval Architecture*, 1851

GALLACHER, WILLIAM, *Revolt on the Clyde*, 1936

GIBSON, J.F., *Brocklebanks, 1770–1950*, 1953

GOODEY, CHARLES, *The First One Hundred Years, The Story of Richards Shipbuilders*, 1976

GRANT, A., *Steel and Ships: The History of John Brown's*, 1950

GRANTHAM, J., *Iron Shipbuilding*, 1868

GREENHILL, BASIL, *The Ship, The Life and Death of the Merchant Sailing Ship*, 1980

GUTHRIE, J., *A History of Marine Shipbuilding*, 1971

HALLIDAY, J.M., *Robert Napier*, 1980–1

HAMER, F.E. (ed.), *The Personal Papers of Lord Rendel*, 1931

HAMMOND, R., *The Making of a Ship*, 1965

HARDY, A.C., *From Ship to Sea, A Chronological Account of the Construction of Merchant Ships From the Laying of the Keel to the Trial Trip*, 1926

— *A History of Motor Shipping*, 1955

HARDY, A.C., and TYRRELL, E., *Shipbuilding, Background to a Great Industry*, 1964

HOLMS, A.C., *Practical Shipbuilding*, 1916

HOPKINS, C.N.G., *Pallion, 1874–1954, Church and People in a Shipyard Parish*, 1954

HUME, JOHN R., and MOSS, MICHAEL S., *A Bed of Nails, The History of P. MacCallum and Sons Ltd. of Greenock, 1781–1981*, 1981
— *Clyde Shipbuilding from Old Photos*, 1971
— *Beardmore, The History of a Scottish Industrial Giant*, 1979

INGLIS, JOHN G., *Inglis, Glasgow*, 1977

JEFFERSON, H., *Viscount Pirrie of Belfast*, 1948

JONES, LESLIE, *Shipbuilding in Britain Mainly between The Two World Wars*, 1957

KRUGER, R., *Launching Ways* (Swan Hunter & Wigham Richardson Ltd.), 1953

LATHAM, TIM, *The Ashburns Schooners*, 1991

LEVY, CATRIONA, *Ardrossan Shipyards: Struggle for Survival, 1825–1983*, 1984

LONG, ANNE & RUSSELL, *A Shipping Venture: Turnbull, Scott & Company, 1872–1972*, 1974

LYON, DAVID, *The Ship, Steam, Steel and Torpedoes*, 1980

LYTHE, S.G.E., *Gourlays of Dundee, The Rise and Fall of a Scottish Shipbuilding Firm*, 1964

MABER, JOHN M., *The Ship, Channel Packets and Ocean Liners*, 1980

MACDONALD, IAN, and TABNER, LEN, *Smith's Dock – Shipbuilders*, 1987

MACDOUGALL, PHILIP, *Royal Dockyards*, 1983

MACKENZIE, PETER, *W.G. Armstrong*, 1983

MCGILL, JACK, *Crisis on the Clyde*, 1973

MCGOWAN, ALAN, *The Ship, the Century Before Steam*, 1980

MAGINNIS, A.J., *The Atlantic Ferry its Ships and Working*, 1900

MARSHALL, J.D., *Furness and the Industrial Revolution*, 1981

MATHIAS, P., and PEARSALL, A.W.H., *Shipping: A Survey of Historical Records*, 1971

MITCHELL, J., *Shipbuilding and the Shipbuilding Industry*, 1926

MOSS, MICHAEL, and HUME, JOHN R., *Shipbuilders to the World: 125 Years of Harland and Wolff*, 1986
— *Workshop of the British Empire*, 1977

MURRAY, A.R., *Shipbuilding in Iron and Wood*, 1863
MURRAY, ANDREW, *The Theory and Practice of Shipbuilding*, 1861
MURRAY, MUNGO, *A Treatise on Shipbuilding*, 1754
NAPIER, DAVID DEHANE, *David Napier, Engineer, 1790–1869*, 1912
NAPIER, JAMES, *Life of Robert Napier*, 1904
NEWMAN, BERNARD, *One Hundred Years of Good Company* (Ruston & Hornsby), 1957
OPPENHEIM, M. (ed.), *The Naval Works of Sir William Monson*, 1913
PAIGE, R.T., *The Tamar Valley At Work, James Goss*, 1978
PARKINSON, J.R., *The Economics of Shipbuilding in the U.K.*,1966
PARSONS, R.L., *The Steam Turbine*, 1942
PAULDEN, SYDNEY M., and HAWKINS, BILL, *Whatever Happened at Fairfields?* 1969
PEARSON, F.H., *The Early History of Hull Steam Shipping*, 1896
PEEBLES, H., *Warship Building on the Clyde*, 1987
PEIRSON, J.G., *Great Ship-builders: The Rise of Harland and Wolff*, 1935
PERRIN, W.G., *The Autobiography of Phineas Pett*, 1918
PICKARD, TOM, *We Make Ships*, 1989
POINTER, M.. *Ruston and Hornsby, Grantham, 1918–1963*, 1977
POLLARD, SIDNEY, and ROBERTSON, BRIAN, *The British Shipbuilding Industry, 1870–1914*, 1979
POLLOCK, D., *Modern Shipbuilding and the Men Engaged In It*, 1884
— *The Shipbuilding Industry, Its History, Practice, Science and Finance*, 1905
POLLOCK, WALTER, *The Pollocks as Engineers*, 1939
POTTS, A. (ed.), *Shipbuilders and Engineers*, 1987
PURSEY, HENRY JAMES, *Merchant Ship Construction*, 1959
RANKINE, W.J. MACQUORN, *Shipbuilding Theoretical and Practical*, 1866
REA, VINCENT, *Palmers Yard and the Town of Jarrow*, 1975
REDSHAW, J.S., *Ships, A Study in Modern Shipbuilding*, 1947
REES, ABRAHAM, *The Cyclopoedia*, 1812 (Section 'Naval Architecture', Reprinted 1970)
REID, J.M., *James Lithgow, Master of Work*, 1964

RICHARDSON, A., *The Evolution of the Parsons Steam Turbine*, 1911

RILEY, R.C., *The Evolution of the Docks and Industrial Buildings in Portsmouth's Royal Dockyard, 1698–1914*, 1985

ROLT, L.T.C., *Isambard Kingdom Brunel*, 1957

ROYDEN, ERNEST, *Thomas Royden & Sons Shipbuilders, Liverpool, 1818–1893*, 1953

RUSSELL, J.S., *The Modern System of Naval Architecture*, 1864

RUTHERFORD, WILFRED, *The Man Who Built The Mauretania, The Life Story of Sir George B. Hunter*, 1934

SCOTT, J.D., *Vickers A History*, 1962

SHIELDS, J., *Clyde Built*, 1949

SMITH, E.C., *A Short History of Naval and Marine Engineering*, 1938

SMITH, J.W., and HOLDEN, T.S., *Where Ships Are Born*, 1953

STEPHEN, MURRAY, *A Shipbuilding History: Alexander Stephen & Sons 1750–1931*, 1932

SUTHERLAND, WILLIAM, *The Shipbuilders Assistant*, 1711

THEARLE, S.J.P., *Naval Architecture*, 1874

TREBILCOCK, C., *The Vickers Brothers: Armaments and Enterprise 1854–1914*, 1977

UDEN, GRANT, and COOPER, RICHARD, *A Dictionary of British Ships and Seamen*, 1980

WALKER, FRED M., *Song of the Clyde*, 1984

— *Steel Ship-Building*, 1981

WALKER, F.M., and SLAVEN, A. (eds.), *European Shipbuilding One Hundred Years of Change*, 1984

WALTON, THOMAS, *Steel Ships Their Construction and Maintenance*, 1908

— *Present Day Shipbuilding*, 1921

WARREN, KENNETH, *Armstrongs of Elswick*, 1989

WILKINSON, ELLEN, *The Town That Was Murdered*, 1939

YARROW, LADY ELEANOR, and BARNES, E.C., *Alfred Yarrow: His Life and Work*, 1923

INDEX